The *Weaving Ourselves Whole* (WOW) experience is the tipping point of an expanded approach to human potential. The tools offered in this book invite and empower the reader to understand and embrace the "medicine" of creativity that is universally available in our own pocket! Weaving, looming, and braiding individual strands to stitch storylines together are the ingredients that lead to personal, team, community, and social transformation through the WOW creative process. While encouraging a deep dive into the exploration of the subconscious, the examples of this expressive arts approach fuel and awaken the imagination, which is said to be the most valued skill for our future economy. Greater wholeness and the power to make a difference in this ever-changing world is the opportunity and the invitation of *Weaving Ourselves Whole.*

Gloria Chance, PhD, Founder/The Mousai Group, Peak Performance Psychologist, Creativity Architect, Saybrook University Board Member

This book speaks to me deeply, connecting me to the essence of person-centered expressive arts. It weaved me into the lived wisdom of the authors on the use of arts for inspiration, healing, and wellness. Each sentence is an inviting thread of imaginative connection to clarity and compassion. As an expressive arts therapist, social worker, and educator, I am amazed by the rich trove of creative activities, engaging guidance, and heartfelt compassion in this book. Each of us needs to offer a space for this wonderful book. I imagine that the WOW seeds are spreading around the globe and planting in our heart fields.

Fiona Chang, PhD, Founding President of the Expressive Arts Therapy Association of Hong Kong, Vice-President of Art in Hospital, Founder and faculty of Person-Centered Expressive Arts Training Program (HKU and CUHK)

The authors of *Weaving Ourselves Whole* have charted an exciting new dimension for those interested in the nature and application of creativity. They have expanded the person-centered approach of expressive arts into new dimensions, basing their experiences of a dozen years of work and a few hundred projects. Their readers will enjoy the results of the transformations they have wrought and may well experience transformations themselves as they delve into the book's fascinating chapters.

Stanley Krippner, PhD, Psychologist, Researcher, Author, Professor at California Institute of Integral Studies

I am in awe and inspired after reading *Weaving Ourselves Whole*! The work of the coauthors based on their creative and transformative experiences is a gift to the field of psychology and to anyone with a desire to explore expressive arts. This book is a guide on how to develop and facilitate a group process devoted to creativity and is sure to help move expressive arts forward into 2023 and beyond. Seeing the photos of the author's creative explorations and the stories behind them are one of my favorite parts.

Kristen Clute, PhD, LMFT, LPCC, Expressive Arts
Practitioner/Researcher

Weaving Ourselves Whole (WOW) is a magnificent work that brings expressive arts to life. The quality of writing is superb. A loving, thoughtful, compelling engagement of the authors with their readers infuses each page. Creativity and guidance to live creatively is given a central place. What comes through is the confidence and faith that you can do this—create a transformational expressive arts circle. WOW will be your steadfast, gently wise companion as you travel that journey. There is a short sentence I find myself saying again and again. This sentence reminds me of the way I want to live my life with others, by saying: "Tell me the story of your artwork." *Weaving Ourselves Whole* offers this profound invitation, this invitation and welcome. Both are so needed by the world right now.

John Fox, Founder, The Institute for Poetic Medicine, Author of *Poetic
Medicine: The Healing Art of Poem-Making*

This groundbreaking book, *Weaving Ourselves Whole,* is a guide for individual and group exploration into the vast potential of our creative expression. The authors interweave extensive professional knowledge and personal experiences to demonstrate that expressive arts and working together in a circle, when woven together, can lead to greater wholeness. This book awakens creativity and invites us on a collective journey to become more fully human.

Scott Barry Kaufman, PhD, Cognitive Scientist, Humanistic Psychologist,
Author, The Psychology Podcast, Professor at Columbia University,
Founder/ Director of the Center for Human Potential

Weaving Ourselves Whole draws you in right from the beginning. *"Fear is a companion of change. And heroism is not the absence of fear, but rather the courage to act despite feelings of fear"* (p. 26). Already the introduction is a WOW. The authors address a most burning must of our time, namely to move away from the egocentric view. Nowadays crisis, conflicts, and suffering are too large to be dealt with on an individual level. The authors claim that we can cultivate a collective mind and a circle that is holding each one of us. Adaptation and transformation need creative emergence. The expressive arts and the notion of an inner circle assist to move the spiral of the creative energy force and to access a greater energy outside of us. A circle is about interconnectedness, a mutual holding together in the circle process of relational, creative tension. This approach validates that we need both: individual and community growth. *Weaving Ourselves Whole* speaks to areas in education, clinical areas, spirituality, social change, and personal transformation.

Margo Fuchs Knill, PhD, Professor, Psychotherapist, Expressive Arts Professional, Poet. Dean of the Division Arts, Health and Society at European Graduate School. Co-author *Poetry in Expressive Arts: Supporting Resilience through Poetic Writing*

Weaving Ourselves Whole is itself a work of art, with all the essential strands for expressive arts circles woven together beautifully by its wise and humble authors. Based on the ancient archetypes of the weaver and the circle, WOW provides guiding principles and rich stories that will enable other groups to deepen their collective journey—tapping into wells of creativity that will nourish group members and the wider world. Highly recommended!

Bill Joiner, EdD, MBA, author of Leadership Agility, Founder/CEO of ChangeWise

Ever think about the wall that keeps you from reaching your paradise? This book, *Weaving Ourselves Whole,* just might be the map and inspiration you need to climb over to the other side. While sharing powerful examples of transformation of those involved in their life-changing circle of creativity and growth, the co-authors show you the way.

Anin Utigaard, MFT, REAT, Co-founder of the International Expressive Arts Therapists Association

We can walk through life on automatic pilot, using what neuroscientists term our "default mode network," or we can choose to be fully alive, living a life of meaning and purpose. Many of us attempt this journey to greater wholeness alone, but soon find the daily grind drawing us back to a life of just surviving instead of thriving. All wisdom traditions teach us that community is essential to spiritual growth and transformation and *Weaving Ourselves Whole* provides a communal creative process that supports us in becoming people who can make a more positive impact in our families, work, and communities. In working with this profound book, you will feel that you are supported by loving hands and hearts of those who have gone before you. We each must do our own work, but we don't have to do it alone.

Judi Neal, PhD, Executive Director, Global Consciousness Institute
Founder and CEO, Edgewalkers International
Author *Edgewalkers: People and Organizations that Take Risks, Build Bridges and Break New Ground*; *Creating Enlightened Organizations: Four Gateways to Spirit at Work*; and the *Handbook of Personal and Organizational Transformation*

Weaving Ourselves Whole

A Guide To Forming a Transformational Expressive Arts Circle

Authors
T. Goslin-Jones, P. Caraffa, H. Carson,
K. McCallum, G. Reinert, & N. Williger

Book Photographer
Pam Caraffa

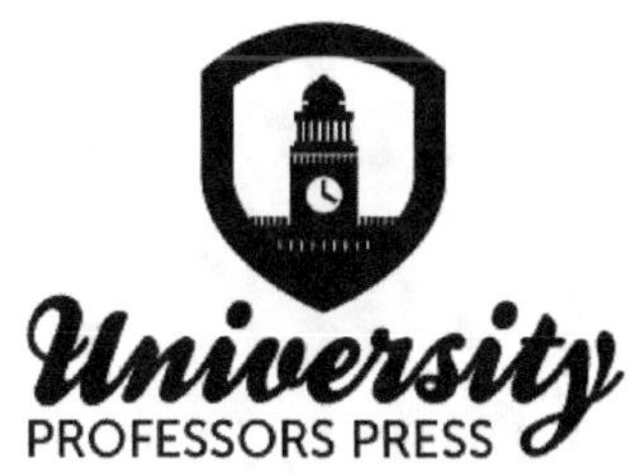

University
PROFESSORS PRESS

Colorado Springs, CO
www.universityprofessorspress.com

Copyright © 2023 University Professors Press

Weaving Ourselves Whole: A Guide for Forming a Transformational Expressive Arts Circle
By Terri Goslin-Jones, Pam Caraffa, Holly Carson, Kim McCallum, Ginger Reinert, & Nancy Williger

University Professors Press. Colorado Springs, CO, United States.

ISBN (Hardcover):   978-1-955737-23-4
ISBN (Paperback):   978-1-955737-24-1
ISBN (Ebook):   978-1-955737-25-8

University Professors Press
Colorado Springs, CO
www.universityprofessorspress.com

Cover Image by Pam Caraffa
Cover Design by Laura Ross

Table of Contents

Gratitude

I believe that creativity is like freedom, once you taste it, you can't do without it. It is a transforming and healing process.
—Natalie Rogers

There is an old French proverb that suggests that gratitude is the heart's memory. We offer this book to the world with gratitude for the creative souls who have gone before us and walked alongside us, inspiring us to experience our life path as a creative voyage. This book would not have become a reality were it not for the devoted support and collaboration of many hearts and minds.

To our dear colleague and editor Dr. Steven Pritzker, we extend our heartfelt gratitude for his belief in our book, his keen editorial eye, and his patience in editing a book co-authored by six individuals with very different writing styles. His knowledge, expertise in the field of creativity studies, and leadership were invaluable in guiding us to develop the narrative of the book into a cohesive whole.

Thank you to our publisher, University Professors Press, and Dr. Louis Hoffman for taking on our first collaborative writing project. We are honored and humbled that he saw the potential of writing about our experience with our Creative Spirit Circle so that others might also be inspired to launch their own creative circle and discover the transformative power of expressive arts and relational creativity.

We thank Dr. Ruth Richards for her trailblazing work in creativity studies and consciousness. Her research and publishing in creativity studies generate a transformative vision of how we might embody "everyday creativity" and awaken our human potential. Her lifework inspires us to be braver with our creativity.

To our colleagues and friends who read early drafts, edited, and offered their ongoing encouragement along the way—Marina Aguirre, Carrie Arnold, Ralph Caraffa, John Davis, Frances Fuchs, Janet Groenemann, Noeli Lytton, Wendy Phillips, Melinda Rothouse, Rodney Sanders, Saybrook University students and faculty, and Anin

Utigaard—we are forever grateful for your inspiration and generous support.

Special thanks to Lyza Fontana for her graphic arts support, creative perseverance, and flexibility. You opened our eyes to new and creative ways to envision our creative circle process that were especially meaningful to all of us. Thank you for sharing your artistic gifts with us and the world.

To our families, we thank you for your patience, love, and support of our creativity throughout the process of writing this book. Thank you for believing in us! Your companionship has infused our creative journey with love.

We extend our utmost appreciation and gratitude to Natalie Rogers whose influence is woven throughout these pages. She was a founder and pioneer in the field of person-centered expressive arts. Her spirit in our work continues to teach us what it means to awaken the creative life force through the creative connection. We hope this book will honor her legacy and mission to contribute to personal and planetary healing by bringing expressive arts to communities, cross-cultural work, and circles of belonging.

Foreword

This book is a treat. It is also a creative challenge—a wonderful challenge that uncovers zest, joy, surprise, emergent creative insights, and psychological depths we may never have known we had. Furthermore, we don't have to do it alone. Picture yourself in a circle with a group of at friends or acquaintances, coming together with the shared purpose of exploring personal growth through expressive arts. This is one part of the *Weaving Ourselves Whole* (or the WOW) process: the connecting, the sharing, the group adventure, and the support. Actually, it is one aspect that this group of six people especially liked over their twelve years together!

Finding insights, together. Picture a group soon to start, each person in their own way wanting a fuller experience of their presence and potential in the world, *individually* and within the *collective.* We have hidden and unconscious depths that can reveal our fullest potential *if we dare to explore them* (see Goslin-Jones, 2010; Jordan, 2018; Rogers, 1993, 2011). This group of authors was willing to try and, more powerfully, try with one another.

They know that expressive arts can offer a moving and motivating way to unfold their deeper selves and seek personal development—*together.* They are, or they hope they are, willing to risk and change in creative relationships with one another. Will it happen? Do they dare? Let us give thanks for the intention, and for the hope we can do it, too, and say a big "WOW"!

WOW! How can it all happen? "WOW" suggests something sudden, amazing, totally surprising—and overall positive—which one never remotely suspected. Could a book do this? Only with you, with me, and with one another. It is a group alchemy. We are individually unique and can offer even more together—indeed in the spirit of holistic and creative emergence, where "the whole is greater than the sum of its parts." Here we explore our own creative spirit and the depths of our unconscious mind (vaster than ever suspected) via an everyday creative process we all have, across many modes of creative expression—verbal, visual, sonorous, in motion, meditative, and more, our alternative languages of life (no experience required).

Remarkable indeed when people find they can join together toward the emergence of something greater. Each expressive arts experience is, by the way, "an invitation" and not a requirement. Further, the circle work is very much about *process,* and learning from lived and shared creative experience. No masterpieces are necessary. Circles are designed and co-led by different combinations of members within a clear creative structure. How much richer the possibilities, adding to an element of surprise.

"*Weaving Ourselves Whole*" evolved from Natalie Rogers' (1993, 2011) PCEA. This inspired new variation on Person-Centered Expressive Arts (PCEA) for an expanded and more general population was developed initially from Terri Goslin-Jones' ongoing work, including her illustrated Creative Living Web (see Goslin-Jones, 2010; Goslin-Jones & Richards, 2018) and a 16-hour Creative Living Circle program she developed and facilitated, post-doctorally. She was honored to have Natalie Rogers as her consultant and mentor during the launch of this program. Two current co-authors of WOW participated in the Creative Living Circle.

The care taken to hone and test this sensitive and deep expressive arts program means a lot to me as a professor of creativity, a psychiatrist, and a colleague of Natalie Rogers, whom I knew for many years. I experienced her dedication, caring, enormous creativity, and sensitivity, whether she was helping clinical clients or furthering social change or structuring her two-year training program for PCEA. This included Rogers' work with the International Expressive Arts Therapy Association (www.ieata.org) described in Appendix A.

Natalie Rogers' (1993, 2011) Person-Centered Expressive Arts (PCEA), as originally designed and as adapted and extended here, honors caring and person-centered principles. PCEA individual and group exploration and growth takes some courage, too, such that safety and openness, unconditional acceptance, trust, and further guidelines are vital. In PCEA, it is also natural that the artistic choices may intimidate some of us. Can we do it? (The five-year-old next door might give it a try, though.) Yet the WOW program is about *process* and exploring, not masterfully creative end *products.* One might start with dance or movement, waving colorful scarves experimentally, and go on to other choices, including meditation, paints, clay, writing, and more. As one author said, it seemed awkward at first, but as time passed expressive arts became more and more a way "to connect and to have fun."

Terri Goslin-Jones in turn used PCEA in her doctoral research and in her consulting work toward healthy change in organizations. She also teaches Creativity Studies and supervises doctoral students in research. One can be sure that WOW, developed for specific clinical and consultation purposes, is now an excellent resource for healing, growth, and even transcendence for us as well.

Perhaps this sounds as if it's "too good to be true"? I would say that reading *Weaving Ourselves Whole* can be healing in itself, as well as revealing. So make a hot cup of tea, sit back, and flip through the book (including pictures). Do not miss the photo of the woven basket, whose origins we can contemplate later.

New routes to "integrative health" and emergence. As for me, I am a Harvard-trained psychiatrist and educational psychologist who has studied creativity ("the originality of everyday life") and practiced some as well—we all do!—for years. I am convinced that evolution equipped us humans with this huge potential so we could both *survive* and *thrive*. I have applied this in education, clinical areas, spirituality, social action, and more. I taught for 25 years full time at Saybrook University in two areas (which I helped establish—with unique colleagues—as Faculty Co-Chair): (1) Consciousness, Spirituality, and Integrative Health, and (2) Creativity Studies.

Put your pointer on the *integrative* in that specialization area called Consciousness, Spirituality, and Integrative Health. Here is healing practice broadly conceived, allopathic and alternative medicine together in complex interaction. For me as an MD, PhD, this means a lot, and creativity is intrinsic to this mix. How do we find our fullest healing possibilities, connect deeply with self, world, and one another? Can we transform our life? (It does happen!) My colleagues and I have written, edited and co-edited relevant books (Runco & Richards, 1997; Richards, 2007a, 2018) and now find that chaos and complexity theory can add further richness (Schuldberg et al., 2022). Two examples: illumination of the magic Aha! Moment (which we all can have if we don't inhibit it) and the surprising *emergence* of the new (first, "the whole is greater than the sum of its parts" and, second, we cannot anticipate it all beforehand anyway; some is hidden from us).

Expressive arts: One of our best medicines? Creative arts and other expressive options are often a big part of mind–body medicine, holistic healing, and whole-person health (see Freeman, 2009; Richards, 2018; Runco & Pritzker, 2011; Serlin et al., 2019). Our best "medicine" or treatment is not solely to fix a malady (yet may we find excellent treatments for them). It is also to take us further and give us more awareness and presence in the moment, meaning in life, values, capability, connection, caring, compassion, and loving kindness.

There is good evidence of the healing powers of creating (meeting criteria of originality and meaningfulness), whether in conventional art therapies or other areas of everyday creative life. At times, it's less *what* we do than *how* we do it. We can be open and non-defensive while being creatively flexible, adaptive, experimental, original in many ways. We may be teaching a class, raising kids, cooking a meal, landscaping the yard, planning a fundraiser, or writing that novel. What we model helps affect the people we work with (Richards, 2018). Would you think living creatively links to healthy aging? (It does.) And what about greater life meaning/or spirituality? (Yes, again; see Pargament, 2011; Richards, 2018; Schuldberg et al., 2022). It is significant that this "medicine" is universally available (and in your pocket at this very moment). Meanwhile, just to have it is empowering. And this medicine is *free*!

Learning from and about our coauthors. Let's hear more now about WOW and the people who wrote *Weaving Ourselves Whole* and who lived this process for twelve—yes twelve—years! Did the co-author participants find new creative depths within themselves and new bonds with the world? Absolutely! I was delighted to meet these participants on Zoom and will share some insights below. They are accomplished in various ways, and yet several did not feel very experienced in the arts when they first joined the Creative Spirit Circle. Again, no experience required.

What they found most amazing: The group's creative synergy and the magic of circle work. Before starting their Creative Spirit Circle, most members loosely knew at least one other member in the group. Group connections emerged "organically" through networking with an intention to start this circle focused on using expressive arts for personal growth. The authors were also brought together through a general recognition that each sought to find other parts of their being and their overall human potential. Variations on this exploration included the "sacred marriage" of anima and animus, both carried within each of us. The group discovered an early affinity with one another but built an even stronger bond as their encounters deepened, and through their continued commitment to expressive arts and circle work.

During the past two years, while writing this book, the six authors encountered several tragedies and challenges, including the death of ten family members. COVID also was a challenge for the coauthors and their families. Some had issues with elder care, health, surgeries, retirement, relocation, and other life transitions, and found an understanding and empathetic group of peers in the Creative Spirit Circle. One person in a challenging situation even mentioned having "the group with her," a sympathy others shared in their own way. Over the twelve years support has grown and is palpable.

What moved me especially was that as much as these individuals enjoyed the expressive arts aspect, they all especially valued their shared experience of creating together. Other topics of discussion included group interactions—for example, an appreciation of vulnerability as a pathway to increased creativity, openness, and belonging. Notably, for us all, relationships have their own dynamic lives, and we continue balancing individual creative initiative and harmonious group space. One excellent chapter goes particularly deeply into relational conflicts and healthy resolutions.

Some ongoing wishes for the authors' circle included developing further links between "creativity and spirituality." This was important. Yet ties deepened beyond that. One person shared how, even after years of mindfulness practice, "I did not expect *collective consciousness!*" Another used a similar term. Another member spoke of "relational creativity" (indeed a dynamic dance and interplay of originality and meaningfulness) and its being "energetic with a common field." Another said how "co-creative" this group had become—"our creative collaborations broke me open," it "blew me away." Others spoke of transcendence linked to humanistic psychology and potential for traits of self-actualizing people (Kaufman, 2020; Maslow, 1971).

Let's take this very seriously. I take these expressions seriously indeed in a world in crisis needing understanding and connection. One might think of Buber's (1970) "between space" or Marks-Tarlow (as cited in Schuldberg et al., 2022) on chaos theory and a joint fractal field for intuition. Consider Wu Chen's paintings of bamboo, called "portraits of the artist as bamboo" or Nobelist Barbara McClintock's unique methods (called art and science by her biographer) in studying the genetics of corn (Richards, 2018).

So much is left to learn about our connection and mutual "attunement" (Kossak, 2021; Siegel, 2007). For instance, do we even understand quantum "entanglement"? Empathy was touted by no less than Charles Darwin as central to humanity as a social species (Loye, as cited in Schuldberg et al., 2022); empathy itself crosses species, as well; plus we are wired for it, with our mirror neurons (Richards, 2018). Whatever secrets are yet to be revealed, the circle work seems to tap into them and helps us create bonds that feel extraordinary.

Can this "WOW" path work for us as well? Every group is different, of course, and the WOW program is exemplary. However, I have seen similar attunement, empathy, mutuality, and more emerge in resonant groups and settings (e.g., Jordan, 2018; Jordan et al., 1991; Richards, 2007c). Nor is age, education, or experience necessarily an issue since we are addressing *human* qualities. Beyond this, the Weaving Ourselves Whole program does have special organizational features that shape sessions while further building shared community, values, and practices. This begins with the metaphorical (and very real) basket that is being woven in the collaboration. The *warp* supports the whole in whatever it attempts; the *weft*—the horizontal part—represents many creative strands and paths. Yet, at the end the entire creation stands as an integrated whole and a symbol of a complex, integrated experience. There are many other structural elements and ritual orderings, too, that bring a special feel to the WOW time together and add to what may come to feel like a special, sacred space.

Another image is also a personal favorite, the wonderful jigsaw puzzle that circle members created—all out of the same intention and preliminary planning, but each in their own uniquely creative way. Then it came together into something more. Here, initially, is a large paper disc cut into many jigsaw pieces. Each group member separately works with one of these pieces as a metaphor for the circle's vision. Finally, the whole composition is assembled as a unified vision. It absolutely seems to work.

It is key that being creative may—at best, all else being equal— help us to become more open, non-defensive, attuned, risk taking, spontaneous, authentic (Richards, 2014), and perhaps even better people. This surely deserves further research. Jordan (2018) discussed relational benefits movingly in *Relational Cultural Therapy*, an approach that has been well received; a third edition from APA Books will soon be forthcoming. There is an ongoing discussion here, however, since a "dark side of creativity" is also well known (Cropley et al., 2010). Yet, a group that is willing to risk openness, honesty, empathy, unconditional acceptance, and a person-centered frame, while facilitating, as one person said, "shedding a false self," may be apt to end up in a better place.

I shared the following quote from relational cultural theory co-founder Judith Jordan (2018; Jordan et al., 1991). The *Weaving Ourselves Whole* authors felt this captured their Creative Spirit Circle experience. Now this new book can share WOW with everyone:

> *Where empathy and concern flow both ways, there is an intense affirmation of the self and, paradoxically, a transcendence of the self, a sense of the self as part of a larger relational unit. The interaction allows for a relaxation of the sense of separateness; the other's well-being becomes as important as one's own.*

* * *

Ruth Richards, MD, PhD
Berkeley, CA, USA
Saybrook University and California Institute of Integral Studies

Introduction

Never doubt that a small group of thoughtful, committed citizens can change the world, indeed, it's the only thing that ever has.
—Margaret Mead

Weaving Ourselves Whole: A Guide for Forming a Transformational Expressive Arts Circle was inspired by the collective experience of an expressive arts circle that has met over the span of twelve years. Together, our group facilitated over fifty arts sessions and continues to meet and create within our circle process. The growth and transformation we collectively experienced over the past decade have been profound, beyond anything we could have imagined. Something generative happens when people dive into the creative process together. Our circle members were united by a mutual desire for personal growth, and a hunger to deepen and explore our creative journeys.

Our Creative Spirit Circle uses person-centered expressive arts to access vaster levels of personal, spiritual, and creative potential within a collaborative and generative group process that shares leadership. We agreed to adopt a shared leadership model that includes co-facilitation for each expressive arts journey.

What do we mean by Weaving Ourselves Whole? Wholeness is moving toward an undivided life, one that integrates the unknown and our potential to grow. Wholeness is becoming more open to and present with life's challenges and responding within an awakened, compassionate heart. This process involves taking care of our mind, body, and spirit. The premise of this book is that expressive arts and circle work, when woven together, can lead to greater wholeness and possibly transcendence.

In the world of weavers, a circular loom is the substrate upon which the weaver threads their creative aspirations and destiny. The weaver archetype appears across cultures and mythology and is symbolic of interconnection and originality. The Creative Spirit Circle has been our creative loom, braiding personal transformation as individual strands and learning to weave and stitch the threads of our storylines together.

The circle process invites participants to tap into shared consciousness and explore new aspects of the known and unknown self. Together, there is a synergistic knowing that is far beyond what each could access or experience individually. The archetype of the circle is activated and awakened through inspirational connection. This brings each participant into a visceral remembrance of being whole rather than broken and an awareness of being held in ancient belonging versus being alone. There is a creative spirit within all of us longing for authentic expression.

The purpose of this book is to encourage others to start a Creative Spirit Circle of their own. This book provides a resource filled with tools and inspiration to serve and guide both helping professionals in the fields of expressive arts, education, mental health, and coaching, as well as students, artists, individuals, and groups who are interested in forming an expressive arts circle to awaken creative potential and support social transformation. *Weaving Ourselves Whole* is both philosophical and pragmatic. It speaks to the wonder and transformational power of creative awakening, weaving conscious creativity with the colorful threads of imagination, ritual, myth, story, symbol, creative expression, and friendship.

Organization of the Book

The first section of the book introduces the field of person-centered expressive arts (PCEA) and the Creative Spirit Circle group process. Chapter 1 describes the field of person-centered expressive arts, a branch of expressive arts developed by Natalie Rogers that combines the use of expressive arts (art, sound, movement, improvisational drama, music, dance, and poetry) with the person-centered theories and philosophy of Carl Rogers, to promote growth and healing. This chapter also explores the theoretical background of PCEA and how to use it in a group format.

Chapter 2 details the Creative Spirit Circle group process and provides guidelines on how to develop and sustain a group of your own. The art of weaving that guides this process entails transforming opposite tensions into a unified whole. The Creative Spirit Circle process balances personal work with a community focus, allowing for both creative expression and psychological safety. These two tensions, when balanced, enable the individual and the group to evolve and symbiotically develop higher levels of connection and consciousness. This generates a haven for peak creativity.

Chapter 3 provides a meeting template to develop and conduct Creative Spirit Circle sessions. The basic structure and principles used for all sessions are described, enabling you to design your own circle meetings.

Chapters 4 and 5 describe how to formulate an individual and collective vision for your Creative Spirit Circle. The collective vision is co-created by all circle members.

Chapters 6 through 15 offer *expressive arts journeys* designed and facilitated by the authors over the course of our Creative Spirit Circle process. Each journey represents a creative threshold, taking the group on a journey of discovery. Many of the journey themes come from the rich traditions of depth, humanistic, Jungian, and transpersonal psychology. Interwoven throughout these chapters are brief vignettes entitled WOW Stories, with photos and/or creative writing. Each chapter ends with a section called Creative Weavings, with suggestions for further reflection, creative exploration, and learning.

Chapter 16, Conscious Closure: The Art of Circling, shares lessons learned and insights gained over twelve years of creating and co-facilitating circle sessions.

Throughout the book, we share stories about Weaving Ourselves Whole (WOW Stories) and discuss how expressive arts and circle work have been transformational for us. Our collective experiences changed the tapestry of the group in unexpected ways, and writing this book has woven the story of our captivating journey together into our lives.

References, appendices, and author biographies complete the book. The appendices are referred to throughout the book and contain additional information and documents for the expressive arts journey. The final section contains brief biographies of each author, introducing you to the creative souls who fueled the fire of the Creative Spirit Circle.

This book was written during a time of tumultuous change and transition, amidst the uncertainties of a global pandemic, global warming, and the threat of geopolitical unrest. A Creative Spirit Circle serves as a potent container that allows us, through the poetic inner eye, to find beauty in our broken world. The manifestation of creativity circles can help heal our world through the power of personal and collective transformation. Creativity circles speak across cultures and heal us to the bone. The underlying principles of expressive arts serve as a healing bridge to navigate social injustice and humanitarian crises and inspire social change. It can help us tap into our collective resilience as we attempt to meet life's challenges with wisdom and compassion. By changing ourselves, we change our world. By seeking wholeness, we find we are all connected as one.

We are excited you found our book and welcome you into our Creative Spirit Circle process. May it ignite your inner spark and encourage you to embark on a similar journey of adventure and growth. There is something precious about having a small group of companions dedicated to cultivating imagination, wholeness, and wisdom. Over time, may your creativity and the circle process guide you to grow in surprising ways. May your creative expression strengthen and nourish a flourishing connection within yourself, your circle members, loved ones, and the larger world.

Chapter 1

Person-Centered Expressive Arts:
Portal for Discovery

*In the Creative Connection process, the power of the
arts to heal and transform is undeniable and magical.*
— Natalie Rogers

Engaging with the arts has been an integral and uniquely human form of expression throughout history. The arts celebrate the cycles of life and capture the beauty and complexity of our experience. Nested within psychology and creativity studies, expressive arts draw upon multiple artistic modalities to explore human expression and development.

As an interdisciplinary arts-based approach for personal growth and social transformation, expressive arts (EA) span endeavors ranging from counseling and psychotherapy to consulting and education. Many artists work to create meaningful finished works such as drawings and poems. EA, however, focuses on the creative process for the purpose of inquiry and self-exploration. In fact, having a goal to develop a specific product, such as a painting or poem, can interfere with the EA process. Creative exploration and self-expression direct attention to *process* over *product*. This is an essential component of the transformative dynamics and healing powers associated with an expressive arts practice. There is freedom in creating without judgment (Goslin-Jones, 2020).

This chapter introduces expressive arts so that circle members can develop a collective understanding and a common language (Appendix A) to design and facilitate their expressive arts circle sessions. Unlike art therapy or artists who concentrate on one art form at a time, expressive arts engage a multi-modal process, integrating multiple kinds of creative expression in a sequential manner. This might include visual and material arts combined with drama and dance or music and writing, as well as meditation. Practitioners offer a variety of multi-modal arts processes that evoke emotions and insights in individuals and groups. Illumination, clarity, and joy in the process of expression act as catalysts for growth. Group members don't need to be artists or creative professionals to participate in a Creative Spirit Circle. In fact, diverse backgrounds contribute to new perspectives and enrich the group's creative experience.

Person-Centered Expressive Arts

The work of psychologist Natalie Rogers, PhD, (1928–2015) influences the Creative Spirit Circle process discussed in this book. As a therapist, artist, teacher, and founder of the Person-Centered Expressive Therapy Institute (PCETI), Natalie entered the field of expressive arts through her work in play therapy and integrated the arts in her private practice with children and adults. In 1974, she experimented with using expressive arts in a series of therapeutic person-centered group workshops while working with her father Carl Rogers, PhD, founder of the person-centered approach to psychotherapy (Goslin-Jones & Herron, 2016).

Natalie incorporated the person-centered philosophy with the integrative, multi-modal process of expressive arts and named her practice the Creative Connection, which she used as a therapist and later as an educator. Initially, expressive arts were used primarily in therapeutic settings. As time passed, expressive arts graduates expanded their work into an international and cross-cultural network that included consultants, educators, and therapists who worked with individuals and groups for social transformation. Both individuals and groups utilized person-centered expressive arts (Rogers, 1993, 2011).

The Creative Connection
The person-centered expressive arts approach invites participants to make choices using a variety of modalities that might include art, movement, sounding, and writing to access inner resources for greater self-awareness. Facilitators provide group process guidelines at the beginning of PCEA sessions to foster a safe and supportive environment. This allows participants to open and expand their creative energy by engaging in the expressive arts. Emerging feelings become resources for further understanding and creativity. This integrative, multi-modal expressive arts process expands sensory awareness and unlocks creative energy that may lead to new awareness. Each person can awaken to new possibilities, and with

these expansions the individual and group begin to shift consciousness (Rogers, 2011).

PCEA as a Portal for Creative Potential

Person-centered expressive arts offer a portal to the collective unconscious and a bridge to our personal creative potential. Natalie Rogers (1993, p. 44) conceived a visual image of this individual and universal force (see Figure 1) of creative energy, which is expressed and integrated by moving from one art form to another. As we let go of expectations and inner blocks, layers of suppressed energy are released and channeled through the container of expressive arts.

As a person moves up the creative energy spiral, the process includes suspending judgment from the inner critic. This permits greater risk taking and experimentation. All the senses become engaged more fully, and the mind becomes more receptive and free flowing. Circle members may then access inspiration beyond their everyday consciousness.

While engaging in expressive arts, participants can become more aware of their creative life force and access this energy to enrich everyday living. This is discussed further in *The Creative Connection* (Rogers, 1993) and *The Creative Connection for Groups* (Rogers, 2011; see Figure 1).

Take a Detour to Explore Creativity

What does it mean to use expressive arts to explore the dynamic possibilities of life versus living life from a linear perspective? Expressive arts can energetically move and integrate creative energy. For example, following a recipe, a map, or directions in a step-by-step procedure is a more linear process, making it harder to pause and reflect on new possibilities. Following specific directions reduces intuitive detours and exploration. Oftentimes, others predetermine or direct us toward a linear path. This happens with societal conditioning, systemic barriers, or choices like staying in a job one despises because it seems like there are no other options available.

Person-centered expressive arts invite you to use color, textures, sounds, physical movement, emotions, and writing to transport yourself into a new domain of experimentation where you can embrace ambiguity and open yourself to original discovery. This process opens intuitive channels, helping you move up the spiral of the creative energy force.

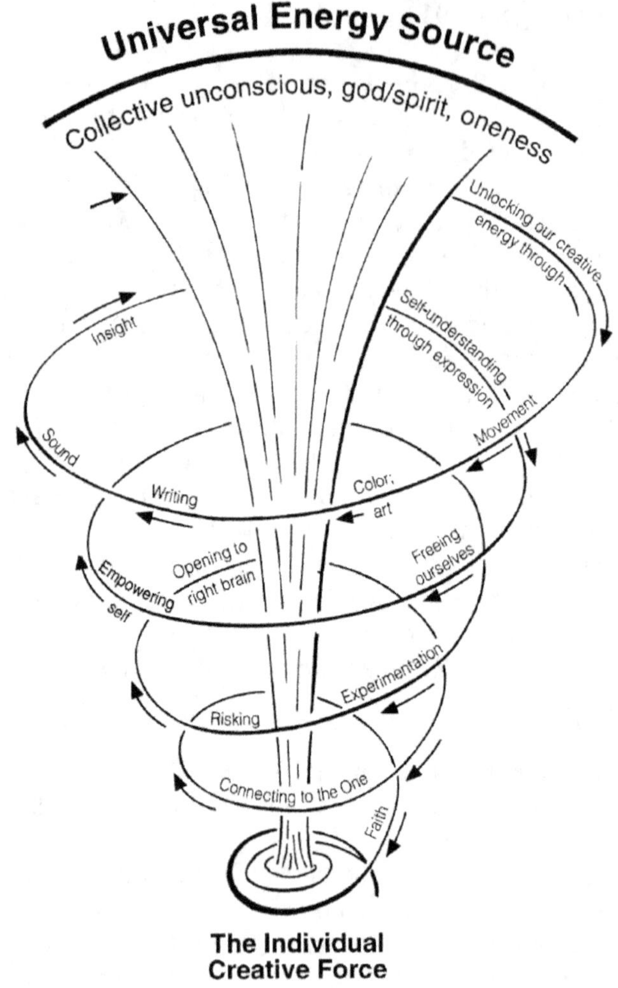

Figure 1: The Individual and Universal Energy Source, Natalie Rogers (1993, p. 44)

When you try something new and enter unfamiliar territory as when you travel to a new location in the world, your body opens, and you expand your sensory intake. With PCEA you arrive in the present moment and travel to a vast, interior world with an intention to attain conscious awareness. An essential part of this experience is listening to your inner voice in ways that facilitate and bring forth your personal creativity. Explore life by asking questions: What would be different if you changed jobs, moved to a new community, left a stagnant relationship, or followed your dreams? The journey inward offers surprises, insight, new ways of expressing yourself, and avenues for personal growth.

From an evolutionary standpoint, we may also learn to access a greater energy outside of us, an energy from our environment and even the collective unconscious. Sharing experiences in a group helps deepen creativity and integrate emerging themes that show up in life. The more we practice this, the easier it gets. Expressive arts circles provide ample opportunity for practice and experimentation. Creative inquiry evolves and begins to transform life, serving as a pathway toward self-actualization.

PCEA Groups as a Life-long Creative Practice

This book proposes that person-centered expressive arts groups can serve as a life-long creative practice for personal growth within an ongoing circle of committed members. When working within such a circle, the group members offer an accepting presence that supports each person's exploration.

The multi-modal expressive arts process engages many aspects of what makes a person unique by activating creative exploration and initiating a discovery process that may lead to greater self-awareness and growth. For example, one PCEA session designed by the authors was on the topic of time and its impact on us. We were invited to bring mementos and symbols of what time meant to us. During the session, we engaged our bodies and minds by walking a path, with different earthly epochs of time shown in drawings spaced around the garden. We then shared a meditation reflecting on time

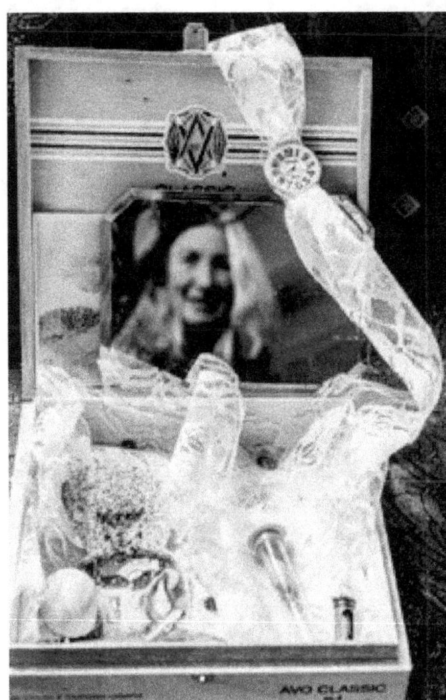

Figure 2: WOW Story, Time Travel, mixed media, Kim McCallum (2021)

before entering a creative expression period. Figure 2 shows one circle member's illustration of her relationship with time during our session.

Kim: In our expressive arts *Time of Your Life* workshop, I contemplated time. This is my time-travel meditation box (Figure 2). I made the box and then used the mirror for time travel today. Noticing the aging in my skin, I imagined seeing my wrinkles as the folds of time versus trying to erase them.

While Kim noticed the folds, unfolding, and impermanence of time, another member attended to the wisdom gained during the passage of time. A third person envisioned space–time as more room for an open heart to flower and for an acceptance of growing older. There was a unique engagement with the topic for each person, and personal realizations emerged from the multi-modal experience.

An expressive arts circle workshop can be designed in numerous ways. Frequently, they include a brief mindfulness meditation to bring everyone away from the busyness of the day and into the present moment. Sometimes, facilitators invite physical movement in spontaneous ways to convey feelings or physical sensations. When the movement feels complete, it may be followed by coloring or drawing with the non-dominant hand, using oil pastels or crayons. An entry into the emotional realm may be as simple as picking an image from a deck of archetypal cards and connecting images to personal feelings or experiences. A writing prompt such as "I am…, I feel…, I need…" might encourage capturing the personal experiences in words. Finally, participants share their experience verbally with the group. Any members who may not be ready can choose to pass.

During an expressive arts circle process, members connect to multiple layers of their emotional realm. Feelings get stirred up and unraveled. Often in life, people avoid or suppress emotions. In the expressive arts process, feelings become a primary source of creative material and an invitation to open to experience, be authentic, and meet life with compassion and empathy.

Early in our time together, one group member shared what an expressive arts circle felt like to her. The image in Figure 3 illustrates her thoughts and feelings. She spoke about the artmaking and reflection portion of circle sessions.

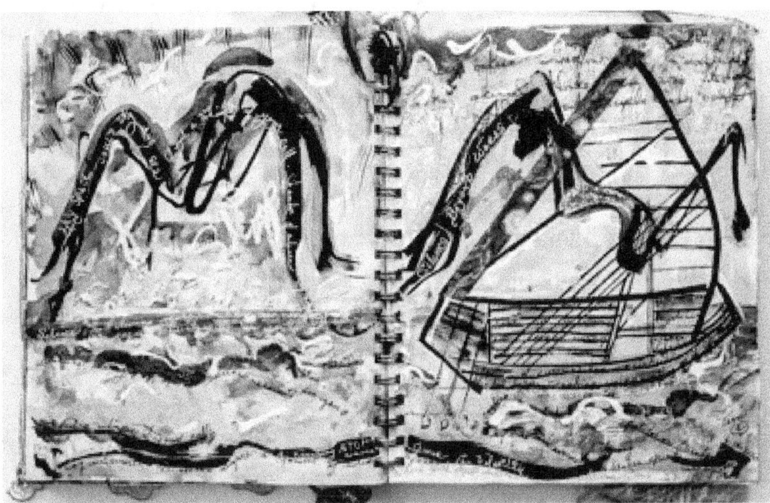

Figure 3: WOW Story, Beyond Words, acrylic, Terri Goslin-Jones (2020).

Terri: The intermodal process of using meditation, movement, and artmaking transports me to an abstract and preverbal, emotional place. My artmaking (Figure 3) reveals my emotions and activates my intuition. As I reflect on my artmaking and begin the writing process, a bridge forms between my logical and intuitive selves, and insights arise.

As Terri described, multimodal expressive arts encourage you to move to a deep internal space and experiment with various art mediums. Different artforms provide ways to reflect upon and digest the journey individually and collectively. It is rare in life to have a safe and enjoyable space to travel inside yourself in the company of a small band of friends.

Possibilities expand for circle members as they experience and express their compassion and empathy to one another. This accepting, nonjudgmental environment fosters a culture of openness for circle members and provides a vessel and invitation for exploration and experimentation. The person-centered process fosters a safe and evaluation-free environment for new levels of awareness to emerge. Being present to one's authentic emotions, which too often are unsupported or suppressed, can reveal truths and new possibilities. Exploring new realities can lead to choices that are more closely aligned with living a meaningful life.

Within the PCEA circle process, specific invitations and prompts help generate focus for group members. Circle members also have the freedom to modify all directions and projects. When presenting an overview of a circle meeting or workshop, facilitators remind members that they can choose different approaches during the expressive arts process. Participants then have the freedom and power to choose a creative process that is personally meaningful. For example, circle members have the option to bring personal art supplies or to work in an art journal while others are working with clay. Listening to one's inner desires and expressing this in an artform is encouraged. Expressive arts include all art modalities as pathways to access our greater potential.

Barriers To Creativity

Inner judgment can diminish and shut down imagination. The inner critic's voice may be strong and inhibit your expression. Many of us have been socialized in a logical, linear, and high-tech manner that diminishes play, artmaking, spontaneity, and messiness. Are you aware of your inner voice? What messages do you hear or tell yourself? Your inner voice may include internalized critics from early life experiences or messages from family members, peers, teachers, and the media. You may have learned and been socialized to adjust so much to your outside environment that you forget who you are on the inside. The pace and noise of the world make it easy to become numb to internal longings and desires. Stepping into the unknown or trying new experiences can often cause anxiety and discomfort. Being immersed in a creative process may trigger a fear of failure and a fear of the unknown. Nevertheless, becoming aware of our internal dialogue and using an expressive arts process can guide us through the challenging times of life by raising awareness and cultivating new skills.

How Does a Circle Develop Freedom and Psychological Safety?

Individuals differ greatly in their readiness and comfort level in exploring their lives using expressive arts. Each person has a unique learning style that includes different ways of communicating, skill sets, and facilitation styles. Groups can increase psychological safety and freedom by co-creating and using circle guidelines. Group guidelines and norms ensure mutual agreement, healthy boundaries, and ways to share compassionate feedback with one another.

Circumstances in the environment and your personal history can inhibit your expression. For instance, you may not feel able to express yourself because it was never encouraged or others said you had no artistic talent. There may be so much going on in your life that you feel you don't have the energy to be imaginative. Expressive arts offer a safe space and a wonderful play space for exploring these conditions. The sessions do not require talent, skill, or energy. In fact, they may *give* you energy if you participate openly, without trying to be anything other than who you are at that moment. You may want to ask yourself some questions to cultivate awareness about the environment that supports your creative expression:

- What conditions foster your creativity?
- What is your experience of working in a group? For example, are you more introverted or extroverted? How does being part of a group help you see yourself and grow? How does a group hinder this?
- When do you feel the most open to new experiences?
- When do you need guidelines or when do you need freedom? What is your tolerance for ambiguity?
- Everyone learns differently. What is your learning style, meaning what helps you learn? Examples might be walking or moving while you think, listening to quiet music, one-on-one conversations with someone you trust, or lots of ideas tossed around in a lively discussion.

Each person has their own way of learning and imagining. For example, some take notes and let things marinate; others need pictures and diagrams; still others find themselves doodling or drawing as they think or listen. Take some time to reflect on what helps and hinders you. If you don't know, pay attention over the next several days to what conditions nurture your growth.

The expressive arts circle becomes a place to experiment, to get to know yourself and other members in your group. The co-facilitators who lead each session extend, invite, and model psychological safety and freedom, but it is truly each circle member's responsibility to foster these conditions for themselves. A multitude of behaviors can interrupt psychological safety, and this typically happens when members do not understand their blind spots. A psychological blind spot is an aspect of yourself of which you are unaware but others can see. Everyone has some blind spots. It could be an unseen bias you hold or a behavior or topic you tend to ignore because you find it difficult or unpleasant.

For example, group members may change the subject or shift the focus by sharing a personal story that is off topic when they are uncomfortable with a topic but unaware of their discomfort. Someone may not realize they are becoming overly directive. Group members who are aware of the undercurrent arising can gently redirect the group back to the agenda and to a stance of welcoming acceptance. All kinds of tensions can be harnessed to generate greater levels of self-understanding and creativity.

As individuals in the expressive arts circle begin to express their feelings and develop greater self-awareness, the group learns to hold the circle's diversity, and the entire group becomes stronger. Personal and group conflict are a natural part of growth. This is apparent in how nature teaches us to handle storms. The earth needs thunderstorms and rain, and you can learn to "dance in the rain" with intention and compassion. When conflict arises within you or the group, you can turn the volume up, get closer, and explore the intensity that is happening inside of you; or you can turn it down and step away for some safe distance. It is like putting on a raincoat to avoid getting drenched; it is your decision to get what you need at that moment.

Additional ways to bring safety to a group include cultivating awareness about the impact of language. When the facilitators describe and verbalize expressive arts prompts, it is important to reduce directives or mandates and to be conscious of language that implies everyone should go forward with the same behaviors and that there is one best way for the whole group. You can use terminology that includes *suggestions* and *invitations,* and you can share circle guidelines verbally and in writing. Offer reminders that everything is an invitation. For example, instead of saying, "Create a symbol of your current feelings using the clay we have provided," you could say, "We have provided clay for you to use to express your current feelings, but if clay doesn't fit your mood, you can use whatever creative expression seems right to you, like writing, dancing, or painting. The important thing is to express what you are feeling in the best way that suits you right now."

Use meditation and other processes that cultivate presence and invite circle members to slow down, listen to their internal voice, and attend to their bodies as a way to take care of their personal needs. Remind them that there is no right or wrong way to make art. We are creating for the process, for the experience of more meaningful ways of knowing ourselves and one another, rather than for the pressure of developing a product with deadlines and requirements.

Sometimes artmaking, movement, and writing activate anxiety in people who have had challenging experiences with their creative process. Even though the facilitator(s) may invite people to create freely, some group members may want detailed instructions and feel very confused by open guidelines and freedom. The awareness and sensitivity of the facilitator to meet the wide variety of needs in a group can be taxing. Circle members rotate facilitation, and as you gain more experience, you will realize confusion about the creative process is generally about different needs and different learning styles. You learn to be flexible and sensitive to the different needs of each group member.

Cultivating a judgment-free zone is valuable. Judgment and evaluation suppress creative energy. Frequently, members do not realize that sharing personal opinions about another person's expressive arts experience can feel like a judgment. For example, a member may intend to express appreciation and say, "Your artwork reminds me of a jack-in-the-box. It looks so happy." However, the person drawing the art saw it as a box of fire that reflected personal passion and anger. They weren't given the space to share a personal experience of their artmaking. The verbal opinion of another circle member can cause personal judgment and self-criticism to arise.

Even though unintended, sharing opinions and saying things like, "I love your jack-in-the-box," might leave a member feeling crushed or misunderstood. It is more effective to simply be present and open in an accepting manner and ask a question like, "What does your artwork mean to you?" or "This is amazing. Tell me the story of your artwork." This type of response allows the circle member to describe their artmaking without external interpretation and guides a person into new levels of awareness through safety, acceptance, and authentic expression.

Meta-Awareness

The expressive arts circle process can be a dwelling space to facilitate "meta-awareness" in everyday living. Meta-awareness is the ability to observe your thoughts, feelings, and physical sensations while they are arising without judgment. You can learn to do this by beginning to watch your behavior, listen to your thoughts, and notice your bodily feelings as you work on your expressive arts project or communicate with your circle group. The group process can deepen this experience because you engage with new experiences through artmaking, physical movements, writing, and verbally sharing your experience with a compassionate and non-judgmental circle that is committed to honoring creative expression.

Participating in this group experience may provide a journey into the unconscious and cultivate new awareness with oneself and other circle members. The individual and the group have a safe place for growth and transformation. You become steadily more awake to all that is arising within you. Over time, meta-awareness may become integrated into everyday life.

Summary

Expressive arts provide a multi-modal process—including mindfulness, movement, sounding, artmaking and writing—for self-exploration, creative expression, and integration in a safe and supportive environment. This book presents ways to develop and sustain an ongoing person-centered expressive arts circle as a powerful way to support health and well-being.

Research indicates that over time using expressive arts can lead to personal growth, healing, deeper relationships, being present, experiencing flow, discovery, and insight bridging to preverbal knowledge (Goslin-Jones, 2010, 2020; Goslin-Jones & Richards, 2018).

Practicing expressive arts increases self-awareness, which in turn facilitates physical, emotional, and spiritual health. Well-being serves as a catalyst for increasing authenticity, empathy, and presence with oneself and others. Engagement in expressive arts is bound to awaken your innate creativity. As your imagination and intuition are activated, you are led toward greater wholeness and the capacity to embody your higher human potential.

Chapter 2

An Invitation to the Creative
Spirit Circle Process

A circle becomes like the universe.
— Yamada Reirin

A Creative Spirit Circle is an open-ended invitation for members to gather the fibers of their inner resources and creative potential and weave them into a web of collective growth. Human beings are social animals. We need one another for comfort and love. We desire input and feedback from one another in order to learn. Young children literally need adults to survive, and older children only partially develop without adult love and attention. Teenagers depend heavily on their peers to help them grow from childhood to adulthood. As adults, we need one another to continue to step across thresholds of change and transformation to grow into more mature beings. And as we develop, we see more clearly how interdependent and co-creative the world really is. Since ancient times, writers have noted that we are fibers in the huge tapestry of life; we are connected to one another in innumerable ways. Not only that, but every action we take is really an *interaction* and may come back to us with desirable or undesirable effects.

A Creative Spirit Circle uses expressive arts to deepen individual and group exploration. Art is relational. In artmaking, we communicate our internal world to others. In a circle, we share our innermost essence with a few other souls. We are set free through the love and synergy that develops within the group. By exploring one another's stories, we are companions in the numinous on a journey of discovery. Some of us have had negative experiences with artmaking in our lives. A healthy circle can heal those wounds. One author had such an experience as a young child. Figure 4 shows her artwork in an early session, as she tentatively played with collage to describe her feelings.

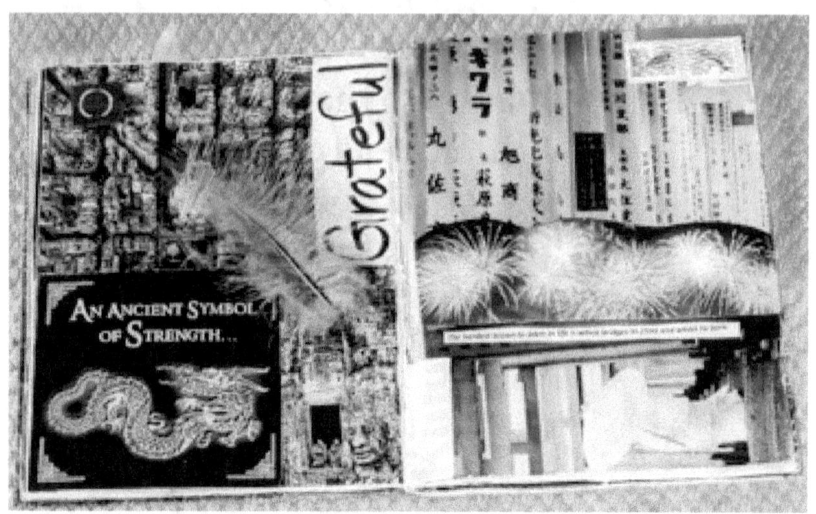

Figure 4: WOW Story, The Zen of Gratitude, collage materials, Ginger Reinert (2012).

Ginger: When I was in kindergarten, my teacher stood me in front of a large flip chart, tied an apron around me, gave me a palette of paints, and told me to paint something. I stood there and cried. I still experience dread when faced with creating art. Yet somehow, each time I manage to come up with my own piece of creativity. I know that expressive arts is not about producing a perfect example of my talents; rather, it is a deep dive into an exploration of the subconscious. I have found that collage (Figure 4), beading, and poetry work best for me when expressing myself, and I am more open to my own creative style.

As Ginger expressed, it is not about trying to erase the past but about facing it and learning to welcome it as a collaborative companion on the creative journey. She also beautifully exemplifies some key elements in transformation: openness to new experience, willingness to explore her inner self, and seeking the media and methods that work best for her. Finally, she did not transcend her past alone but in the company of fellow travelers.

There are many forms of community: family and friends, work and faith, along with innumerable interest groups. The word "circle" differentiates between a collection of people focused on a task outside themselves and an intentional collaboration among those focused on personal growth (Bolen, 1999). A circle also illustrates interconnectedness, a mutual holding together of some of the paradoxical aspects of life—being alone while being together and the fact that focusing on and sharing one's individual growth with others fuels collective evolution. A Creative Spirit Circle encourages one's hidden and sometimes wild self to emerge and integrate by providing psychological safety.

Circles are open to everyone. Rather than requiring artistic skills, the process invites you to be highly sensitive to yourself and to your peers. John O'Donohue (2000), poet and author, pointed out in his book *Eternal Echoes* that "The human heart is a theater of longing" (p. xxv). Most people desire to express multiple voices in their internal theater and to connect with the many external souls in the playhouse of life. There are joys and challenges in joining a group, whether it's a book club, a band, a poetry reading, or a circle dedicated to creativity and personal growth. If you have been part of a volunteer group or a formal work team, you likely have experienced both the positive and frustrating feelings that result from group work.

This chapter examines the natural tensions that commonly affect groups. It suggests ways to address the challenges and harness the gifts of circle work. In addition, it outlines the special needs of a group focused on creativity and personal transformation.

A Creative Spirit Circle Has Numerous Benefits

One can create alone, but it's difficult to grow as a person without being in relationship with others. There is evidence that individuals create better if there is both alone time and meaningful interaction with others (Pollack & Cabane, 2017). Human interaction is a basic human need (Baumeister & Leary, 1995) and contributes to greater contentment, faster healing, and a deeper life with more opportunity for transcendence. Strong, healthy relationships with others are vital to healthy growth and expand the potential of individuals and the group.

"Relational creativity" (Goslin-Jones, 2020, p. 479; Goslin-Jones & Richards, 2018), a central practice of this book, utilizes authenticity, empathy, originality, presence, and personal qualities to encourage openness and mutuality with others. The Person-Centered Expressive Arts (PCEA) practices introduced in Chapter 1 offer a safe and supportive environment for authentic exploration and interactions. Expressive arts create a bridge that brings forth what is inside each person so that the invisible becomes visible. Circles magnify this process because members act as mirrors for one another. Circle members witness each person's experience and provide divergent vantage points for them to consider.

Being part of a Creative Spirit Circle brings new concepts, as well as the rich life experience of each group member. The circle offers generous sustenance and encouragement from others when one feels lost or stuck. A key aspect of the circle process is witnessing each person's journey and creation. Feeling that you are truly heard and accepted allows you to share your thoughts and feelings more fully. Everyone has blind spots. Feedback from trusted circle members brings blind spots into the open. The circle sheds light on individual shadows and reflects the light and dark within us in a prism of possibilities.

Circles function best if a pair of facilitators guide each session. Co-creation is stimulating and fun. Co-facilitators meet before the group session to discuss their ideas and to plan the workshop flow. Brainstorming and planning the sessions is generative and part of the joy in our circle process. Each person brings a different style and history, and the partnership of co-facilitation produces vibrant possibilities for each circle session. Co-facilitators notice and respond to more of what is happening in the group than a single leader. Facilitators weave the group together, lacing vibrant and broken connections into a whole fabric of shared meaning. Because leadership is shared and rotates, the group grows, entwining its members into unexpected new patterns (Bethurst & Monin, 2016).

What is Personal Growth and Transformation?

Throughout this book, we use phrases such as personal growth, creative growth, conscious evolution, transformation, individual development, and spiritual growth. In modern society, these terms often refer to simply building skills or knowledge because we are already "grown-up." Expressive arts and circle work, however, follow the theories and research in the field of psychology and presume that there are stages to adult development that result in changed mindsets. Personal growth goes beyond adding new knowledge or skills to the mind as a fixed container. It's about changing the container, the way our mind works, and expanding the way we know and understand the world. This enlarges our capacity to take in and work with greater levels of complexity (Kegan, 1994).

Creativity is a path that opens us to develop to our higher potential. Creativity expert Ruth Richards identified 12 key benefits of creativity: dynamic, conscious, healthy, non-defensive, open, integrating, observing actively, caring, collaborative, androgynous, developing, and brave (Richards, 2007b, p. 290). Transformation happens when we notice new things in life that we didn't notice before, things that cause us to step back and reflect. Richards (2018) advocated: "With new discoveries, entire new areas of the creative palette (of life), once dim or hidden, can suddenly open up and become brilliant with figurative colors and possibilities" (p. 39).

As we integrate these new threads of experience, we construct decisions differently, based on our new understanding of the world. In the process of restructuring our understanding of the cosmic loom of life, we gather the braids of our own being, adapting as we go. The growth steps are usually small in nature and many in number. One of our circle members discussed the benefits of exploring her creativity within the expressive arts circle process. This is an example of one small developmental step: that of learning to attend to one's inner creative voice without needing external validation.

> In my professional work, I was quite creative, but focused on what was beneficial to my clients. In our circle, I discovered the importance of cultivating my inner creative energy. The circle offered delight in personal exploration, a new experience for me. Though it seemed like wasting time originally, I realized there was joy in creating and discovering more about myself. This led to exploring photography as a creative endeavor.
>
> As a photographer, I noticed similar patterns within myself. I rejected images because others didn't value them. Finally, I realized I don't need others' approval to know what is valuable for my creative outcomes. It doesn't matter what others think. If I allow inner creative energy to arise and be heard, it is of value to me and it may be of value to others. (Pam Caraffa, personal communication, February 1, 2022)

Such growth within our circle is made possible through the process and practices that we have adopted, described in this chapter.

The Creative Spirit Circle Process

The authors formed a Creative Spirit Circle hoping to awaken creative potential and expand their paths of spiritual development. The experiential process of our circle exceeded expectations—it was playful and joyful! Our experience was expansive, supportive, and transformative. We discovered new patterns in ourselves and new ways of weaving our lives separately and together so that we were wiser and more complete. Therefore, we named the book *Weaving Ourselves Whole: A Guide for Forming a Transformational Expressive Arts Circle.* This section describes the process we use to encourage creative expression in service of both individual and collective health and growth.

With a clear and shared intention, creative circles can be delightful and surprising. Typical tensions that arise in action-oriented groups — such as the drive for results or competition for status — may not be as prevalent when shared leadership is adopted. However, it is natural that tensions arise. For example, individuals have different needs and different learning styles. Some members may need more time for group dialogue, and other members may need greater reflection time. There may be times when some members struggle with creative expression, while other members experience a sense of freedom and want to take greater risks. Healthy groups learn to balance the energies and tensions that arise, using PCL practices.

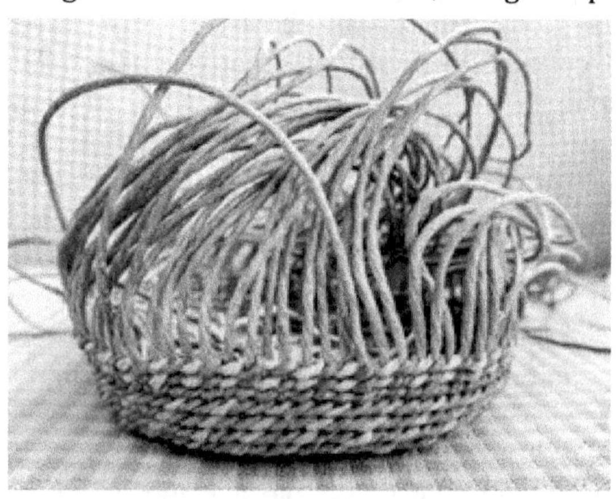

Figure 5: Author Art, A Basket Weaving Begins, waxed linen, Pam Caraffa (2018).

To continue our weaving metaphor, in weaving a basket, there are two basic types of threads. As shown in Figure 5, the structure of the basket is determined by the *warp* threads, which is the weaving term for the threads running from bottom to top.

The weaver determines the length and nature of warp threads before starting because they provide structure for the container being built. Weft means "to weave" in old English, and weft threads are those spiraling horizontally around the basket in Figure 5 in dense rows. They manifest the designs, textures, and colors of the piece and form the creative expression of one's imagination within the structure of the warp threads. As you build a basket, your energy provides the right amount of tension so that it forms a whole both strong and pliable. When the basket is finished, you cannot see the warp threads, but it would have no form and substance without them. It is the same with the need to establish a coherent relationship at the very beginning of a Creative Spirit Circle.

The Creative Spirit Circle process developed by the authors is shown in Figure 6. Our process lies within what is called an *enso* circle. We chose this metaphor because the form of the open circle is quite simple, yet the idea of creating a structure that both supports its members and is an open environment is difficult to grasp.

As a symbol, the circle is an archetype of wholeness. Enso circles are also symbols of teaching, and a metaphor for the journey toward enlightenment. They represent balance and offer a sense of completion. Yet within an enso, there is an open space for creation. There are endless unique expressions by each artist who composes one (Seo, 2007). Like an enso, the Creative Spirit Circle is an artform that has the potential to transform the way we understand ourselves and the world around us. The remainder of this chapter describes the various elements of the process contained within the Creative Spirit Circle enso.

The warp tension in a circle is called *relational tension*, illustrated in Figure 6 by the vertical bands between "Community" and "Individual." There is a natural tension between connecting with others in community and being on our own because relationships often involve challenges and individuals usually have personal insecurities. When we successfully work to balance community with our individual selves, we relax, our hearts open, and our creativity flourishes. Relationship tension addresses questions like:

- How can I express my uniqueness in this community or circle of members?
- How can I connect with circle members, so the experience is beneficial for all of us?
- How can I stay grounded and responsive to my emotions and inner world while simultaneously expanding my capacity to include more of the universe around me?
- Early in your circle experience, take time to reflect on how you feel. Are you comfortable and creative, or do you need to share a concern and allow the group to help you express more of yourself in the circle? This same approach applies to the second tension, discussed next.

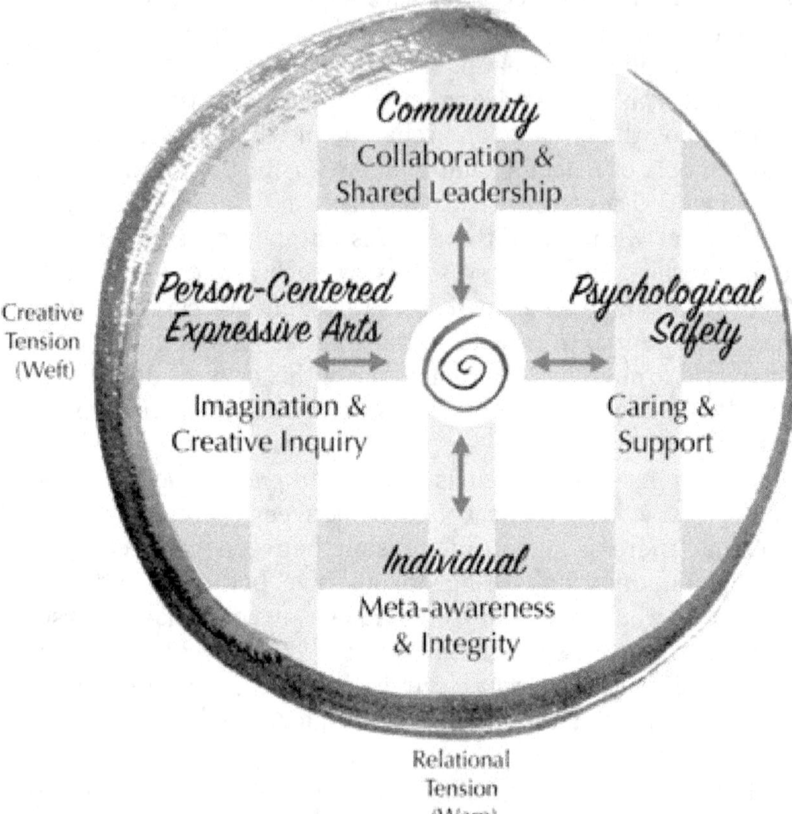

Figure 6: Creative Spirit Circle process: Personal and Circle Evolution is a Function of Working with Relational and Creative Tensions.

The weft tension, illustrated in Figure 6 by the horizontal bands between person-centered expressive art and psychological safety, is the natural "creative tension" between the pure, uncensored imagination that is within each of us and the need for sufficient psychological safety for creative energy to emerge spontaneously. Creative tension relates to such questions as:

- How can I explore the feelings, ideas, and intuitions emerging in my imagination without censoring myself? This exploration is called *creative inquiry*.
- How can I tap into my wildest ideas without losing myself?
- How can I create from my heart without being afraid of others judging me or my creation?

It takes time and experimentation for each person to find their unique response to these questions. Sometimes a person needs more safety, sometimes more wildness. Sometimes one needs to focus on being more authentic; at other times the focus may need to be on receptivity and offering support to the group.

As in a beautiful basket or tapestry, there is an art to balancing these tensions. Relational and creative tension offer new levels of awareness. Creative energy and synergy can arise from tension, and this can enhance the form and structure of the work. The circle process for the structure of the expressive arts journeys described in Chapter 3 helps each person and the collective circle find an integrative balance that expands creative expression. Over time the group members evolve as individuals and as a collective.

Relationship Tension is the Thread Between the Individual and the Circle

The tension between warp and weft threads necessary to weaving reveals the deep "both/and" character of life. It is the braiding of both the warp and the weft that makes a strong, whole basket. It is the entwining of you and me, the inclusion of each of our points of view, that moves us forward and creates something wonderful and new (Bethurst & Monin, 2016). As described previously, the warp threads in a weaving are the strands that anchor the structure. They hold a great deal of tension and are the container for the imaginative, energy-filled creation of the weft design.

The same is true of relationship tension. A Creative Spirit Circle is a community with a mutually agreed-upon purpose and set of values that weave the individual members together over time. Your circle may adopt the values described in this chapter or set your own values and behavioral norms. The values and norms established for your group provide a strong, healthy relational fabric in which creative tension can thrive and support circle relationships. We co-developed our vision, described in Chapter 4, for our Creative Spirit Circle so that we would be weaving the same overall tapestry, though each in our own unique ways. A mutually held vision has been a major contributor to our well-being and to our longevity since we established our circle in 2011. The vision and the norms guide both individual and collaborative behaviors in the circle process.

The vertical relationship tension (warp) axis of Figure 6 illustrates a balance between personal inner experience and the reality of being part of a circle. As an individual, you are responsible for learning about yourself and being true to your experience. Over time, you will learn about and practice meta-awareness and integrity and hold yourself accountable to the values agreed upon by the circle. As described in Chapter 1, meta-awareness refers to the ability to stand a bit outside of yourself and pay attention to what you are thinking, feeling, and behaving, and to observe how your behavior and presence impact others, without judgment. Mindfulness practices offer a skillful way of learning how to do this, which is why every session begins with a brief meditation. We also encourage meditation practice between sessions.

Integrity—the state of being whole and undivided—means that you endeavor to be authentic and honest with yourself and others. Of course, this is not easy when you are also attempting to grow and change. How can you be true to who you are now and who you want to become at the same time? Primarily this entails just being open and honest about conflicting thoughts, feelings, and behaviors as they arise. No one is expected to be perfect, ever. Being true to yourself involves simply doing the best you can with where you are at the present moment while honoring the experiences of others.

The well-being of your circle becomes central to you as you witness each other's journeys and experience the power of relational creativity. Members are jointly responsible for building a collaborative container that supports shared vision and values while fostering group accountability. An abundance mindset sustains a focus on personal growth and presumes there are more than enough possibilities and resources as we open our minds to see them.

An abundance mentality allows for innovative solutions to challenging situations. For example: "We can, and we will, figure this out." "There is enough (material, space, care, and love) for everyone." Threads may break as you tug too tightly, yet the flexibility of the basket and the practice of twining allows you to mend the tears and add new twists. In basketry, twining means interlacing fibers. If a fiber breaks, you add a new one by threading it into the existing weave in a seamless manner.

It can be easy for a person or a group to lose focus on personal growth and shift, for example, to simply making art or to a competition about who is most creative. The processes and structure described in this book aid in keeping the focus on creativity for the sake of individual and collective growth. Personal growth is unique, and a Creative Spirit Circle can enable you to be creative in your own way. The process offers opportunities to experiment. Your creativity will thrive with the unconscious and conscious nutrients that the group provides.

A key circle practice for creative collaboration and growth is person-centered listening (PCL; C. Rogers, 1965; N. Rogers, 1993). The purpose of PCL is to help members see and hear themselves more clearly. It is a discovery process for the person who is sharing their expressive arts experience. The practice of PCL includes the following guidelines:

1. Listening empathetically and being present for another person's expressive arts process is an honor and is sacred. You are giving the rare and precious gift of being creative mirrors for one another so that each person can see themselves more clearly.

2. You are providing the space for your circle colleague to be seen and for everyone to hear their experience for the first time.

3. Being present and using PCL is a receptive process that encompasses congruence, empathy, and unconditional positive regard (described in the Creative Spirit Circle Guidelines in the next section). Your role is to listen deeply, not to share your feedback, commentary, or personal stories.

4. PCL provides another way for the person sharing to learn from experience. As the creator shares their creation, self-reflection occurs in a way not possible if the creator did not share.

5. Ensure that a memory keeper is recording key messages that can be shared in the session notes.

A more detailed version of the person-centered listening (PCL) guidelines is in Appendix B. We recommend that you make copies of this and use the guidelines to build a culture of person-centered listening as you begin your circle.

One of the most valuable aspects of the Creative Spirit Circle is shared facilitation of meetings. It takes a while to learn how to balance the needs of both the individual and the group, as well as the creative tension between pure imagination and psychological safety. Sharing the design and facilitation of each meeting between two members enriches each session and makes the work easier. Even more, collaborative leadership recognizes that, in our biological and psychological world, individual organisms, and people, only survive when in relationship with their environment and with one another. As the environment changes, so, too, does the individual. Rachel Carson (1998) expressed this sense of interconnection in *The Edge of the Sea*:

> Nowhere on the shore is the relation of a creature to its surroundings a matter of a single cause and effect; each living thing is bound to its world by many threads, weaving the intricate design of the fabric of life. (p. 14)

No one is alone in following or leading, and circle members influence one another by virtue of being together. Each person influences the other simply by being present. This makes it impossible to know who is the weaver and who is the thread, and thus who is leading and who is following at any given time (Bethurst & Monin, 2016).

The co-leaders follow the basic structure described in Chapter 3 to design each unique experience for the whole circle. The structure and the creative modalities chosen (for example, a session might include movement, clay, and writing) help the leaders balance the relationship and creative tensions in such a way that there is a sweet spot of freedom for everyone to create and evolve into their next selves. Shared facilitation allows each member of the circle to fully participate in creative endeavors.

Creative Tension is the Thread Between Pure Imagination and Psychological Safety

Creative tension is illustrated by the horizontal threads, the weft, in a weaving design. Creativity refers most basically to any occurrence of something novel coming into being, whether that is an intuition, a feeling, an idea, or a product. Circle members focus on cultivating their individual creative force and enhancing their experience of life.

Using PCEA to balance pure imagination and creative inquiry with the psychological safety of caring and support allows creativity to emerge spontaneously without a particular goal and without judgment or censoring. The desired outcome in any expressive arts journey is that circle members engage in self-expression and explore new ways of understanding themselves and others through creative inquiry and artmaking.

We focus on the process, not the product, on expressing thoughts and feelings and building self-understanding. There is something so freeing about expressing yourself creatively with no worry whatsoever and developing an artistic creation that will not be evaluated by others. These sessions are a way to learn more about our emerging selves, for circle members to bear witness to and celebrate that emergence. While the process certainly can result in "better art" over time, that is not the intention. The purpose is to increase meta-awareness, self-reflection, and creativity for the sake of becoming a more whole human being in the midst of everyday life.

Artistic expression and creativity are fueled by immersing yourself in imagination and engaging your playful self. Use free association and whimsical observation to experiment spontaneously. The movie *Alice in Wonderland* reminds us of our potential for zaniness when Alice's father tells her, "You're mad, bonkers, completely off your head. But I'll tell you a secret. All the best people are" (Burton, 2010).

Allow yourself to shape and be shaped by your experience and artmaking in the circle sessions, to wander imaginatively to see where your heart and soul take you. In the expressive arts field, this process is called "poiesis" and implies a letting go of expectations and control to see what emerges. The experience of learning comes from the act of creating (Knill & Atkins, 2021). The creator is being re-formed through the process of creative engagement. Let go of knowing and outcome to allow your unconscious to influence you, to allow arising symbols and archetypes to point the way to undiscovered possibilities. Creative engagement includes the use of multi-modal expressive arts, life events and relationships with circle members.

A related concept, "de-centering," specifically describes the act of leaving the immediate focus of concern and entering the world of imagination to gain new perspectives about yourself (Knill & Atkins, 2021). You may cross the threshold into your circle through the de-centering process. De-focus from any immediate concern and your egoic energy, and re-focus on play and your subconscious world. As you practice re-focusing your attention, you will become more and more present to emergent thoughts and feelings without judgment. As you allow yourself to be vulnerable in your safe circle, you will become more attuned to all your senses—including intuition—and will be able to turn the high-beam lights of your curiosity onto your inner self with less fear. After you have de-centered, you may become present to your inner imagination, and poietic artmaking can occur. Allow your hands and body to follow the suggestions of your inner voice without censoring or judgment. Allow your heart and soul to weave what it will.

Then, what is called the "third" may show up, a creative work that is frequently surprising (Knill et al., 2004; Knill & Atkins, 2021). Something new emerges that is different from replicating someone else's art or making your art with a predetermined plan. Your expressive arts process is spontaneous and accesses your intuition. The image, poem, or dance that may result from the process reflects your soul at the time of creating. An artwork formed in this way may speak to you in meaningful ways if you ask what the work can tell you about yourself and your thoughts and feelings in the present moment.

Part of creative tension is paying attention to your inner life. If you focus predominantly on the creative product and external results, your energy is going outward and is likely censored based on fear and assumptions about external reactions and expectations. For example, you may ponder how you and your creation will be evaluated by circle members and perhaps others outside the circle. This frequently causes censorship and a disconnect from your inner life because the energy is going toward an external product rather than toward you as the creator and what the creation means to you. It is also possible to disconnect from your inner self by maintaining too much focus on the techniques of artmaking. In either case, your weaving may be tight and predictable. Person-centered expressive arts involve dancing with your inner life and engaging the art materials in a playful way. The art process is held lightly and used in service of exploring your internal messages and mysteries so that you weave something that speaks to you.

At the other end of the weft—the creative tension thread—an excessive focus on psychological safety tends to submerge the self that wants to evolve. When we focus on feeling secure, we tend to create what we think others may like or what we already know rather than explore what is in our hearts. It will also be difficult to develop if you only focus on the superficial, "top-of-mind" ideas you have. Loneliness arises from holding back and not expressing what is in your heart. Therefore, you and the others in the circle cannot experience your authentic self.

The paradox of safety is that it requires the courage to let go of control and surrender to the creative process. Following your heart and expressing your desires, wherever they may lead, helps you and others develop authenticity. Trust is often more of a choice and mindset than a feeling; creativity can feel like a leap of faith. The weft is meant to dance to the rhythms of your soul. The potential for creativity and growth increases when group members feel secure.

Fear is a companion of change. Everyone feels it. Sometimes fear is in the shadows, denied or ignored. Sometimes it is front and center and temporarily immobilizing. Or it may be somewhere in between. We naturally fear what we might not understand, and change is inevitably something new and hard to grasp. If you feel nervous or afraid of making artwork with others or sharing it, please know that it is completely normal to feel that way. Any personal change you make is an act of heroism because it requires a leap in the dark. Heroism is not the absence of fear, but rather the courage to act despite feelings of fear. The same can be said of someone who grows and changes.

What can you as an individual do if you feel insecure, afraid, or tense about making art as part of a circle? Some of the responsibility falls on the group itself, and there are Creative Spirit Circle guidelines (Appendix B) to support psychological safety. Some things to consider:

1. Remember that you chose to join a group that is focused on personal evolution. This is generally unsettling, so everyone is probably feeling a little uncomfortable right along with you.
2. Know that both creativity and personal evolution depend upon being open to experience. In your everyday life, try something new that you would like to do but that is slightly uncomfortable for you. Do this more frequently if you find it is helping you experience more of life. With the circle experience you could:
   a. Give yourself permission to reflect and listen to others during the first session of sharing. You can share a word about how you are feeling, or you can pass and say that you are not ready to share at this time.
   b. Take a deep breath and a smaller step in artmaking. Make a simpler artwork: for example, put together a simple collage of pictures from a magazine, make an abstract drawing of colors and/or lines that fit what you are feeling, or take a cellphone picture of something that reminds you of the session's topic.
   c. Take a deep breath and a smaller step in sharing your art: show one thing you are comfortable letting others in the group see. Then, next time, bring one thing you

> are slightly uncomfortable sharing. If you feel safe after that, share a little more the next time.

3. Be open with the group about your discomfort. Say how you are feeling. It would be surprising if others don't have the same feelings. It is likely you will find support and ideas from the others in the circle.
4. Read the short but classic book *Art and Fear: Observations on the Perils (and Rewards) of Artmaking* (Bayles & Orland, 2001).
5. If you don't feel supported, you can ask the group to discuss safety and risk taking and revisit the circle guidelines. Ask for what you need.

We invite you to experiment in the group and in your life with feelings and ideas that make you somewhat uncomfortable. Try new and different creative modalities to express your uniqueness and learn new things about yourself and the world. Become your own vibrant and highest self by tapping into what feels chaotic and give it life and voice. Balance the creative tension in the expressive arts circle with inquiries such as, "Where am I right now?" and "What in me wants to express itself?" Then hold space for whatever emerges in your circle.

The Creative Spirit Circle process emphasizes the child-like endeavor of seizing whatever is available for pure creation. All visual arts, fiber and material arts, woodworking, sculpture, music, drama, writing, and movement techniques are at your disposal to express whatever is surfacing inside you. The co-facilitators of a specific expressive arts journey will suggest and offer a combination of expressive arts processes for that session, but you may choose to alter this in a way that supports your current introspection. All expressive arts session designs are invitations only, not directives. Focus on the creative process rather than its outcome, on what's playing inside you rather than how the creation shows up externally. That means the expression may be tentative or explosive, unpredictable or confusing, lovely or ugly, complete or messy, and all these expressions are welcomed wholeheartedly as the beginning of something new or the emergence of a submerged part of yourself.

To balance all that potentially chaotic imagination and expression, psychological safety and empathy for all members are required for creative growth to occur. Trust is the primary prerequisite for creative expression because it enables you to listen without judgment to your internal voices and explore your personal creative process in relative peace and with joy. All members of the circle agree to embody the principles and practices of safety so that each individual may fearlessly turn inward and express what they have discovered to the group.

Creative Spirit Circle guidelines support both safety and creativity during the circle process. They are adapted from the PCEA guidelines developed by Natalie Rogers (1993, 2011) and informed by her father Carl Rogers' (1965) original person-centered theory of psychotherapy. You have the option to choose what supports your process. Guidelines include:

1. Everything is an open invitation. There is no right or wrong way to make art. No experience is needed.
2. Be aware of your feelings as a source for creative expression.
3. These experiences can stir up many feelings. Expressing your emotions can be helpful in releasing feelings, heightening self-awareness, and gaining new insights.
4. Be aware of your body and take care of yourself.
5. Be aware of and support the group process.
    a. Pay attention to how frequently you speak or don't speak and balance it so that everyone is contributing. Ask questions of those who are very quiet.
    b. Honor differences among circle members, including experience, backgrounds, and views, including seen and unseen diversity.
6. Use person-centered listening:
    a. Focus on yourself first. Most psychological "help" that others experience comes more from your presence, and how you embody your own personal work and less from what you do or say for others' sake. The purpose of the circle is, first, for you to grow and become more creative and, second, for you to support others doing the same.
    b. Avoid giving unsolicited advice and trying to fix one another. Focus on listening.
        i. You may ask questions for better understanding or to encourage a person to share more of themselves and their work.
        ii. If a person specifically asks for input, feedback, or suggestions, give your honest opinion in a positive way: For example, "Have you thought about… ?" rather than "Stop doing…."

    c. Practice congruence: Be the genuine and real person you are. Practice being as honest with yourself as you can about who and how you really are.

    d. Practice empathy: Everyone has a different perception of the world. Try to understand each circle member's thoughts and feelings as *they* (not you) experience them. Walk in their shoes, in the way *they* would walk.

    e. Practice giving unconditional positive regard to yourself and others: To grow and be creative, it is necessary to accept yourself as you are. To be a contributing member of an expressive arts circle, accept each member as they are. You may not approve of some of your own or others' actions, but you genuinely care for yourself and one another.

7. If you choose to observe instead of participating in a specific activity, keep an open mind and heart and honor the process of each member.

8. Everything that happens in the expressive arts circle is kept confidential.

9. If a member repeatedly ignores these guidelines or influences the group with negative behavior, the group holds them accountable quickly, firmly, and kindly. Use positive language that says what might be done rather than what not to do: "Let's listen for a while to what she has to say" or "Remember, we're here to listen to what he is experiencing; we don't need to give him any advice unless he asks for something specific" rather than "Stop interrupting" or "Don't tell someone what they should or could do."

Summary

Throughout life there is a delicate balance between individual growth and being part of a larger community. We thrive in creative immersion yet often struggle with the desire for psychological safety and support from our community. In the circle process, individual growth and community growth arise from the topics you choose to work with in your expressive arts journeys. This in turn leads to a richer and more expanded tapestry of life for each circle member, along with a deep mesh of interrelationship for the group.

Circle members share leadership: Two members co-facilitate each session. Together we fashion the warp and weft of our shared experiences. As you plan sessions, integrating PCEA facilitation practices into your design moves the group more deeply into their evolving selves. The pace of sessions will tend to be slower and more thoughtful than a typical meeting. There will be more silence. The unique interlacing between individual creativity and circle inquiry requires and yields time and space for reflection. The Creative Spirit Circle process enables members to generate something new in each session. This contemplative approach and the expressive arts process knit the creative energy that resides within you and shapes an expanded sense of self.

Chapter 3

Crossing the Threshold: Working Together

The idea in the heroic adventure is to walk bodily through the door into the world where the dualistic rules don't apply.
— Joseph Campbell, 2004, p. 114

For a Creative Spirit Circle, crossing the threshold refers to the archetypal concept of advancing into the heroic journey of mystery and a sphere of "magnified power" (Campbell, 1973, p. 77). The word *threshold* is the space in which something begins or changes. Water turns to ice below the threshold of 32 degrees Fahrenheit. A couple kiss and hold hands in the doorway of their first shared home to signal the beginning of a life committed to each other. When you cross a threshold, you move between moments in time and space, between the old and the new, the known and the unknown.

A literary example of crossing a threshold comes from the book *Lord of the Rings*, when Frodo leaves his Bag End home and the Shire, and travels to lands completely foreign to him. During circle sessions, you leave your ordinary world and cross into a creative adventure. The circle creates both a safe space and companionship for entering the inner unknown. A Creative Spirit Circle offers preparation and tools for unleashing the imagination and a place of power greater than in everyday life. You leave behind the dualistic rules Joseph Campbell mentions because you enter a both/and rather than an either/or way of thinking. You embrace paradox and contradiction.

Crossing a threshold is a numinous experience in which we welcome vulnerability and a willingness to change. Thresholds are magical because they are liminal spaces, neither inside nor outside, a third place where both/and creates a unique opportunity. Ideally, as you evolve, all of life becomes a threshold, and you become more present to each moment as it unfolds. Here's what circle member Kim McCallum shared during a 2015 session:

> As a doctor and leader, how do I get to retirement? Is my baby, my business, ready to move on without me? Our treatment center, and the nonprofit, both emerged from my passion and commitment. I enjoyed mentoring others, watching them grow. If I leave, I must accept that things will change; I will no longer continue on the same path, my vision will be diluted and altered as others guide it. Others will and should have their own view. I have much sadness but am grateful for the experience; I feel happy to create space for new passions, lucky and vulnerable as I move on and focus on letting go. I expect to learn many lessons as I shift my attention inward, outward, and onward.

This chapter is a guide to planning circle meetings and implementing norms and guidelines as your group develops. A specific framework underlies every session which, along with the principles and practices described in the first two chapters, enables safe and creative passage through emotional territory and across both exciting and challenging boundaries. Like the strong warp threads in a basket, the framework is held stationary, while the experience and meaning (the weft threads) of each session vary greatly. This framework aids in cultivating individual and communal creativity. When you consistently meet as a group, the circle process and framework expands your individual and collective capacity for journeying inwardly.

Forming Your Creative Spirit Circle

When forming a circle, consider inviting 5–8 members. The only requirements for participating are a desire to create and to grow as a person. A small number allows each person to contribute meaningfully to the group dialogue portions of each session, while also making it easier to find individual space for each person to create during the expressive arts journey portion of your sessions. Finally, because your group is more than just your meetings together, a small group allows you to hold dear your circle's individual and collective relationships within the larger sphere of your lives.

How Do You Create the Right Group of Members?

An expressive arts group can be organized in all stages of life. Diversity of experience, gender, race, sexual orientation, religion, and physical ability contribute to developing new perspectives and enriching the group's experience. Group members do not need to be artists or creative professionals to participate. They may come together based on common interests such as student life, parenting, co-workers, social activism, and their mutual desire to express creativity and explore their greater potential.

The authors' Creative Spirit Circle was formed based on our shared professional interests in psychology, consciousness studies, and a desire to use expressive arts for personal growth and transformation. We did not all know one another when our group formed. Two members participated in Terri Goslin-Jones's, PhD, *Creative Living Circle* coaching process, launched in 2011. After this experience, there was a desire to develop an ongoing expressive arts circle where members would share the planning, leadership, and co-facilitation roles. Through informal networking, we formed our circle of six members that has continued to meet for over twelve years.

In the circle process, everyone's thoughts and wishes are included, and the group arrives at mutual goals and a shared vision for the future. This need not be complicated; during one of your first circle gatherings, you can discuss and develop your vision. Chapters 4 and 5 offer a process for developing your personal vision and a vision for your group.

A circle vision can be very rough and tentative at first and develop over time as the group evolves and comes to know itself. Don't be concerned if you only have vague agreements or only a few ideas and clumsy language during the first meeting. Your vision will become more complete as your circle gains experience and becomes more interconnected. If your vision seems fuzzy to you, consider having a second vision session after several more meetings.

Creative Spirit Circle Vision Example
The authors developed the following Circle Vision in 2011, and it is still active today:

> We will embody a collaborative, generative process that reflects shared leadership. Our creative spirit circle will use expressive arts to access deeper levels of our creative potential. Together we will engage in an infinity circle that embraces, develops, and launches our creative potential into the world.

Frequency, Location, and Time for Circle Sessions
Two early decisions for your new circle include the frequency and length of sessions. The authors meet roughly 5–8 times each year for a half-day for our expressive arts journeys. Each expressive arts journey is generally 3.5–4 hours to accommodate the framework outlined below. This includes 20–30 minutes of social interaction at the beginning of each meeting. Over the last five years or so, we have read roughly two books together each year and met over dinner for a dialogue about the books and their impact on us. Book discussions have enriched and expanded the topics for our circle meetings.

The place and frequency of meetings must also be established. The group should agree on a time and rotating location for your circle meetings. Balance the facilitation and hosting among your circle members across meetings. Planning for circle meetings includes details such as snacks, art supplies, topics, and meeting location. The authors have, so far, enjoyed sessions hosted in their homes as well as incorporating creative exploration in gardens, a zoo, a museum, a place of worship, and a labyrinth.

How We Prepare and Structure Our Time Creating Together

The subject matter for each circle meeting is tailored to the collective interests of the group. In a fascinating way, each topic organically opens new channels of exploration for circle members. Prior to the circle gathering, two people volunteer to co-lead the session on a topic they think would be provocative for the circle. Within a couple of years, you may have a list of desired topics and volunteers and your decision process may become more organic, choosing what best suits your evolving desires for growth. You may also find yourself creating several sessions on one theme.

Facilitators choose forms of artistic expression that complement the topic of the session. For a session to be truly multi-modal, you may have 3–5 artistic modes in play each time, such as movement, sculpture, music, and writing. Meditation and writing typically occur in every session, as they provide a fruitful vehicle for inner reflection and then documenting what emerged during the session. Circle members are encouraged to keep a journal of their writing and artwork and to take photographs of artwork from each session. Every expressive arts journey unfolds in a unique way depending on the topic. For instance, our Mindfulness and the Artful Journey session

(Chapter 8) uses a sensory-rich tea ceremony, drawing, movement, sandtray sculpture, and writing as modes of creative expression.

The facilitators develop the circle plan and general guidelines, introduced to the group as possibilities and invitations. The workshop topics provided in Chapters 4–16 offer examples to inspire your group's creativity. These sessions can be adapted and customized or may generate new areas of focus for your group.

Before Each Circle Session

Facilitators plan each session ahead of time, including the written handouts, materials, and the physical layout for the experience. A week or more in advance of the meetings, they email an agenda and suggestions for contemplation, generally including the creative inquiries described later in this chapter. Sometimes the leaders/facilitators provide a short introduction to the topic in the email, especially if the topic is complex and members might need time to ponder possible artistic expression and supplies to bring.

The facilitators think through every aspect of the experience so they can offer multiple modalities of expression and sensation to support the theme. They also request a volunteer to be the memory keeper, the person who takes notes during the check-in and conscious closure portions of the meeting (described below). Someone takes photographs of the artwork created during the session and of the session itself and includes them with the notes. These notes and photographs have proved essential to amplifying the impact of a session and for keeping a journal as a collective memory of Creative Spirit Circle experiences.

For example, a session entitled The Queen Within included a field trip to the International Chess Hall of Fame, which had an exhibit on the queen game piece, her history, forms, and stories. The facilitators sent information on the exhibit ahead of time, along with a page of information on the archetypal role of the queen in human history. The circle met at the host's home near the exhibit and began the session there. They walked to the museum to view the exhibit together and then returned to the host's home for the expressive arts journey, which included creating a crown as artmaking. One member took several photographs of the exhibit and of each member's artmaking process that explored the archetypal energy of the queen. The memory keeper took notes, gathered the collection of photographs, and sent a summary to everyone after the meeting.

Gathering Together
When you plan your circle meetings, you may want to schedule the first 30 minutes to socialize, connect with each other, chat, and share food or a beverage. Even though this is an informal time, it is the beginning of the sensory and psychological experience. For instance, facilitators may greet circle members with certain artifacts to be used that day. Choose special music and play it in the background. Consider what other senses you may want to stimulate with aromas, sights, touch, or taste.

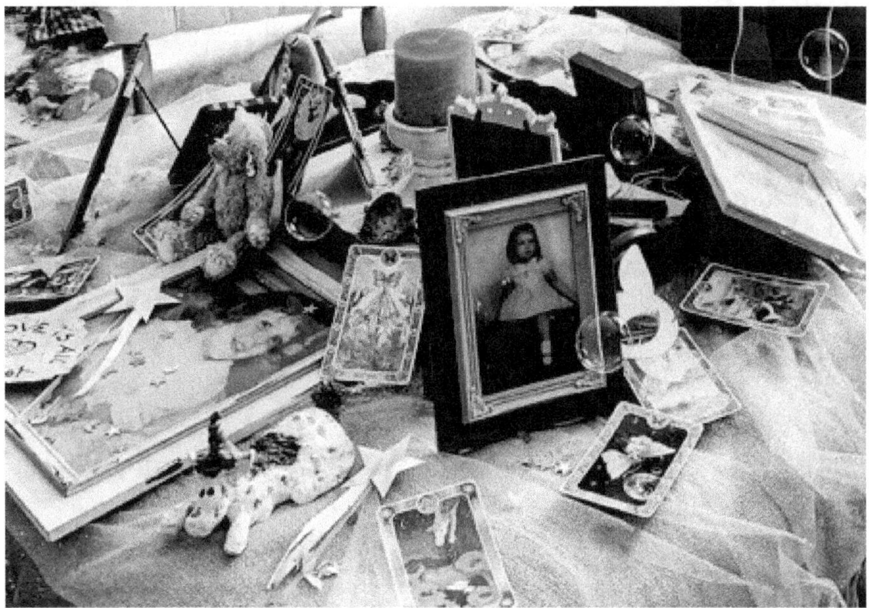
Figure 7: Most sessions have a centerpiece or altar for candles and symbols of the topic.

Often, a centerpiece or altar is created, around which to share the opening ritual and creative inquiries portion of the session. Figure 7 shows the altar created for the Wonderment session. The authors brought photographs and other childhood tokens. We blew bubbles to evoke a playful mood; one is in the top right corner. As you gather and connect during the first part of your circle, you leave the cares of your day and the world behind. This is an opportunity to reconnect with other circle members and shift your mindset toward imagination.

Session Framework

Every session uses the same framework, and each section of a session has a specific purpose in forming a rich and creative experience for everyone. We invite you to use this framework consistently, not only to make the work of designing a session easier, but also to allow its ritual use to entrain you. Being entrained means that you synchronize, or fall into a comfortable rhythm, with something. This enables you to relax because you know what the experience will be like in its structure. The familiar rhythm draws you to become entranced, fully attentive to, and excited by what the topic means to you. Each section of the circle framework includes a description, along with a rough allotment of time. While there will be at least one example given for each section below, Chapters 4–16 are full of additional ideas to inspire you.

Intention and Purpose

At the beginning of the session, the facilitators share the desired outcomes in a way that invites immersion into the subject matter. When members have a good sense of what the session will be like, it is easier to relax and fully engage. In a recent session entitled Wild, Wonderful Water, a facilitator said:

> Our intention is to become aware of water and attend to its role in our lives. Water is a vital part of the earth and of us. During this time, we will focus on the impact and meaning water has on our lives and on our being. What role does water play in your life right now? What emotional meaning does it have for you? How can observing and experiencing water guide you in your personal evolution?

Invariably, sharing the topic elicits a few comments and questions from circle members, so 5–10 minutes may be needed to complete this section of the session.

Creative Inquiries

We suggest co-facilitators write several questions to engage members in the session topic. These questions may be sent out ahead of time with the announcement of the session to stimulate thinking, feeling, and imagination around the theme. These questions are also listed in the handout shared during the session. For example, Wild, Wonderful Water questions included the following:

- What was your first experience of water?
- Think about a meaningful experience with water.
- Where are you frozen or washed out?
- Are there places where you may be overflowing?
- Where are you flowing free?

This part of the framework usually takes 2–3 minutes per person as members have had a chance to read and think about the questions before the session.

Introduction

So much of daily life can separate us from the whole of our being as we endeavor to complete tasks and fulfill needs. This part of the session invites your heart, mind, body, and spirit to join in the circle. The co-facilitators might briefly clarify the meaning of the topic using a poem or quote. Or they might offer a brief exercise that invites everyone to join into the spirit of the theme in a more visceral way. For Wild, Wonderful Water, members were invited to stand in a circle and use a small spray bottle to sprinkle water on one another and extend a greeting, "Welcome to our watery world."

During this time, the co-facilitators provide an overview of art supplies and logistical considerations. Circle members can begin imagining how they might enter their personal expressive arts journey later in the session. Allow about 5–10 minutes for this section.

Opening Ritual & Invitation

This section utilizes rituals to welcome every aspect of ourselves more fully to the experience. Facilitators may light candles at this time or invite members to move or dance freely, to use drumming or drawing—anything to help circle members enter the creative space and invoke creative energy. Opening rituals serve the same function as preparing a loom for weaving or choosing and preparing the materials from which you might make a basket. Rituals that involve moving your hands and/or body are especially powerful to ready yourself for an imaginative engagement. This is a good time to embody the purpose of your session and to create an environment conducive to energetically embrace the topic for a few hours.

While conceptual engagement in the topic is important, having a sense of your emotional and bodily response is just as vital. Energy psychology is a relatively new field focused on well-known evidence in physics that everything in the universe is energy and that energy is always moving, though sometimes so slowly it can only be detected by the most sensitive scientific instruments. We humans contain that same energy within our own bodies, minds, and emotions. Our biological and neurological systems operate with minute currents of energy and are influenced by the energy of both other humans, creatures, and larger social and environmental elements (Feinstein & Eden, 2008). Our bodies are like scientific instruments, exquisitely attuned to energy of all kinds. This new knowledge helps us understand that activating all our senses can develop energetic pathways that connect us to and expand our creative potential.

This is the benefit of the intermodal expressive arts process. A multi-sensory experience may include meditation, visualization, music, movement, and visual arts. The topic comes alive for each member. For example, in the circle session on Wild, Wonderful Water, members were invited to engage their five senses and experience four forms of water to engage their senses. They listened to the sound of a brook, watched a video of waves, smelled and tasted water, and felt liquid, frozen, and vaporous water. This activated many memories for each person. Allow about 5–10 minutes for this.

Check-In

During this time, invite each person to share their thoughts about the topic or a relevant aspect of it. Members could, for instance, share an answer to a creative inquiry that captivated them. Sharing one's thoughts aloud in a group is a significant way of engaging with the topic. Frequently, you will hear yourself say something you didn't pay attention to before you said it, or you may have an idea that would not have previously occurred to you.

The memory keeper will take notes of what is shared by each person in this section and in the conscious closure section. Note-taking is another form of deep witnessing. It can be quite powerful to read what you said. So much happens during the session, and reflecting after the fact on your experience and on what was shared frequently brings fresh perspective. Allow about 2–3 minutes per person, or 15–20 minutes total for this.

Lecturette

For some sessions, you will know the topic well and only need a common framework for your discussion. For instance, we had a meeting about Love Connections. We all intuitively knew what we were talking about with this topic. But language may be used differently, so the facilitators wrote a two-page description, sent out ahead of time, of the different types of love—agape, romantic, filial, etc.—so that we could all speak the same language of love in our conversation. During the meeting, the facilitators quickly reviewed those pages and asked and answered a few questions.

At other times, the topic may be new to all or some of the group and require more explanation. For instance, as described in Chapter 9: Dreams and Individuation, some members knew more about dreams than others, so the facilitators emailed a written handout ahead of time for the group to read. Then during the session, they spent about 30 minutes in a dialogue to ensure a basic understanding about dreams and individuation. Allow 15–30 minutes for this section.

We encourage you to expand on the Lecturettes offered by the authors in each chapter. Include your own inspiration, readings, and creative musings. The research that supports each workshop topic is a meaningful and creative part of the planning process.

Crossing the Threshold

At this point in the session, members are invited to transition from the group experience to a personal inner journey via a brief mindfulness meditation. The authors frequently create their own mindfulness meditations to invite members into the present moment of their awareness of the topic at hand. You may want to create your own meditations, and any of the meditations described in this book may be adapted to your purposes.

You may also invite members to choose from among a number of quotes or sayings, or to randomly choose a card from a deck of animal totem cards, god or goddess cards, lines of poetry, astrological cards, and the like to act as a catalyst for the imagination. This portion of the session allows us to cross over our expressive arts threshold as mindfully and with as much heart and spirit as possible. Allow 10–20 minutes for this element.

Expressive Arts Journey

Description. Give your circle members an explanation of how they might work with the materials and supplies provided. For instance, we chose watercolor as the artmaking material for Wild, Wonderful Water. The facilitators invited members to make a picture that illustrated their current relationship with water. They could use watercolor alone or combine it with collage materials. They could also use different materials brought from home, such as photographs or sculpture materials.

Materials and Supplies. Each session will have its own needs for materials and supplies. Facilitators may provide basic materials and supplies relevant for their session or invite members to bring what they want to work with. Chapters 4–16 each contain examples of what might be used. For instance, if drawing is the primary mode of expression, you may provide paper and a collection of colored pencils, crayons, or other markers. In the TV show *Star Trek: Next Generation*, Season 6, Episode 7, the character Guinan said, "That's the wonderful thing about crayons. They can take you to more places than a starship."

Guidelines and Process. Offer guidelines and a flexible structure. For instance, you might suggest using the outside of a shoe box to convey how members think they appear to others, and the inside of the box to convey how they feel on the inside. You may invite members to work with materials in a specific way but, as noted previously, they always have the option to follow their intuition and modify the guidelines.

Artmaking. The expressive arts journey and conscious closure are the heart of your time together as a group. Everything else is preparation. Facilitators prepare a place for each person to sit and work, either at a table on their own or with others, or in separate spaces or rooms. All members respect each other's privacy and focus silently on their own work. Facilitators set up art supplies on a table for easy access and allow each person to select the materials they desire.

When you begin your artmaking process, allow ideas and expression to flow without censorship. Seek what your heart and spirit want to share. *Shosin* or "beginner's mind" (Suzuki, 2006) is a useful practice at this point. That is, allow your mind to be open as if you were just starting to learn a new subject. You may discover parts of yourself that rarely communicate. Express and explore what is emerging from your body, heart, mind, and/or spirit. Use the materials at hand in whatever way comes to you. Don't worry about whether your artwork will be complete by the end of the allotted time. You are simply expressing yourself, so whatever shows up is valuable. Knitters will tell you that they frequently leave with the sweater half done! And remember what Maya Angelou (1982) said: "You can't use up creativity. The more you use, the more you have" (p. 34). Allow 45–60 minutes for artmaking.

Writing Reflection. Facilitators invite everyone to use the last 10–15 minutes of individual time to reflect and write on their artmaking experience, to mark and digest what has happened so that they remember and integrate it. Frequently, the facilitators will offer writing prompts, which members have the option of using. There are times when poems and insights arise from the expressive arts journey. Members will be invited to share some of their experience during conscious closure (see below) as this will also help ensure memory and insight. Yet it is beneficial for each member to personally reflect before interaction with the group. Allow about 15 minutes for writing.

Conscious Closure and Integration

During conscious closure, you will return to your circle with your partial or completed artwork and written notes. Private time for exploration is essential, and so is sharing what you have experienced and learned. Members take turns, for roughly 8–10 minutes each, sharing their artmaking experience and insights about the overall session. For instance, during one of our conscious closure sessions, one of our members spoke about her creation (Figure 8):

> **Holly:** I am amazed by the power of creating collectively. I feel like this exercise has been a beautiful container for my creativity to flow. I made a string of prayer beads for meditation (Figure 8). It's a metaphor for the spiritual journey. As I created it, I thought of a moving river and how this is a metaphor for Spirit. It flows from the edges to the center.

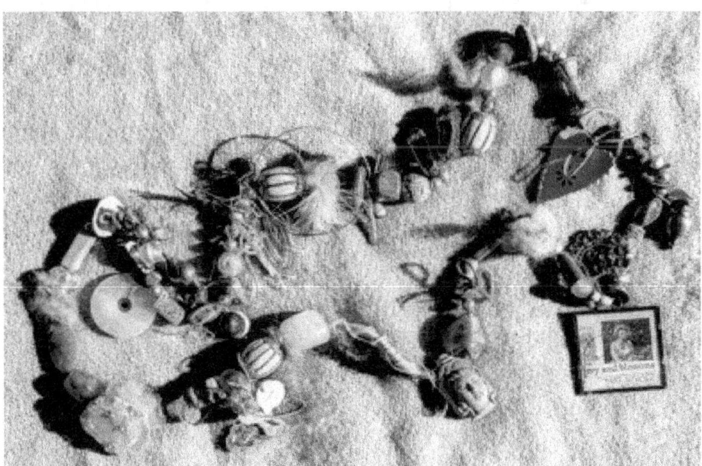

Figure 8: WOW Story, River Spirit, mixed media, Holly Carson (2011).

A variety of artwork emerges from expressive arts journeys. While Holly made prayer beads, others made a symbolic wall hanging, necklace, or talisman. During conscious closure, you may show your creation, discuss your creative process, or talk about insights or learnings from the artmaking experience. Group members may have a lot to share or only a little. Members listen nonjudgmentally and bear witness to the person who is sharing. The listeners hold space for you to be seen and to hear you share your experience for the first time, which may add its own insights. You are sharing something close to your heart, something about the current "edge" of your growth as a person. This is not a casual conversation. It requires generous sharing and generous listening. Ensure that the memory keeper takes a few notes regarding what each person shares. The notes are distributed to all members after the meeting and frequently inspire further creative expression. The group dialogue adds an additional layer of discovery and insight.

There may be times during your expressive arts journey, that you move through mystical moments. Mystical states include an experience of unity, transcendence, or an experience of sacred presence. The circle provides a safe, welcoming, and supportive group container for transformative experiences. At the end, thank each person for sharing. Close your meeting with a planned ritual such as reading a poem, blowing out candles, and/or another type of brief closing ritual that suits the topic. Allow about an hour for conscious closure.

In summary, the timing of each section of a session varies. Develop a plan with estimated times for each topic and reserve at least 3 hours. Use the agenda as a guideline; at the same time, it's best not worry too much about the exact time and allow things to evolve. If a session ends up with little time for conscious closure, then the group learns to adapt the earlier portions of future meetings accordingly so that the expressive arts journey and conscious closure sections have sufficient time.

Creative Weavings

During the session share handouts that offer suggestions for personal integration of the topic. Handouts can be shared even after the session has ended. Sometimes the art created during the expressive arts journey is complete. Sometimes further imaginative expression emerges after the session. Often, the impact of the session continues for days or weeks afterwards. You are invited to include a few bullet points with ideas for circle members on how to continue to work with the topic. Each of the expressive arts journey chapters suggests ways to weave the session focus into daily life.

After the Meeting
The memory keeper completes the notes, gathers photographs of the artwork and the experience, and combines them into an email to send out after the session. This maintains a journal record of your sessions: the topic, who facilitated, the art modalities utilized, notes, and photographs. When you read the circle notes, surprises can show up and frequently inspire further creative expression.

Surveys

Surveys and short written questionnaires (Appendix E) are a way to gather individual views about circle experiences and future topics. A survey and questions are offered in the addendum to explore your circle's structure, process, and practices. It is beneficial to periodically offer a brief questionnaire to ascertain what is working, what might need to change, and to discern circle members' desires for the future. This allows the group to continually refresh and re-energize the process and framework. Feedback from circle members provides information to guide the group in designing generative and meaningful meetings over many years.

Summary

Expressive arts journeys incorporate multiple senses and forms of awareness—what Daniel Siegel (2018) calls "The Wheel of Awareness." In each session, you access some or all five senses of touch, taste, smell, sight, and hearing. You may even tap into your "sixth sense" of awareness of the interiority of your body and your "seventh sense" of awareness of your mental activities—thoughts, feelings, memories, intuitions—through meditation and mindfulness. Finally, you may visit your "eighth sense" of awareness: your interconnectedness with circle members, others, and nature. Creative expression engages your whole body, heart, mind, and spirit. Expanding your "Wheel of Awareness" to include all eight senses enables creative expression to be a superhighway to personal growth.

The remaining chapters in this book are framed as expressive arts journeys and follow the format outlined in this chapter. The first two,

Chapters 4 and 5, are journeys to help circle members describe the vision for their individual participation in the circle and then develop a collective vision for the circle as a whole. The other chapters describe a variety of expressive arts journeys you may use or modify for your group.

Chapter 4

Weaving a Personal Vision for Creative Living

It is up to us to re-enchant this planet earth. Up to us to midwife at our own re-birth.
— Will Ashe Bacon

Intention and Purpose

In the previous chapters person-centered expressive arts and an overview of the Creative Spirit Circle process were discussed. This chapter launches your first expressive arts journey and focuses on developing a personal creative expression that can be used for growth, transformation, and even transcendence. When you think of joining a Creative Spirit Circle, what do you imagine is possible? Why are you in this circle? You may have a clear idea, or you may simply be curious about ways you might tap into your fuller potential. In this expressive arts journey, you will investigate creativity in multiple areas of your life and imagine how you might develop as a person.

In his book *Transcend: The New Science of Self-Actualization,* psychologist Scott Barry Kaufman (2020) discussed how moving toward wholeness and full realization of our potential is an "ongoing journey of discovery, openness, and courage in which you reach higher and higher levels of integration and harmony within yourself and the outside world" (p. 257). A Creative Spirit Circle provides a process and pathway to pursue the integration and journey toward self-actualization described by Abraham Maslow (1998) and later expanded upon by Kaufman (2020). The characteristics of self-actualization are grouped into four categories: exploration, love, purpose, and transcendence. This movement toward growth requires ongoing exploration throughout life.

Abundant imagination and synergy are likely to emerge within a creative spirit circle devoted to exploration for the purpose of transformation. While personal growth in early levels of adult development may be largely individual, higher levels of adult development require multifaceted dialogue and relationships with others. Bill Joiner and Stephen Josephs (2006) described the early levels of personal growth as "heroic" in nature because desires are based on individual needs for belonging and on group safety, expertise, or success. After those early individual capabilities are established, the "post-heroic" levels focus on learning how to navigate and respond to an interconnected world with wisdom and compassion.

A Creative Spirit Circle can aid growth at each level, informing and supporting individual development at earlier levels, while cultivating and enabling interdependent growth at later levels. An example of early growth is learning to welcome another's different view of the world and even feedback about your behavior without becoming defensive. This can be a difficult step for anyone and is eased by a supportive group. Different worldviews can expand possibilities.

An example of advanced growth is being able to respond to feelings in the moment rather than realizing later what was happening. Perhaps you were thinking about plans for the day or what you were going to share with the group and at the same time noticed one of your circle members was withdrawn and sad. At an early level of growth, you may have been unaware of those sad feelings and remained focused on the task. But now you notice the sadness after the fact and go back to ask your friend how she or he is feeling. Eventually, you learn to attend to and ask about those feelings the moment they occur. It's not just the outcome of something that's important, but how you interact with others and respond to their journey.

Chapters 4–16 follow the format described in Chapter 3. Since this is your initial session, here are suggestions for how to begin.

Facilitators/Leaders

Choose two circle members to serve as facilitators/leaders. The facilitators will plan and host the Creative Spirit Circle, as well as distribute the agenda. This session for Weaving a Personal Vision for Creative Living includes reading material and some questionnaires for circle members to complete before they gather.

Prework: Ask participants to read the following passages and complete the following exercises prior to the personal vision session.

1. Read *Weaving Ourselves Whole*: Chapters 1–4.
2. Complete the Creative Living Plan© (CLP), Appendix D. You will be invited to share parts of your CLP with circle members in this first session.
3. Bring a symbol that has special meaning for you and represents your intention or focus for your CLP© (e.g., a stone, shell, paintbrush, photo, spiritual symbol, or quote).

Creative Inquiries

- What is your current "lifework"? What legacy do you want to leave the world?
- What change(s) would you like to see in your life in the next year and beyond?
- When do you experience your greatest sense of vitality and creativity?
- What practices connect you to your higher self, to a higher power, to divine energy?
- If anything were possible, what would you be experiencing in your life and in this Creative Spirit Circle?

Introduction

The first part of this circle session focuses on your individual journey using the Creative Living Web, Creative Life Map, and CLP©. This is a process to weave together a personal vision for a more creative and fulfilling life.

- Creativity is rooted in the daily experience of being a co-creator, family member, friend, spiritual seeker, lifelong learner, and worker in the world. The Creative Living Web process, Figure 9, will help you develop your *whole* self. As you explore the Creative Living Web, you are invited to think about a personal vision for your life and consider how your circle can support each member. Some circle members may want to explore every dimension of the Creative Living Web while others may be drawn to one or two areas. What resonates with you as you consider each area? If nothing comes to mind, you can leave one of the areas blank or reflect for a while to see if something emerges.

- **Family Life**: How could you strengthen family bonds? For example, do you want to deepen relationships with family members by supporting members in various life stages such as graduation, birth, relocation, marriage/divorce, retirement, or eldercare?

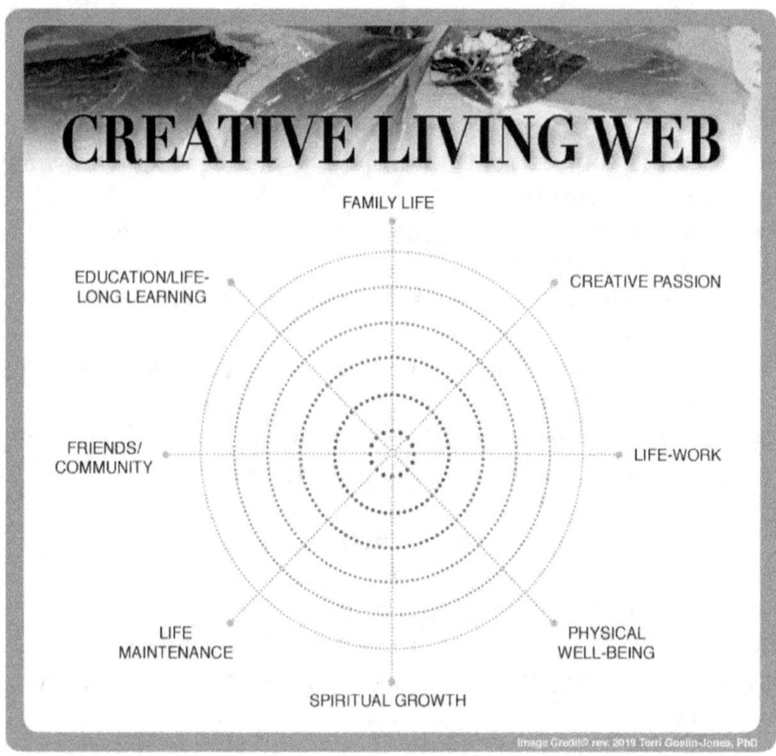

Figure 9: Creative Living Web (Note: Copyright Goslin-Jones [2011/2020], *Encyclopedia of Creativity*)

- **Creative Passion**: Develop or revise a plan for a form of creative expression. What endeavor(s) would you most like to try (e.g., playing music, improvisation, innovative thinking, building a boat, hiking/mountain climbing, horticulture, sailing/surfing, writing poetry or a novel, travel, social activism)?
- **Lifework**: What is important in your work life? Choosing a field of work? Completing a degree? Finding a new work role? Life–work balance? Being a full-time parent?

- **Physical Well-being**: Develop or revise a plan for exercise, nutrition, sleep, and overall emotional and physical well-being. What does your body currently need?
- **Spiritual Growth**: Cultivate a spiritual practice such as mindfulness, acts of compassion, gratitude, prayer/meditation, or silent retreats.
- **Life Maintenance**: Maintain mental well-being while caring for your finances, home, transportation, and belongings. Develop a plan for managing the details of your life.
- **Friends/Community**: Identify priorities and commitments to support your friends and community. Is your social life working well for you? Do you feel supported by and supportive of others?
- **Education/Life-long Learning**: Are you planning for further formal education? Would you like to learn new skills such as community gardening, fly fishing, poetic medicine, how to play a musical instrument, digital literacy, college degree(s), or advanced certifications?

During this first Creative Spirit Circle, you have an opportunity to learn more about one another through the lens of creative exploration. Consider the facets of your life you would like to include in your personal vision for the next few years. How can circle members support one another's visions? What would enable you to deepen relationships with the other members of your circle? The power of your circle can assist you in your creative journey toward self-actualization.

Opening Ritual and Invitation

Prepare a low table or bench that serves as an altar, centerpiece, or shrine where group members sit during the session. Add symbols that will be important to your group. For example, flowers symbolize connection to nature. Small figures or statues represent community. A universal symbol such as a sculpture of the sun, moon, and/or the Earth brings nature into the circle. Candles bring light to the darkness and represent opportunities and openings. Provide a candle for each group member and ask them to light it. Invite the members to place symbols of their personal creative focus/intentions on the altar.

Check-In

Person Centered Listening: Let Your Life Speak
Invite each person to share parts of their Creative Life Map© with
another circle member using person-centered listening (Appendix B).
Discuss the summary highlights with a partner. For example, give an
example of how you are weaving life lessons into wisdom. What
overall themes emerged in your map? Listen to one another with
openness, empathy, and curiosity.

Lecturette: Appreciative Inquiry and Your Creative Living Vision
This section introduces the process of Appreciative Inquiry, which
facilitators can share with the group. What is Appreciative Inquiry and
how does this inform your Creative Spirit Circle? The basic
assumption of Appreciative Inquiry, developed by David Cooperrider
(2017), is that life is a web of strengths linked to infinite capacity.
Imagination enlivens possibilities. We are alive, dynamic, and
transformed moment to moment. As George Bernard Shaw reminds
us, "Life isn't about finding yourself; life is about creating yourself."

Appreciative Inquiry is used as an exploratory process to focus on
strengths rather than weaknesses and to look for the best in people
and groups. Ask questions like "Which potentialities within me do I
most wish to spend my limited time cultivating, developing, and
actualizing in this world?" (Kaufman, 2020, p. 258). Appreciative
inquiry can be used in conjunction with your Creative Living Plan to
develop your potential in the following ways:

1. **Appreciate** the best of what is. Envision the greatest potential
    of your life right now and the positive impact this could have
    on your Creative Spirit Circle and your community.
2. **Imagine** what might be. Envision a valued and vital future that
    is grounded in your creative potential.
3. **Dialogue and Design** what could be. Select one or two areas
    from your Creative Living Web that will launch your vision and
    dialogue about your plan within your Creative Spirit Circle.
4. **Create** what will be. Use arts-based inquiry and expressive
    arts to enliven and embody a new way of being.

You can use appreciative inquiry and your Creative Living Web to
consciously create your life and grow into your fuller potential. This
process offers a wholesome way to use your strengths to explore

challenges and vulnerabilities that naturally arise. A provocative proposition for your life can bring your fullest potential into your vision: A provocative proposition is a statement that bridges the best of "what is" with your intuition of "the best of what might be" (Cooperrider, 2017; Cooperrider & Whitney, 2005). It is provocative because it moves you past what you know, questions your assumptions, and imagines transformative possibilities to bring your desired future to life. "Why do I choose to be here? What will I bring to this group?" You may choose to formulate a proposition for the next year or so, or you may focus on one or two areas described in the Creative Living Web.

Creative Spirit Circle Author Example of Provocative Proposition
The Creative Living Web© and circle process emerged from the provocative proposition that Terri Goslin-Jones (1999) developed while offering Waking Up workshops using Appreciative Inquiry and arts-based inquiry processes. While any provocative proposition may push you out of your comfort zone, one that is focused on your overall life may cause you to re-examine and change your life in some major way.

Developing a provocative proposition is spurred by a desire for growth and development. We offer the following example of evolving consciousness as one possibility. This provocative proposition planted the seeds for the Creative Spirit Circle process, and over the years evolved into this collaborative book. Our circle process and book are examples of what may emerge when a group joins together to envision and co-create their dreams. We understand that most people may choose a simpler and narrower proposition. Start in the place that feels right to you.

Premise: Consciousness is evolving at lightning speed.

Question: What if it was possible to understand each person's perspective and soul and use what is emerging from each person's life to grow universal peace, love, understanding, and beauty?

Provocative Proposition for My Life:
My work and life have grown from a seed and a glimmer of understanding that each person's life is a unique and colorful piece of fabric in the quilt of humanity. Our world needs each

perspective, color, texture, and thread to create the strength, the creativity, and the resilience of humanity.

I am a thought leader and an explorer in this quest. I am a pathfinder. It is my job to discover the wisdom and creativity in every individual that I encounter, to unleash the deepest purpose for living and evolve the human spirit. I will bring life to this provocative proposition every day of my life (Goslin-Jones, 1999).

As this example illustrates, a provocative proposition (a) stretches and challenges you, (b) invokes possibility while remaining grounded in reality, (c) excites you, and (d) offers a positive, life-affirming stance. It is your vision for the most enticing and meaningful way you will engage with your future.

Formulating Your Provocative Proposition

Before you join your circle in this first session, draft a tentative provocative proposition that represents (a) your focus on a specific aspect of your Creative Living Web or (b) an aspiration/hope you desire from engaging with your circle. For example, it may be that you personally want to focus on a healthy lifestyle. Someone else may want to develop a new area of interest such as music or learning another language: "Within the next year, I will develop and express my love of music in new ways. This might include taking music lessons, joining a band, or writing my own songs." Another example: "Within the next six months, I will be more in tune with my body. I will be more fit and regularly enjoy nature. I will bicycle 10–15 miles on local cycling trails and enjoy how my body feels."

Alternatively, you may wish to imagine the overall potential for your life. If anything were possible, what would you be experiencing in your life? Use this session to imagine how your circle could help you formulate your life's provocative proposition. Whichever way you choose to go, you can explore and expand your creative potential over time using expressive arts and your Creative Living Plan.

When formulating your provocative proposition, ponder and respond to the following questions:

1. What is your premise? What is your greatest desire for a creative life? How would you like to expand yourself now?
2. What if it were possible? What would be the impact on you and on others?

3.   Describe your provocative proposition for your life.

WOW Stories

The following are personal vision examples from the authors' first Creative Spirit Circle in 2011. As time went by, we developed a personal vision at the beginning of each year. Some members developed a provocative proposition (Goslin-Jones, 1999) while others preferred to use a word or phrase to illustrate their vision. The statements below are notes from our very first meeting and describe where we started. This expanded over the years.

Nancy: Use creativity to find and get back in touch with new parts of myself. Participate in a circle to connect to others in more intimate ways.

Pam: At this point in my life, I have found it helps to share and receive feedback from others. So, I want to be part of a group to cultivate being more present and compassionate in the world and to express myself in new ways.

Ginger: To use expressive arts to focus on finding a new richness in my life. My intention is to find peace, *to be*, to slow down. I want to find completion on a personal level.

Holly: I want to use creativity to reconnect with myself, and with my spirituality, and to be in a group that offers support as believing mirrors to one another. I want to be in a circle that fosters accountability and provides time to partner, to encourage, and validate our creativity.

Kim: I am interested in reawakening my right brain with a desire to grow during this next phase of life. I want to have a creative practice and habits that support me to live fully and happily as I age.

Terri: I want to be "engaged" in a person-centered process that uses expressive arts to expand each person's potential, to deepen my expression of my creative spirit, and to contribute our creativity to the world.

Crossing the Threshold: Inner Guide Meditation

The next stage of the circle process invites members to transition from the group experience to a personal inner journey via meditation to connect with an inner guide. Invite participants to create their own space and to sit with their feet on the floor. Then read the following meditation very slowly, in a calm and relaxed voice:

Tune in to your breath. Relax. Breathe. Feel your chest move in and out as you inhale and exhale. Listen to your breath. Relax your face, *your* eyes, your mouth, your tongue, your cheeks, your jaws. Breathe deeply. You may notice a softening sensation move slowly around your head, down your neck, into your shoulders and across your shoulder blades. Plant your feet on the floor. Imagine you have roots growing from your feet through the floor and into the earth. Thoughts will arise; notice them and then let them go. Breathe deeply. Every exhale brings you deeper into relaxation. Let your breath carry this relaxation down your arms, your chest, your stomach and middle back, melting into your pelvis and bottom, and down your legs into your feet. Know that you are safe, right here, right now.

With each inhalation breathe in the fullness of your life. With each exhalation, relax more comfortably in your body. Become aware of your imagination. Find a path that takes you to the dwelling place of your intuition, and your creativity. You access your imagination through intuitive feelings, words, pictures, sounds, and smells. Your imagination is expansive and suggests a world charmed with possibilities.

Each of us has an inner guide, an intuitive part of ourselves that reflects a higher wisdom and deeper levels of creativity. To contact your inner guide, invite inner wisdom and intuition to join you. As you breathe into this moment, think about qualities you admire in people you know, those whose wisdom makes a difference in the world. Let the qualities of this special person or persons live inside of you as your inner guide. Imagine taking a walk to meet your inner guide. Use intuitive feelings, words, pictures, sounds, and smells to meet this person.

Walk on a special, secret path and reflect on and remember moments when you felt your inner guide's presence before. You might experience appreciation and deep love. Soon you come upon a gate or an archway that leads into your inner sanctuary. You might hear a voice or smell a special scent. There may be a shift in energy. Look around and notice your surroundings. This is a sacred place. What is this sacred place like?

Notice your breath. Relax and feel fully grounded in your body. Your inner guide is with you; you sense and feel the wisdom, intuition, and creative spirit. You observe your surroundings and the experience of being with your inner guide. What smells do you notice? Are there any flavors that come to mind? What sounds do you hear? What is your inner guide wearing? What is your inner guide offering you? There may be a question you would like to ask. You can ask anything. Your questions are answered, and there may be a special message for you. As you listen to the messages, put your hands on your chest and feel your heartbeat. This gesture carries the message into your heart for safekeeping. (*Pause for 10 seconds or more.*)

Know that all is well. Rest. Breathe. Be aware of your inner wisdom. Soon you will leave your inner wisdom guide. Before you leave, your guide will give you a ritual of return, a symbol, or a small gift to help you stay connected. This may be an image, movement, or simple intuition. Listen and accept your gift for your return with gratitude.

As you look once more at your inner guide, visualize your surroundings. Convey your goodbye, knowing that you can come back here anytime you want. Mindfully begin your return journey, walking back through the gate or archway onto the familiar path. Realize your inner guide is always available. (*Pause.*)

As you focus on your breath, begin to move your fingers and toes. Slowly move your head from side to side. Breathe deeply and fully, preparing to open your eyes and come back into this room. Take your time, holding onto the magic of your journey. Softly open your eyes and come back to the present.

Take a few minutes to jot down the details of this journey in your journal. I'll let you know when 10 minutes have passed. When your writing is complete, go to your art space and express your experience through art.

The facilitator offers the following description as an option for artmaking.

Expressive Arts Journey: Inner Life/Outer Life

Description

This artmaking experience provides time to reflect further on messages from your Creative Living Web and inner guide explorations. Set up small empty boxes or other containers on an art table. Ask each circle member to choose a container that symbolizes their current life and/or desires for the future. Circle members may also bring personal supplies such as images, words, quotes, book titles, or letters that reflect parts of their hopes and desires for joining a Creative Living Circle.

Suggest that the circle members consider the interior of the container as a metaphor for their interior life, while the outside may be what they express to the world, how they are viewed in the world, and their desires for future creative endeavors and external influences. Invite each person to explore the inside and outside of their life through the added lens of and experience with their inner guide.

Ask what key messages or insights emerged today. Suggest that members add quotes, words, phrases, or images to the box that reflect recent insights: "As you express your inner and outer life, what is emerging for you as a provocative proposition? Express this in an intuitive and visual way using your box."

Materials and Supplies

- Containers such as wide-mouthed bottles, card boxes, cigar boxes, flowerpots, gift boxes, jewelry boxes, shoeboxes, and/or shadow boxes
- Collage material, magazines, newsprint, quotes, papers
- Glue
- Nature items: leaves, feathers, rocks, sticks

Guidelines and Process

Facilitators prepare a place for each circle member to work, either at a table alone or with others or in separate spaces or rooms. Set up art supplies on a table for easy access and allow each circle member to select the materials they desire. Invite each person to select a place to work individually on their box.

The instructions for this expressive arts journey are the same for every session in this book, unless otherwise noted:

- Take a few deep breaths to relax and become focused on the present moment.
- Gaze at your materials and tune into your intuition and how your body feels.
- Consider your feelings, thoughts, and intuitions and what they suggest you might do with your materials.
- Begin working by allowing your body and intuition to guide your actions almost unconsciously.

Remember to let go of preconceived outcomes. It doesn't matter if you finish your box/container or if it looks good or not. All that matters is attending to what emerges in you as you follow your feelings, thoughts, and intuitions about your inner and outer life. Allow your intuition to direct your artwork. You may find that you are creating something expected, or you may be surprised by what emerges. Either way, this is an opportunity to capture your desires for the future in a new way. Taking time to use expressive arts involves slowing down. There may be surprises as you reflect your thoughts and feelings in your artwork. Allow about 45–60 minutes for everyone to work alone.

Writing Reflection

After the artmaking, provide approximately 15 minutes to reflect and write about the experience. Facilitators may need to check in with each person to remind them to allow sufficient time for this reflection. This part of the intermodal journey is important. Writing is a means to step back, digest, and integrate what has happened. Some questions to consider as you write are:

- What has been meaningful to you about this experience? The prework may have informed your artmaking significantly. If that is the case, consider not only your artmaking but also your Creative Life Map, Creative Living Web, symbol, inner guide meditation, person-centered listening, and provocative proposition.
- What do you appreciate? What is exciting?
- What are you struggling with?

- Are there any new messages/insights from your inner guide and your artmaking that inform your provocative proposition? What have you observed about yourself?

Each of the expressive art journey chapters will include one or more author examples of work created during the artmaking time and reflections shared during conscious closure. Figure 10 shows an example of Holly's artmaking and reflection while developing her personal vision.

WOW Story

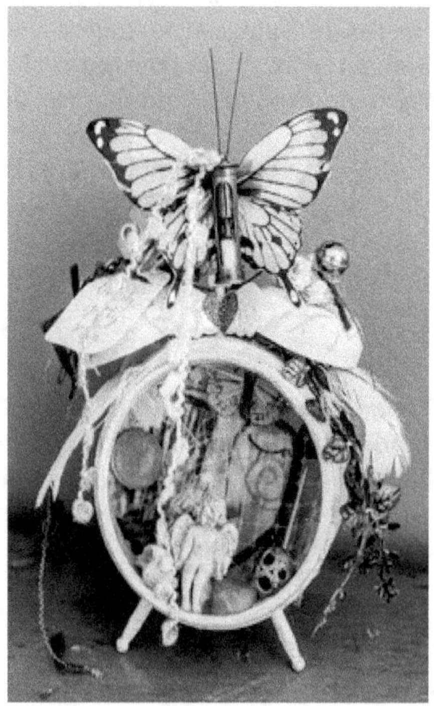

Figure 10: Timeless, mixed media, Holly Carson (2021).

Holly: My *Timeless* shadowbox (Figure 10) is heart centered and expresses my creative "heart opening." The experience of my heart opening feels vast, sacred, vulnerable, wild, and holy. I love the soulful eyes of the interior angel and of the butterfly in my artwork. They are contemplative, inquiring, seeking, and reflective. My shadowbox represents creative courage, creative connection to self and others, and self-compassion. There are parts of my shadow box that represent reaching out, ascent/descent, going deeper. I wrote a poem called "Timeless" for my reflective writing, to go along with the assemblage. My creativity takes me into the flow of deep time.

Key Message: I want to embrace my creativity in a way that is contemplative, spiritual, and more willing to take creative risks. I want to walk a creative path that is heart centered, receptive, and connected with others. My creativity is evolving through heart-centered consciousness and compassionate loving kindness.

Conscious Closure

Conscious closure is the practice of rejoining the circle to discuss the creative process and experience. Invite circle members to share their artwork and a draft of their provocative proposition or any other expressions that emerged. Choose a memory keeper, who will take notes on key information. Notetaking is another form of witnessing and provides ongoing documentation for your circle sessions.

Encourage other circle members to listen non-judgmentally and bear witness to each member (see person-centered listening skills, Appendix B). Some key listening guidelines for this time of sharing include speaking from your heart and listening with openness and curiosity. It can be helpful to develop a ritual of passing something, like a stone or talking stick for each person to hold when they are talking about their experience. Using a talking stick symbolizes empowerment and the equality of each member and is an invitation for a slower rhythm, creating space for a sacred dialogue. The tradition can also be comforting to the person holding the stone or stick because it is symbolic of the cumulative energy and wisdom that is gathered from all members. If a circle member isn't ready to speak, they can pass and continue in a listening mode.

Early on, the facilitators may want to offer a time frame for speaking, such as five minutes per person. Members vary in their need for time. Some may benefit from a question such as "Is there a message that emerged from your artwork?" or "What did you notice about the interior of your container compared to the exterior?" Others may need a reminder of the time limit.

New ideas frequently emerge as a group listens to insights and images shared by other members. To deepen the collective understanding, invite an open dialogue for any new insights. Close with a few open-ended questions:

- What was meaningful to you about this experience?
- What do you appreciate or value?
- Were there any surprises or insights as you listened to each other?

Closing Ritual

Read a closing poem such as "Terton" by Sarah Ruhl to close the circle. Consider a renewal ritual to send each member off on their new journey. For example, bring a sage bundle to the session and light it with a match. Wave the sage and its smoke around each person individually, front and back, to bless their journey. Express gratitude for your new visions and invite circle members to blow out their candles.

Summary

A personal vision enables you to imagine your desired future and begin to weave it into your life journey. The many threads of your Creative Living Web fashion themselves according to what is most important to you. If you reflect on your provocative proposition each day, you will find yourself weaving daily actions together in a way that transforms desires into reality. The artwork and provocative propositions developed in this session will also inform the next circle session when your group begins to lace together the Creative Spirit Circle group vision.

Creative Weavings

This section offers invitations and ways to further integrate creativity into your life journey. There is no pressure to do all of these things. Choose what inspires you.

- Keep your artwork and provocative proposition visible over the next few weeks. Research in expressive arts (Goslin-Jones, 2010) shows that artistic messages often continue to surface as the artist interacts with the art piece over an extended period.
- Develop a plan for your circle members to meet in pairs or triads between sessions. Use PCL skills with each other to deepen your understanding of each other's Creative Living Plan. Include artwork and provocative propositions. Ask, listen, and respond to questions like: (a) if a miracle occurred in your life in one year, share what you would be experiencing, (b) share two to three things that need to happen to create this future, or (c) talk about how you can support each other to embody your creative dreams.
- Share your Creative Living Plan with your friends and family members.

- What further ways might you embody your provocative proposition or a key insight? Some examples include: a book title, dance, dream, improvisation, child's play, poem, podcast, song, or speech. (Note: You could share these expressions with the circle and work on them over time. They may even become topics for future circle sessions.)
- Establish a weekly creativity date to engage and celebrate your provocative proposition.

Chapter 5

Envisioning Your Creative Spirit Circle

Now is the time when we must renew ourselves and live as if we and all of life is sacred, and as if everything we do makes a difference.
— Jean Houston

Intention and Purpose

After you develop a provocative proposition for your individual development (see Chapter 4), the next step is to share the proposition so that group members can understand and support one another's growth. This begins the process of weaving individual visions to guide your Creative Spirit Circle's collective vision. It is easier to embrace a vision your group has co-created.

The goal of this session is to emerge with a draft vision statement and guidelines for how your group will work together. You might decide on the first few circle meeting topics, who will lead them, and the types of expressive arts modalities to be used, along with the frequency, length, and location of meetings. Chapter 3 offers meeting guidelines that your circle may want to adopt.

Distribute a circle survey and pre-session suggestions before your circle meets to explore group needs and preferences (Appendix E):

- Complete the survey and return it to the facilitators before the session.
- Refine your provocative proposition and bring it for the check-in. You may want to expand your vision with artwork.
- Bring musical instruments such as small drums, chimes, tambourines, maracas, singing bowls, or gongs.

The group coordinator can share the results of the survey prior to your visioning session so that members are prepared for a dialogue about the circle parameters. The following inquiries are offered for reflection:

Creative Inquiries

- Step a year into the future: What is your circle like? How are you working together?
- Is there a metaphor or symbol that reflects your vision for the group? For example: butterfly/metamorphosis, turtle/presence, plant/growth and roots, moon/universal cycles, mementos of travel and exploration, or photos of family and friends.
- What challenges do you anticipate? For example: inexperience with expressive arts, navigating time commitments, group dynamics, collaborative leadership, or group decision making.
- How might you personally grow to step into your vision?
- What group characteristics and actions would support your transformation?

Welcome and Overview for the Circle Meeting

This meeting focuses on sharing your refined personal provocative propositions and drafting a collective vision and group norms for your circle work. As Jean Houston discussed in a recent interview (Aizenstat & Houston, 2022), "The greatest form of creativity is the re-creation of yourself." She also recommended the value of forming a community of practice for enhancing and magnifying personal growth and creativity (Houston, 1982). Rainer Maria Rilke (1993) said, "You must give birth to your images. They are the future waiting to be born. Fear not the strangeness you feel. The future must enter you long before it happens. Just wait for the birth, for the hour of the new clarity."

Opening Ritual and Invitation

There are two parts to this opening ritual: (a) five minutes of playing percussion instruments and (b) five minutes of silent meditation. While playing music and while in silence, a facilitator may ask circle members to contemplate:

1. What changes are emerging in your life? In your body? Mind? Spirit?

2.   What are you welcoming into your life?

For the first part of the ritual, invite members to choose a musical instrument and to sit in a circle, indoors or outdoors, on chairs or on the ground. Ask them to tune into their bodies and feelings and to strike the instruments in a way that demonstrates how they feel physically and emotionally. Continue to play together for about five minutes. Encourage members to experiment and express their own rhythm.

For the second part of the ritual, invite members to relax their body and mind and sit or walk very slowly in five minutes of silent meditation. The meditation clears and quiets minds in preparation for the check-in.

Check-In

After the meditation, invite circle members to share their individual vision/provocative proposition. They may show artwork created from their personal visioning process. Each person's life experience and vision for the future is a vital part of the whole circle. The person speaking is a Wisdom Speaker. Consider using a talking stick and assigning the person to the left or right as the Wisdom Listener. After the circle member speaks, the wisdom listener reflects key messages and asks a question or two to deepen the wisdom speaker's experience.

Each person will have 10 minutes to share their provocative proposition. If time permits, other members may ask questions. After each person has shared their vision, ask them: "Is there a gesture that supports your provocative proposition?" Invite circle members to mirror the gesture before moving on to the next wisdom speaker. This bodily mirroring of a mental image of the future adds meaning to the proposition and anchors the desire to fulfill the vision. (Note: Ask someone to be the timekeeper.)

Lecturette

Why is vision important? Beliefs shape our actions. If we have a clear belief, our actions may change to make the belief a reality. When the future is approached as a framework of possibility or a loom upon which dreams can be woven, then we carry forward the best of what we already have and open to new and unknown possibilities. When our mindset expands, we see many potential realities and can choose a life path that serves our greater potential (Zander & Zander, 2000).

The Value of Shared Vision

Envisioning and co-creating a desired future for your circle is a powerful way to begin your journey together. Boyatzis et al.'s (2015) research with groups found that relationships that included a shared vision also shared compassion, and positive emotions are transformative for the individuals involved. Also, the group's learning and growth capacity were increased by being open-minded and having a clear group vision (Lord, 2015).

Open-mindedness is the experience of reflection and using authentic inquiry rather than arriving at quick conclusions or dismissing certain viewpoints. Open-mindedness and curiosity impact the capacity to learn, while shared vision provides direction and motivation for you and your circle members to grow. It is beneficial to revisit your vision every two or three years, if not every year. The benefits of increased learning capacity from the combination of your initial shared vision and your efforts in keeping an open mind will result in new ideas and novel ways of seeing the world.

A shared vision represents group members' honest intentions to work collaboratively toward a mutual aspiration (Lord, 2015) versus a situation where members conform to an idea of the way things are supposed to be. The overarching purpose for a Creative Spirit Circle is for members to grow toward actualization. Everyone will be uniquely different. The vision acts as glue and bonds members on a shared path of growth and transformation.

Considerations for Creating a Strong Personal and Circle Vision

A strong vision is free-standing. If the vision is "peace on earth," peace comes with its utterance. When "the possibility of ideas making a difference" is spoken, at that moment ideas do make a difference. Speaking the vision transforms the speaker and the listener. For that moment the "real world" becomes a universe of possibility, and the barriers to the realization of the vision disappear (Zander & Zander, 2000).

As your group develops its shared vision consider these guidelines developed by Boyatzis et al. (2015):

- Start by sharing values that are important to you. Identify the values your group wants to adopt as guideposts.

- Approach your visioning exercise with a positive attitude. What do you hope for? What desirable future will the vision make possible?
- There may be times when something you want is not chosen by the rest of the group. Decide when it is best to just let it go and when it is important to share your different view.
- Discuss the challenges as they arise so they don't become hindrances to the group vision. For example, if someone does not like the circle name others have suggested, ask what name they would like. Or if you don't feel prepared to facilitate, you may choose to do that later, after a few meetings. The key is to speak up, and for others to respond with questions, be flexible, and remain open.
- Invite members to discuss how they imagine their ideal self rather than seeking to meet anyone else's expectations of them. A powerful vision is not about what you "ought to do"; it is about what your circle desires.

Your Creative Spirit Circle Vision

In the next part of the meeting, you will work together to draft your circle's vision. The group will dialogue about questions such as: "Why are you here in this circle? How will we support one another?" The following example of a Creative Spirit Circle vision to launch your group can be customized and modified over time to meet the unique needs of your group. As noted previously, the authors' Creative Spirit Circle vision is:

> We will embody a collaborative, generative, process that reflects shared leadership. Our creative spirit circle will use expressive arts to access deeper levels of our creative potential. Together we will engage in an infinity circle that embraces, develops, and launches our creative potential into the world.

Your collective vision could be much simpler: for example, "Our Creative Spirit Circle will serve as a dwelling for each of us to find a creative outlet we love. Together, we will learn how to use creativity to enrich all aspects of our lives." Your choice will depend on diverse considerations such as the age range of your group; gender identity, race, and ethnic diversity; family and work status; and other aspects that support your collective needs and desires.

Just as a tapestry is woven over time from many individual threads that constantly influence each other, your group's collective ideas will show you how to weave your needs and desires into one vision. It is not you or I that creates something new; it is the interweaving of all of us and the synergy that develops within our circle. The diversity of your circle group implies continual movement and change as each unique view is introduced. This allows an enriched view of the world to emerge for each of you. As you consider your circle vision, listen to one another's purpose for being here and the insights that arise during today's expressive arts journey.

Crossing the Threshold

Cross over the expressive arts threshold as mindfully and with as much heart and spirit as possible. For this session, first read a poem such as "Everything is Waiting for You" by David Whyte (2012). Follow this with a minute of silence. Next, discuss the enso circle and how it is a metaphor for creative spirit and the circle of life.

Creative Spirit Circle as an Enso Circle… Circle of Life

The enso circle is a symbol in Zen Buddhism representing simplicity, imperfection, togetherness, and the circle of life. It is traditionally drawn as a meditative practice with a singular brushstroke to express a moment when the mind is free and the body creates. In a Creative Spirit Circle, each person's brushstroke of life is their unique expression. Drawing or painting an enso circle is an exercise in exploring the beauty and imperfection in life. The enso circle reminds us that insights are embedded in even our simplest and most primitive artwork. This Japanese artform symbolizes togetherness within the circle of life, oftentimes leaving an opening for possibility and the interconnection of all things (Seo, 2007).

Crossing the Threshold: Drawing an Enso Circle

Divide into groups of two or three people. Have small pieces of paper and brushes/markers available for each circle member. Invite each member to draw an enso circle.

- Reflect on your Creative Living Plan (Chapter 4). Are some areas of your life underdeveloped or incomplete? What might they be?

- You may feel that some exciting puzzle pieces of your life circle are about to be found. What could they be?
- What imperfections or vulnerabilities do you hope to invite into your artmaking?

Allow 25 minutes for the enso circle exercise. After completing the enso circle, dialogue with your partner(s). Next, circle members move to a space for personal artmaking about the group vision. Suggest that circle members carry the artmaking and reflections from this exercise into their individual expressive arts journey.

Expressive Arts Journey: Circle Vision

Every journey has a secret destination of which the traveler is unaware.
— Martin Buber

Description

Reflect upon all that emerged during this expressive arts journey. What did you experience in your body during the percussion ritual and during silence? How does your personal vision intersect with all the other visions you witnessed today? What do the lessons about shared vision suggest is possible for your group? Did the poem and enso circle influence your intuition and imagination? Paint, make a collage, and/or write on your puzzle piece in a way that reflects your personal and group vision.

Compiling these puzzle pieces can bring order to separate parts of ourselves as well as the group. We don't have to know all the steps. There are times in life when moving pieces around is required to see the bigger picture. The circle holds each of us. Like a puzzle, the pieces come together, and a full picture emerges. Life is a puzzle; it manifests over time.

Materials and Supplies

- A large piece of 200–300 lb. watercolor paper cut into a large circle that becomes a puzzle, with a puzzle piece for each person
- A firm surface such as a wood substrate or thick cardboard to glue puzzle pieces after they are completed by each circle member

- Gel medium, or Mod Podge
- Glue sticks
- Paint—finger paint, acrylic
- Magazines, quotes, symbols, yarns, threads, buttons, other ephemera
- Newsprint, flipchart paper for circle visioning notes

Guidelines and Process
Facilitator Preparation
Before the session, the facilitator traces a large circle on watercolor paper and draws shapes on the paper for large puzzle pieces. Cut the circle paper into enough pieces for each person to have one piece. The puzzle pieces will be put together again into one large circle that serves as a metaphor for your circle's vision. Take photos of each puzzle piece and the circle in its blank state.

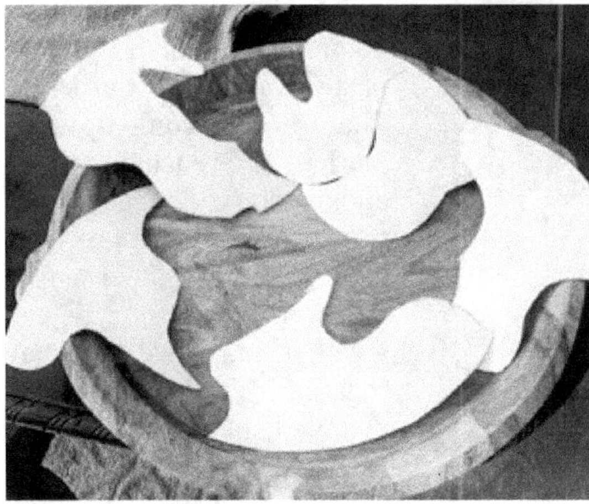

Figure 11: Blank puzzle pieces waiting to become expressive art (2022).

Figure 11 shows how the facilitators prepared the puzzle using a circle and cut-out pieces with a number on the back. Each person picked a puzzle piece and used their imagination to develop a visual symbol that would contribute to the collective circle vision.

Prepare a place for each circle member to work. Set up art supplies on a table for easy access and allow each circle member to select a puzzle piece and materials that will be used to reflect their personal and group vision. Invite each circle member to complete their puzzle piece in an intuitive way that feels true and complete for them. Allow 45–60 minutes for artmaking.

Writing Reflection
Allow 15–20 minutes for circle members to reflect upon their experience during this visioning session. The following questions can inspire their reflection and writing:

- What is calling you as you contemplate the creative potential of your group?
- As you envision the next few years, what do you see?
- How may your group collectively manifest your circle vision?

WOW Stories

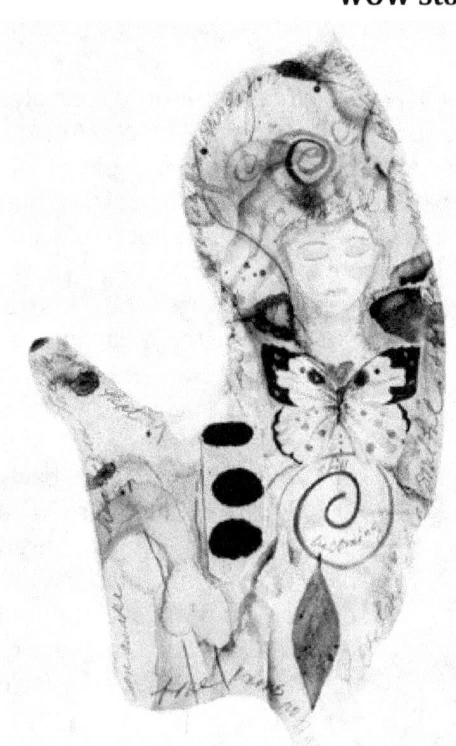

Figure 12: Transcendence, mixed media/watercolor, Holly Carson.

The following are three examples of the authors' experience when they designed their individual puzzle piece to explore and then contribute to the collective circle vision.

Holly: For my symbol of our collective vision, I painted a woman who is part of a tree (Figure 12). The branches come up from her hair and reach into Spirit and mystery. She embodies transcendence. We are on a creative, mystical voyage, a deep, night sea journey, a voyage that we journey together. Our colors complement one another. Our Creative Spirit Circle is earthy, organic, and mystical. As a circle we are unfinished and still becoming. We are contemplative, engaged in deep, holy listening. We value silence and we listen with the ear of our hearts. We are in a continual process of circling, spiraling in and out, receiving and giving back. It is all holy.

Nancy: As I worked on my puzzle piece (Figure 13), I drew six enso circles to represent each person in our Creative Spirit Circle. We

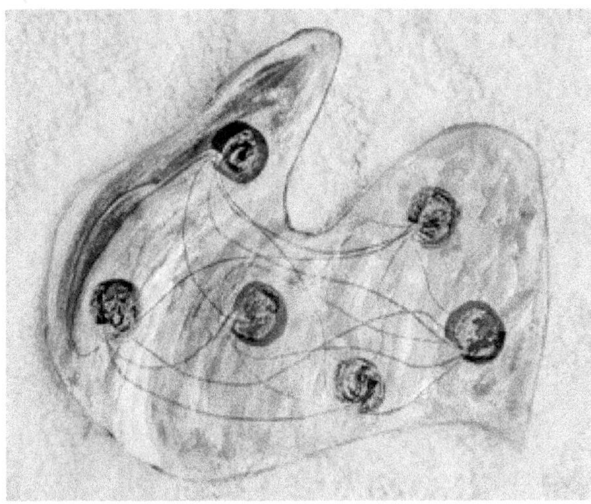

are a coat of many colors. The circles reflect our uniqueness and our connection. It occurred to me that there are pieces within the pieces. The wavy lines in my puzzle piece reminded me of flexibility, yet all the pieces fit together to make the whole. This is representative of

Figure 13: Congruence, pastels and collage, Nancy Williger.

my experience of being in our Creative Spirit Circle. Each person is a unique entity, yet our combined vision forms a collective whole. This poem emerged from my puzzle piece for our vision.

Pieces
Even the pieces have pieces
Complexity lies in the connections
How rare to find a collection of people
With edges flexible enough to fit
Our differences - yet give support
Enough to form the coherent whole.

Kim: After seeing our puzzle pieces together as a whole, it feels like we are living together in the music and mystery of life. We share parallel journeys. From the enso circle, I learned that I want to bring in more sunlight and mountains, which for me means nature. For our group vision going forward, perhaps we can explore how being and creating in nature helps us learn more about our collective inner natures. My phoenix drawing (Figure 14) represents living a long and mystical life and beginning again with each journey. Part of my vision for our circle is to use expressive arts to go deeper, to build on each experience and find fresh inspiration for our lives.

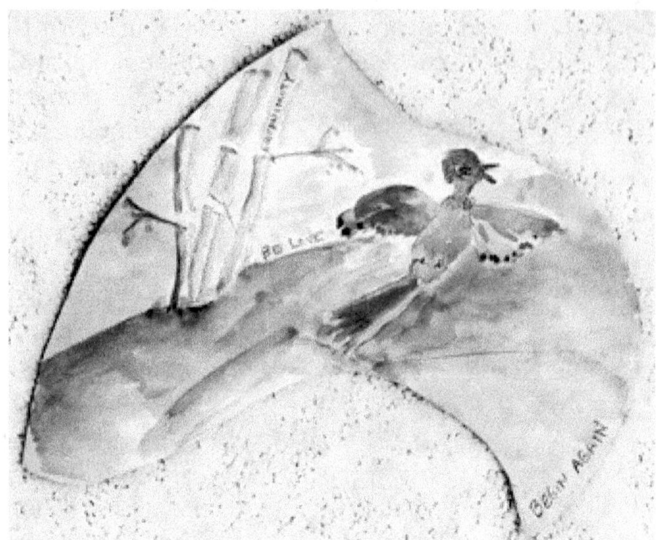

Figure 14: Phoenix and Bamboo, watercolor, Kim McCallum.

Conscious Closure

During conscious closure, circle members share their artmaking and reflections about their circle vision as described in the author example. This dialogue will also clarify how to organize future meetings.

Circle Vision Dialogue

Each person has about five minutes to talk about their puzzle piece and to share suggestions and insights about the vision. After all circle members discuss their vision puzzle piece, you may want to photograph the individual pieces to honor and document the contribution and uniqueness of each person. Then put the pieces together until the vision puzzle is completed.

Stand back and view your vision puzzle in its wholeness (Figure 15). Begin a group dialogue with the questions: As we bring these pieces together, what do you see? How do you feel? Take notes on newsprint paper as people speak. After a few or all have shared, ask: What does the whole puzzle suggest about our collective vision? If we stand in the future one or two years from now, what is that future like in our circle? What are key learnings and insights today that might create our desired future?

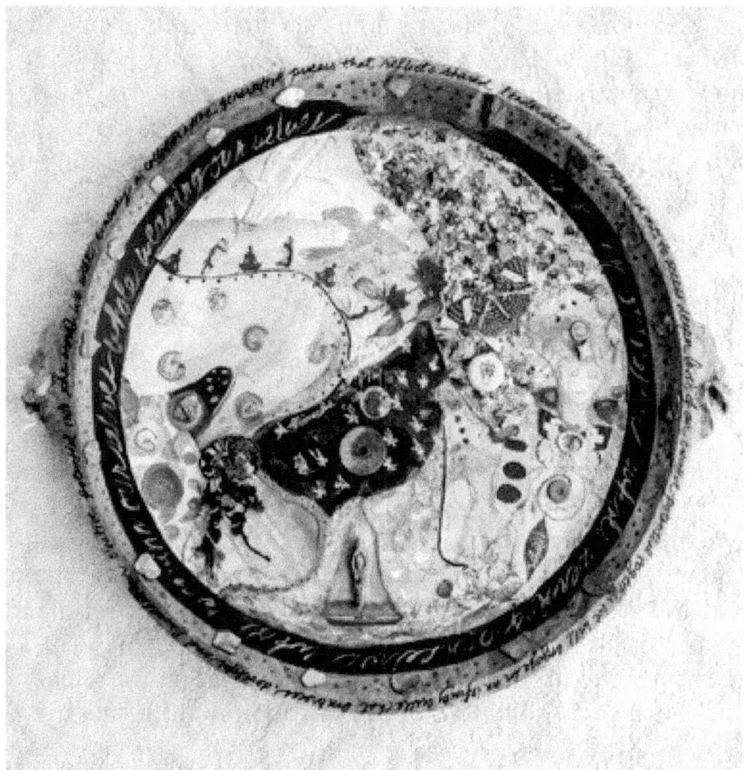

Figure 15: Weaving Ourselves Whole, Mixed Media, Authors' Vision.

After a dialogue about these questions, ask for suggested wording for your circle vision. It may come together easily. If it does not, the facilitator of this session may draft a vision statement based on everyone's input. It is also possible to use the authors' vision statement as your group's vision if it fits closely with everyone's wishes. Whatever choice you make, you may decide to modify your vision after your circle has spent more time together.

Organizing Your Circle's Norms and Guidelines
Discuss and decide upon the circle's meeting time, topics, and member roles. Your circle may modify choices at any time, but it is important to discuss the logistics for your group based on your survey results. Who will be invited to participate in your circle? Decide how often you will meet, how long, location, what topics to start with, who will design and facilitate the next session. You may find it best to develop an

annual plan for your circle meetings or to schedule just the next couple of sessions and amend your dates as you go.

View your circle of puzzle pieces one more time. Do you want to leave it as it is and glue and weave the pieces together? Do you want to continue embellishing your vision with additional artmaking or does your group feel complete? Take a few minutes to decide how you will finish the image of your collective vision.

Closing Ritual

Use the four elements in nature (earth, fire, water, air) to close your visioning session. Dig a small hole in the earth (at your meeting location) or use a bucket of dirt, matches, and one of each of the following for each group member: a strip of paper and a pen, a small candle, and a small container of children's bubbles to blow. Ask each circle member to write a fear about your group vision or process on a strip of paper. Place the strips of paper in the hole and light them with the matches. Cover the ashes with dirt to extinguish the fire and as a metaphor for overcoming fear. Each of you can light a candle to illuminate your path and propel you into your future. Finally, give each person a small container of bubbles to blow your intentions into the air to give them life.

Creative Weavings

- Place a copy of your Creative Spirit Circle vision in a prominent place where you will see it frequently. Read it often and reflect upon how your circle will embody the vision.
- Share the photos of the group's artmaking and the visual image of your collective vision.
- Think about topics you would like to explore with your group. Use a topic for inspiration and create a painting, sculpture, weaving, poem, or other artwork to express your feelings and thoughts about this topic.

Chapter 6

Finding Your Center

Life is a train of moods like a string of beads; and as we pass through them they prove to be many colored lenses which paint the world their own hue, and each shows us only what lies in its own focus.
—Ralph Waldo Emerson

Intention and Purpose

What holds life together? Life is a journey punctuated by inspiring and challenging events. There are many colors and hues to life when viewed through an individual's unique experiences. At the same time, there is rhythm and stability across the lifespan. The intention of this expressive arts journey is to use poetry and beading to symbolize how your life story is evolving and attend to the meaning of these patterns.

Creative Inquiries

To find your center and "let your life speak" (Palmer, 2000), begin by listing some of the key events that have shaped your life. Review your Creative Life Map from your visioning circle session (Chapter 4) for ideas. Use words or phrases to capture the first thoughts about the major highlights/challenges in relation to your family life, creative passion, career/lifework, physical/emotional health, and spiritual development. Consider peak experiences, episodes of misfortune, and the wisdom gained from your life experiences.

- *People*: Who are some of the significant people in your life now and in the past? Consider births, deaths, joys, and challenges.
- *Places*: What places hold meaning for you through the chapters of your life?
- *Events*: What are some major life events that made you who you are?

- *Creativity*: What inspires your creativity? In what ways do you express your creativity?

Introduction

This Creative Spirit Circle includes meditation, stringing beads, and writing poetry to symbolize and integrate lessons from your life journey. Why are poetry and beading used?

Poetic Medicine

"Poetry provides guidance, revealing what you did not know you knew before you wrote or read the poem" (Fox, 1997, p. 3). Fox, founder and president of The Institute for Poetic Medicine, wisely said, "Poetry is a natural medicine that extends solace and relief, gives cathartic voice to suffering, reveals insight, and shows us what it means to be human." Poetry offers an intimate voice for healing and growth and emerges from the rhythm of your heartbeat to paint the picture of your life experiences (Lyon, 1999).

Contemplative Beading

In this circle, beads are strung together as a contemplative ritual to explore how your life journey is an integral part of a larger universal life force. Beads have a variety of symbolic meanings across cultures and are available in many different colors, shapes, and sizes. Selecting beads slows the mind down and at the same time is visual and tactile. Stringing beads together is a multi-sensory meditation. Beading is a process that engages the hands and heart. Each bead serves as a symbol of significant life events.

Opening Ritual and Invitation

Open this circle with a brief meditation. When you prepare the circle, give each member paper and pencil. Have a few art supplies in the middle of the circle such as colored pencils, oil pastels, or colorful markers. Save a few minutes after the meditation for circle members to make a quick drawing and to write a few notes. They can use their drawing and notes to inform the expressive arts beading journey.

Meditation: Find Your Center

Sit comfortably in a chair, allow your face to soften, your eyes to lower. Take in a few deep breaths and allow your breathing to settle.

Draw your attention to any sounds in your environment. Welcome the sounds as they arise and depart. Some may be pleasant, others less so. Some sounds may be neutral. Notice that the sounds bring your focus to the present and to this moment.

When you are ready, see if you can imagine a favorite place. This could be from any time in your life. Allow yourself to time travel to this special place. You may be alone or with friends or family. Are there any images or smells? Are there any sounds or sensations that arise?

Imagine you are moving around your favorite place. Explore the environment in this memory. Wherever you are, invite your internal guide to show you who you are at your center. Your guide helps you to see your strengths and purpose.

Spend the next two to three minutes in silence following your breath. Hold yourself in warmth and kindness. When you are ready, allow your eyes to open. Come into the present moment. Take five minutes to capture your experience in either a simple image or a few notes.

Check-In

Circle members are invited to write a poem using an online poetry template, "Where I'm From" (Lyon, 1999), before they arrive at the circle session. There are numerous poetry examples online to use as inspiration. If someone prefers not to write and read their poem, they can take a different approach or pass when it is their turn to check in. Providing prompts and a poetry template usually offers enough structure for timid writers to discover their inner poet. At the same time, it is important to offer options and the freedom to choose different forms of artistic and verbal expression.

Writing a poem about your heritage is a way to ponder life and describe events that have been important to your development. George Ella Lyon is a poet, teacher, and former Kentucky Poet Laureate. She wrote a poem called "Where I'm From" and then developed a template to inspire her students to write personal poems about their heritage and childhood memories. People from around the world were inspired by her poem and shared their life stories.

Writing poetry about how you grew up and telling stories about your life is a way for circle members to learn more about one another's backgrounds. Writing and reading poetry in a group is intimate, and hearing each other's voice is deeply personal and removes barriers. The following poem is an example written and read to the circle by author Kim McCallum.

WOW Story

I am From
Kim McCallum

I am from pet bowls
From Crazy Mixed up Salt and iPads
I am from a century old home with 4 stories
the house with many souls
I am from seagrass, daffodils and pear trees
and old oaks whose limbs I remember as if they were my own.

I am from Thanksgiving feasts at home and trips to Seaside
From Gilmores and Wills
I'm from Opera, Theater, baseball, and movies together
And from adventures abroad

I am from everything is love
and the early bird catches the worm
And a spoonful of sugar helps the medicine go down
I am from abundant Christmas morning presents
I'm from Indianapolis and Britain

I am from Cinnamon toast and rhubarb
From early immigration to New France
and the first miracle in the New World
I am from the Colonies and the Revolutionary War
 jumping on trains, planting and opening schools
and family albums in my living room

I am from healers and seekers
From spinal cord sections and feminism
From Rock and Roll and walking on the moon
From Universities and Starbucks

And getting breakfast for our
children's friends when they sleep over

Lecturette: Finding Your Center with Poetry and Beading

Writing a poem is a way to describe memories, questions, challenges, and dreams. Poetry explores life experiences and is a way to tell the truth from different angles using imagery and verbal associations. The language of poetry in expressive arts is founded on the principles of authenticity, caring, and love. Your authentic voice speaks from your heart, the place where emotions and words are born. At the same time, some of life's experiences are so traumatic and difficult that you may be speechless and at a loss for words. Poetic writing is a way to resurrect and give voice to important experiences literally and metaphorically.

This precious life does not last forever. Our time is fleeting, and poetry throws us out of rote behaviors. Writing and listening to poetry is a way for spiritual energy to flow through your body and onto the page, bringing your unique voice to the world. The poem does not need to be in a specific form; it just needs to speak the truth. Through writing, you can hear and speak the storyline of your life in transformative ways. By finding and expressing your poetic voice, new perspectives for the most difficult and the most joyful experiences of the life journey emerge (Knill & Atkins, 2021).

Beading

Beading provides a contemplative doorway and is a creative arts process used in therapeutic healing programs (Archibald & Dewar, 2010). Working with color, shapes, forms, and symbols engages the subconscious and allows insights to develop based on personal creative expression. Self-knowledge expands through physical movement, artmaking, reflection, and writing (Rogers, 1993, p. 3).

Beadwork can be a form of meditation through the practice of counting the beads and continuing to return to your breath. Beads are chosen with intuition and intention. Beadwork can help redirect your thoughts. An experience of concentration and stillness develops with the slow, conscious movements of viewing and selecting beads that are then strung together. This practice can be a powerful tool for self-reflection. Beading is a metaphor for life. It is about making choices. Beading is used by many cultures to make artwork, jewelry, talismans, and meditation beads. Beads can be touchstones of self-expression which become portable altars. Meditation beads or portable altars may be used to begin the day, stay in the present moment, close the day, organize your practice, or celebrate special moments in your life (Wiley & Shannon, 2002; Winston, 2016).

Crossing the Threshold

To cross the threshold into the expressive arts journey, choose a favorite poem to read to circle members. Invite circle members to repeat lines from the poem that are especially meaningful to them. A couple of examples include Rumi's "Guest House" or Joy Harjo's "Remember." These poems can be located online. The Academy of American Poets at poet.org is a generous website with many options.

Expressive Arts Journey: Let Your Life Speak

Description

Each circle member chooses beads based on personal inspiration. Any small object with a hole in it can serve as a bead. Organize beads, old jewelry, string, and wires on an art table that is accessible to everyone. Circle members may also bring family beads, charms, vintage jewelry, talisman, feathers, and objects from nature for personal and shared use. Small paper plates can be used to select and gather beads for stringing. Then the beads are assembled into a chosen form that may include artwork, dreamcatchers, jewelry, keychains, talismans, meditation beads, or portable altars.

Materials and Supplies

- Amulets, charms, and assorted beads of different sizes and shapes
- Containers or paper plates to hold and organize the beads
- Needle nose pliers and crimp beads to secure the beginning and end of the string
- Fast-drying glue
- Small objects made of a variety of shapes and materials such as coins, glass, mirrors, seeds, shells, stones, wood, feathers, keys
- Scissors and soft-flex wire, string, or leather for stringing

Guidelines and Process
Some considerations as you begin:
1. What is your intention for the beads? Examples:
    a. Are you reflecting and stringing together significant events from your life journey?
    b. Are you creating a metaphor and representative of a birth, death, dream, or letting go?
    c. Will the beads be reflecting freedom from addictions, compulsive behaviors, or trauma?
    d. Will the beads be used to welcome less illuminated parts of yourself?
    e. Will the beads be used to celebrate new chapters and special life events?
    f. Will the beads be used for contemplation and a doorway to your spiritual realm, a way to allow something unknown to emerge?
2. What form and shape do you want for your beads? What shapes, colors, textures, and materials are you attracted to? Consider the length and strength.
    a. Do you want to use it as a keychain and daily metaphor of crossing thresholds?
    b. Do you want a visual connection to the future such as a dreamcatcher?
    c. Do you want to wear it as a bracelet, bolo tie, or necklace?
    d. Do you want to experience the beads in meditation and as a tactile connection that can travel with you, such as prayer beads or a portable altar?
3. Select beads that represent and offer a metaphor for your intention. Choose the stringing material that supports the way you want to use your beads. Cut the stringing material four inches longer than the size you want for your finished creation. This will give you space to secure the beads with knots and closures. Beads and equipment may be found online or at craft stores. Wiley and Shannon (2002) are bead artists and provide written directions on the art of beading.
4. After you complete your beading process, reflect on your creative process and messages that may be embedded in the beads.

Writing Reflection
Select question(s) from the following list that inspire you. Use free writing for your reflection and integration. After about 15 minutes of free writing, re-read what you wrote and highlight key information. Is there a poem, blessing, or key message embedded in your writing?

- In silence, experience your beads in a sensory manner that includes touch, vision, and intuitive communication.
- What might you hear, see, or smell intuitively as you experience your beads?
- How would you describe your beading creation? Use adjectives, adverbs, colors, emotions, feelings, symbols.
- What parts of your life speak to you through the beads? What do you want to hold on to and what might you want to let go of or change?
- What messages are coming to you that you want to recall from the beads about your past, present or future?
- What messages/insights have emerged about your creative process?

The following are two examples of the writing that emerged from the writing reflection. One example is a poem, and the other is a portable altar and free-writing prose.

WOW Stories

Unity
Pam Caraffa (2011)

Symmetry, not symmetry.
Inside, outside.
Tangible, intangible.
Flow, full stop.
Mystery, known.
Color.

Walking the inside is not the same
As walking the outside,
yet it is the same journey —
meeting in the one,
the pearl of great price,

the jewel of Atman,
the lotus flower,
where all things join.

Color.
Nothing, everything.
Seeing all, seeing nothing.
Showing off, keeping secrets.
Holding on, letting go.
Separate yet together.

Color.
Doing, being.
Resonating, cacophony.
Love, hate, fear, joy.
Earth, sky, sun, moon.
Breathe in, breathe out.

Terri: I asked Ginger to help me string and tie my beads together (Figure 16) because I was struggling with the technical parts of manifesting my creative idea. Then I noticed I was taking her away from her beading process and was afraid my questions were intruding upon contemplative space for everyone. There are times when I am pushy, but I don't realize it until later. I have this creative energy bursting out of my body. From this session, I grasped a key awareness: I desire collaboration with my creativity, yet I never want to impose my

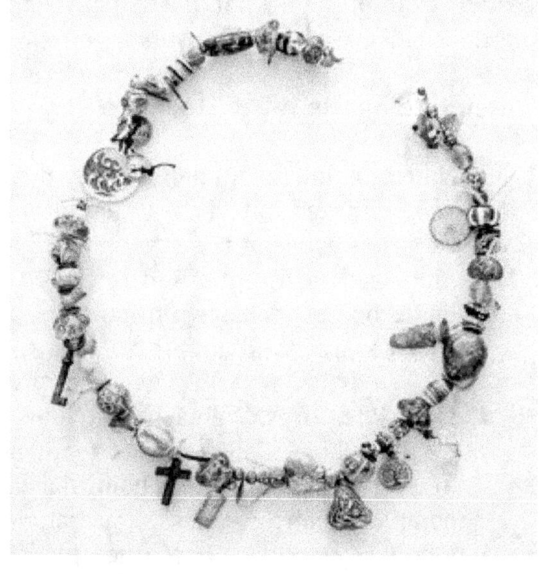

Figure 16: Portable Altar, beading, Terri Goslin-Jones (2011).

process on others or interfere with their creativity.

As I strung the beads together, a portable altar emerged, yielding messages in shapes, colors, and inscriptions. *Breathe* invites spiritual energy into my physical plane. *Focus* is an area where I need continued growth. *Imagine* shows I am constantly learning how to transform spiritual energy into understanding and actions in my life. The center of my portable altar holds a charm of my wise woman (bottom right), who carries emotion, depth, soul, and my inner child. Each talisman on my portable altar reflects a discovery or chapter of her travels. These insights can now travel outside of me, where previously they were messages locked inside.

Conscious Closure and Integration

Gather your members into a circle and ask each member to bring their beads and writings for a closing dialogue. The conscious closure and integration segment of this session provides an opportunity for each member to share their chosen beading project and expressive arts process. Circle members listen and ask questions that guide participants into deeper levels of personal awareness. The following are two examples of what participants shared during the author's conscious closure and integration.

Conscious Closure: WOW Stories

> **Nancy:** I slowly and deliberately put each bead on the string. I was amazed at how meditative and comfortable the experience became. I created a red necklace because I need more red in my life. Red is a bold, vibrant color. The small beads on my necklace remind me of all the people in the world, each separate and unique.
>
> We have an individual identity even though we share similar features. We each contribute our own unique features to the whole. Some of our features are more similar than others; some stand out being larger and heavier and more complex. There is a lesson as each person contributes to the whole. My necklace has larger, focal beads, and people are like that too. Some people seem larger than life and receive a lot of attention; even so they are better with a supporting cast. Beads are from the earth and offer a connection to the earth. I

feel a deep connection to other people and to the Earth after making this beaded necklace.

Holly: I was amazed by the power of creating with beads, and how this expressive arts process became a container for my creativity to flow. I made a string of prayer beads to use for contemplative prayer and meditation. As I open to life's river and sacred flow, I become more fully alive.

My creative process opens me to the flow of spirit; a subterranean river that flows through everything. My string of prayer beads begins and ends with a heart. My spiritual path is ultimately one of the heart and learning how to love and be loved.

Holly also wrote a blessing poem as a blessing for herself and others. Though we only include a few poems in this book, they frequently emerge from the expressive arts journey, because poetry is such an evocative and eloquent form of expression. When you are deep in the creative process, you enter the edges of the unconscious. Poems emerge to illuminate ideas and feelings lying fallow within our center.

Flow
Holly Carson (2011)

May you be carried by the
River flow of Spirit
Into miraculous mystery
Ever surprised by the wonder
Of your unfolding
In her redemptive waters
Deep currents of intuitive knowing
Let go and let it flow
You are an artist of being alive.

Closing Ritual

In closing, ask each person to select and string a couple of beads on a beading string that is symbolic of weaving together the insights of the whole group. The string of beads can be brought to future circle meetings, added to over time, and used as part of future circle rituals that cumulatively reflect insights in the form of poetic lines from circle members.

Summary

Hands and heart connect while writing poetry or stringing beads into a tangible form of poetic self-expression. Beads are touchstones and reminders to be present to your life journey. Poems are beacons from the unconscious, highlighting aspects of your essence.

As you use artistic expression to reflect on what's happening in your life, you reconnect with an aspect of yourself that you may have forgotten. There is an opportunity to develop greater self-awareness. While stringing beads and writing poems, you open to a threshold of contemplation, not only in the finished product but also to the creative process itself and what it may illuminate in you.

Creative Weavings

- String beads together for special passages in your life. Write a line of poetry for each bead.
- Collect words, thoughts, synchronicities in a daily journal. Write a weekly poem to express your experiences.
- Collect beads when you travel and string them together as symbols of life's adventures. Write a line of poetry for each bead that you add. Your life adventures string of beads and poem collage will grow over time.
- Ask family members to write a "Where I'm From" poem and make a poetry book that includes your extended family.

Chapter 7

Self and the Sacred Circle

We shall not cease from exploration. And the end of all of our exploring will be to arrive where we started and know the place for the first time.
—T.S. Eliot

Intention and Purpose

This expressive arts journey introduces the circle as a symbol of wholeness and a reflection of the self. The circle is a captivating universal symbol representing eternity, wholeness, the self, the infinite, timelessness, and cycles of life. The similar Japanese enso understanding of the circle is illustrated and discussed in Chapter 2. In this Creative Spirit Circle, labyrinths and mandalas serve as pathways to wholeness.

Creative Inquiries

- What meaning do circles have in your life?
- What is an important example for you of experiencing the "circle of life?"
- When has your life come full circle?
- What is inside your circle? Outside your circle? When have you expanded your circle?

Introduction

Circles abound in the natural world in flowers, seeds, plants, and the food we eat. Toss a pebble into still water and circles pulse outward. The moon and sun illuminate the sky in circular patterns. Life cycles are associated with circular rhythms. We refer to the everlasting circle of life that is carried on through generations. Circles represent something with no beginning and no end. Circles are eternal.

Labyrinths and mandalas are described as sacred circles and symbols that hold the capacity for unity. Creating a mandala or walking a labyrinth is a source of reflection with the potential to unify your experience of inner and outer reality. Sacred circles are reflected throughout many cultural traditions, including Aztec and Mayan time wheels, Buddhist mandala sand paintings, Celtic crosses, and the rose windows of Gothic cathedrals.

The labyrinth and mandala offer ancient pathways to explore different aspects of the self and the sacred circle. During the meditation as you cross the threshold, you will have an opportunity to set an intention for your labyrinth and mandala exploration. Before the meeting, journey leaders can arrange a circular space or altar as a symbol for the group members and the sacred circle that you have formed together. Include elements from nature that reflect earth, fire, water, and air, and have a candle for each person. Ask members to bring a circular object of personal significance. This might be a shell, a stone, a keepsake, or token.

Opening Ritual and Invitation

Sit or stand in a circle around the altar. Ask each person to light a candle. Invite each circle member to share the significance of the circular object they added to the altar. Then suggest that each person raise their arms to shoulder height and make a circle with their arms. What does this circle feel like? Is there another circle you would like to make with your body?

Check-In

Creative inquiries bring symbols from the unconscious into the conscious realm. Ask members to select and respond to a question from the creative inquiries.

Lecturette: Mandalas and Labyrinths

Using the beach as a metaphor, imagine you are close to the water, standing in the sand. In your mind, turn around in place. Imagine you are touching a stick to the sand and drawing a circle. Notice how the circle you draw organizes the empty space into pairs of opposites:

inside/outside, here/there, and near/far. In a circle, the center is always present. Circles bring order to life (Watts, 2000).

Mandala

"Mandala" is a Sanskrit word used to describe a sacred circle representing the inseparable nature of the physical and spiritual universe. A mandala is a container for meaning. It is often seen as a representation of the universe and a collection point for universal forces (Holbrook & Comer, 2017). There is a pattern of wholeness within each person that can be illustrated when creating a mandala. It is a form of visual artmaking that can contain inner awakenings and reflect the psyche. Creating a mandala serves as a meditation tool to focus our attention and establish sacred space (Fincher, 2010; Mulchay, 2013).

Carl Jung described the mandala as an instrument of contemplation and a path to individuation through formation and transformation. He called it "Eternal Mind's eternal recreation." In his book, *The Archetypes and the Collective Unconscious* (1969), Jung stated that there is an urge in every person to manifest the energy of the central archetypal self, becoming what one is. This is not ego but the Self. There is a geometric element to the spiritual, emotional, and psychological work here that focuses one's attention.

The purpose of using mandalas in artmaking is to encourage introspection that may create awareness of meaning in life and enhance the integration of unconscious material. Mandala drawings reflect the psyche and express what may not yet be available in words. The contemplation and/or the creation of mandalas is believed to reduce stress. To focus on the image is a way to simultaneously find stillness and expansion (Watts, 2000). Think of how a kaleidoscope displays its beauty as a mandala.

Labyrinth

A labyrinth is a symbol found in various forms around the world going back 3,000 years. From prehistoric times through the Romans and Medieval Europe, the archetype has played an important role in spiritual symbolism. The concentric path of the labyrinth leads to a center point and has been described as the longest path within a confined space. Moving through a labyrinth can be a metaphor for a spiritual journey, a way to travel an interior path. In a labyrinth, there is a beginning threshold to pass, a middle path, and a resting place at the end (Artress, 1995).

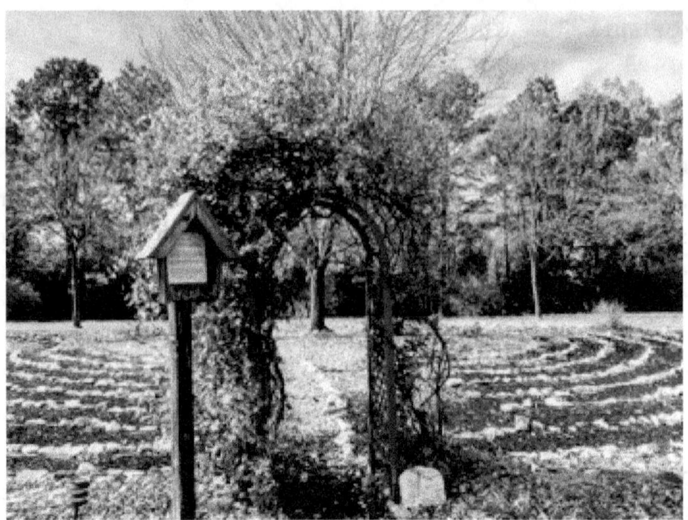
Figure 17: Labyrinth in St. Louis, Missouri.

The labyrinth offers a meditation process and is a universal archetype representing the spiritual journey. Figure 17 shows the labyrinth the authors walked. By following the circular path into the labyrinth, the traveler has time to settle and journey inward to seek quiet, calm, and peace or to contemplate their life cycle. During the walk out of the labyrinth, the unwinding path is a symbol of integration and empowerment to move forward in life with a fresh worldview.

In this expressive arts journey, you will walk a path of reflection with the intention to integrate mind, body, and spirit. The journey invites an open mind and a receptive heart. The zigzags of the labyrinth represent life's challenges and transitions. An enduring message of the walk is that change occurs moment by moment.

A labyrinth offers a framework and a way to walk in wholeness even during an upheaval happening outside the physical space. Wholeness includes not only light but dark, not only ease but struggle, not only order but chaos. The process of walking a labyrinth and participating in your Creative Spirit Circle requires moving through moment-to-moment changes. When faced honestly, reflecting on inner life can surface emotions that become creative energy toward growth and change.

Crossing the Threshold

The next part of this session includes a movement meditation to cross the threshold and walk through the labyrinth. Before a circle facilitator reads the meditation, provide an overview of the expressive arts journey that includes: (1) meditation, (2) use of a colored pencil to "walk" a paper labyrinth, (3) walking a physical labyrinth, (4) artmaking to create a mandala, and (5) reflection and writing. Remind circle members to finish the labyrinth walk in their own timeframe and then return to the circle space for artmaking and writing.

Meditation
The following meditation may be read by a facilitator.

Sacred circles are reflected in the labyrinth and the mandala. They are a place to explore balance, healing, and wholeness. Before we enter the labyrinth, we will summon the four directions of nature:

North is the direction of the earth. The garden's dirt represents the natural form of the earth and our human body. Facing north, we call for awareness of our bodies and for healing, rest, and balance. We call on the wisdom that resides in our bones.

East is the direction of air. The winds, atmosphere, and breath are its natural forms. Facing east, we call for awakened vision and new beginnings.

South is the direction of fire. Flames, lightning, electricity, and life itself are its natural forms. Facing south, we request awareness of warmth and daylight. We seek change that will call our greater potential out of hibernation; we emerge from the shadow and into the light of action.

West is the direction of water. Oceans, lakes, streams, rivers, wells, and body fluids are its natural forms. Facing west, we call for awareness of our emotions and feelings. We offer intimacy and trust in our relationships. We seek self-reflection and understanding, authenticity and compassion with Self and within our community.

A facilitator may read a poem such as "What In Your Life Is Calling You?" by the Terma Collective (Artress, 2006, p. 133) before the group begins their labyrinth walk.

Walking the Labyrinth with Your Finger
Download a labyrinth image for each circle member from an online resource. Members use the labyrinth image and colored pencils or

markers to "walk" in and out before going to the physical labyrinth. First, they use their non-dominant hand to follow the path and then switch to their other hand. This is a way to shift from automatic and unconscious behavior to present-moment awareness. Then invite members to walk an actual labyrinth.

Labyrinth Walk as a Moving Meditation

You can construct a labyrinth outdoors using masking tape, string, or markings on the beach. To find a labyrinth in your area, review the *Labyrinth Society* website. Walking a labyrinth is an active form of meditation using the entire body. Walk in single file and in silence to and through the labyrinth. There is no right or wrong way to walk a labyrinth. This process is a moving meditation. Walking this path is a way to move beyond limited states of consciousness to a deeper place of awareness.

Lauren Artress (1995, 2006), author and leading force in the worldwide labyrinth movement, offers guidelines for labyrinth walking. As you enter the labyrinth, focus your attention by asking a question, repeating a sacred word or mantra, praying, or reciting a poem. Consciously let go of expectations and control. As you walk through the labyrinth, notice your breathing, quiet your mind, shed your worries, and consciously release negative energy. You may meet others on the walk coming and going. If they are behind you and moving at a faster pace, step off the path for a moment to let them pass, or you can pass other travelers as you walk at a pace that is natural to you.

When you reach the labyrinth's center, you may wish to stand or sit in reflection and ground your labyrinth walk with a brief stop or word of gratitude. Then revisit the intention or question that launched your walk. You might ask for a symbol or word that anchors your journey into the interior of the labyrinth. The symbol or word may become a focal point for your return walk and used in your expressive arts. Like an enso circle, the end is also the beginning.

Expressive Arts Journey: The Sacred Circle of Life

Description

After the labyrinth walk, return to your gathering space for artmaking and writing. Mandalas can be made from clay, collage, food, flowers, hand-drawn circles, sand, paint, or weaving. Set up a table with a variety of the supplies listed below. Each circle member can also bring supplies they may want to include in their mandalas.

Materials and Supplies (optional examples)

- Circular objects with which to trace
- Clay, collage materials, colored pens, paint, crayons, thread, yarn
- Food items (edible food mandalas)
- Paper, paper plates, printed mandalas, protractors
- Sand for mandalas

Guidelines and Process

Create your own mandala by selecting from the mixed media supplies on the art table. Were there colors, images, or symbols that emerged on your labyrinth walk that you may want to express in the mandala? Did you carry out a word, a blessing, or an insight that you want to embed in your mandala? Use colors and shapes that symbolize your flow of life.

Writing Reflection

For this session, a facilitator might want to give each group member a handout before the expressive arts journey begins with these questions, and the instructions beneath them, to inspire the writing reflection.

- What was your intention for the labyrinth walk?
- How is your circle of life evolving?
- What do all the twists and turns of the path represent to you?
- Is there a phrase, word, or title that captures your experience?

Select some questions from the list above and write your response in a freeform, spontaneous way. Then highlight words or phrases that offer insights and lessons. You may want to conclude your writing with a poem or blessing.

Conscious Closure and Integration

Gather in a circle for conscious closure and integration. Place your mandalas in the center of the circle and spend a few minutes quietly absorbing each mandala. It is best not to comment or offer feedback or interpretations about the work. This is a time to appreciate the artmaking and to honor the sacred nature of each mandala.

Then invite each person to share their experience. Circle members may choose to speak spontaneously about their mandala or labyrinth walk, or they may read something they wrote.

WOW Stories

Kim: As I began to walk, I thought about the back and forth of my body— my brain, lungs, and lymphatics. How do I welcome my soul into my body and stay with light energy, my intention? This is a corollary of what my body has to do with my soul. How do I feel my soul in my body? I was feeling very alive and energized. I shifted into a meditation on love. I thought of all the people I love in my life. I walked slowly because I was feeling so happy. As I changed directions, I was reminded of changes in my body and how my blood is constantly flowing.

Terri: When I returned after the labyrinth walk and started to draw my mandala, I had a panic attack. I'm supposed to know what I'm doing! But I started from the inside and got mixed up. It's so like me; I'm always inside out/backwards. My intention was, "How do I walk my center?" I walked past Ginger and thought I was going to the wrong place but then reminded myself, "You can't go wrong with the labyrinth." I was walking in stride with soulmates.

The middle place in the labyrinth was a captivating surprise. I sat on each tree stool around the tree to understand different views and new perspectives. Walking out of the labyrinth was a whole different experience for me. I felt the aging in my body, as if I was moving through my stages and age without getting stuck. I want to appreciate the wisdom that comes from the aging process.

Pam: Creating a mandala (Figure 18) from scratch felt like a risk, since drawing is not my strength. A fire engine went by while I was drawing, as did people talking. I was reminded that chaos is always in the mix of life. There is structure in the four segments of the circle, but the crayon swirls and wavy edges create a dance with chaos. This feels like my psyche, both chaotic and ordered. I feel vibrant, interconnected, and more comfortable with complexity than ever before. It is a revelation to have drawn this spontaneously, without forethought and then to realize that it is an accurate portrayal of how I feel!

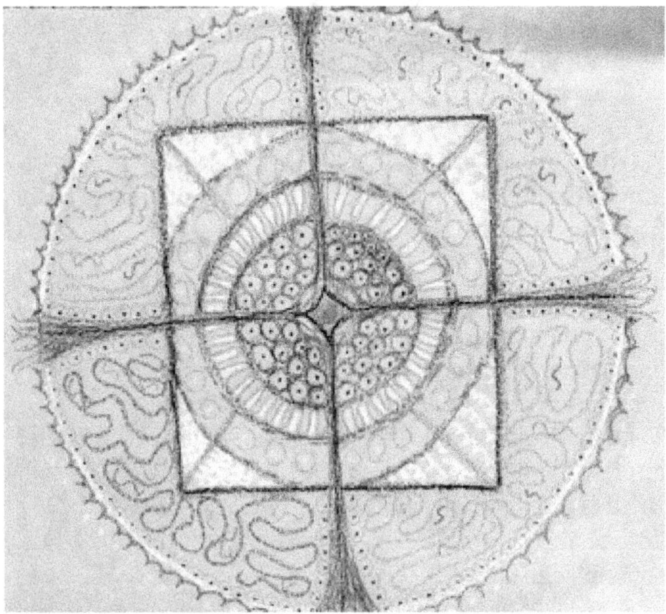

Figure 18: Order and Chaos, crayon, Pam Caraffa (2013).

Closing Ritual

Come together in a circle and join hands or stand close to one another. Ask each person to say one word or phrase representing what they want to remember from this session. After everyone has spoken, ask members to share anything else they'd like that relates to today's experience. Circle members then remove their sacred circle symbol from the altar and blow out their candle.

Summary

In this journey, labyrinths and mandalas were explored as conduits for illumination and wholeness. Your circle is another form of the sacred circle reflected in the labyrinth and the mandala. Your process offers a structure like a labyrinth, a consistent, spiral structure and group process that guides your travels as you explore consciousness. In your expressive arts journey, you travel inward and actively explore your inner life. Then you travel back into your creative spirit circle, and for a short time your personal unfolding path becomes the central focus as you discuss your experience. You share the unique insights of your life, and at the same time you walk side by side with the sojourners in your group. You learn from one another. You grow individually and transform as an intertwined circle.

Creative Weavings

This section offers ways to continue exploring and integrating sacred circles into your life.

- In your art journal, write about experiences on a day that make you aware of circles in your life, literally and figuratively.
- Spend a few minutes a day drawing an enso circle or a mandala as a mindfulness meditation.
- Take a mindful walk to locate and reflect on the circles that appear in nature and in your neighborhood.
- Read *Walking a Sacred Path* by Lauren Artress (1995).
- Locate and travel to labyrinths for a sacred walk as the seasons shift.

Chapter 8

Mindfulness and the Artful Journey

When you touch one thing with deep awareness, you touch everything.
> —Thich Nhat Hanh

Intention and Purpose

This expressive arts workshop explores integrating mindfulness practices into the creative process. In this way the present moment is welcomed into the artful journey, deepening the creative experience.

Creative Inquiries

- How do you embody mindfulness and cultivate presence in your creative practice?
- Where do you find yourself being "mindless" and on autopilot?
- How might mindfulness enhance your creativity?
- What does mindfulness bring to your inner and outer artful journey?

Introduction

We live in a hectic world. Our minds are pulled in multiple directions, and we can feel scattered, distracted, and overwhelmed as we move through our day. Mindfulness, defined as present-moment awareness, invites us to explore and cultivate presence, non-attachment, equanimity, acceptance, and non-judgment into every area of our lives. Mindfulness can enhance, motivate, and even shape our creative process.

Through the artful journey, life is lived to its fullest, embracing the totality of life's experiences including your creative passions, career, education, relationships, spirituality, and your physical well-being. All these areas are part of a Creative Living Web© that comprises a unique way for you to be the author and artist of your life.

Cultivating mindfulness and creativity is a way for you to consciously develop your creative potential in all aspects of your life. Buddhist monks established an early link between mindfulness and creativity. This can be observed in their beautiful works of art, created mindfully while in meditation: calligraphy, flower arrangements, poetry, sand mandalas, and tea ceremonies. Even the act of drinking tea can be an art symbolic of awakening, balance, harmony, and peace.

Opening Ritual and Invitation

Invite your circle members to tea. Suggest that they listen, slow down, smell the tea's aroma, feel the temperature, and enjoy the sensation of a sip. Through this process they can nourish themselves, coming into being with the tea, with themselves, and with one another.

The Chalice of Now: Tea Ceremony
The tea ceremony is a ritual to inspire greater awareness of the balance and connection between friends and the human soul and nature. The tea ceremony and meditation invite and evoke sensory awareness, while also serving as a transition into presence with oneself and other group members. The very act of preparing and drinking tea can cultivate gratitude and being present in the moment.

To prepare for the tea ceremony, arrange a variety of teacups with various types of tea and a pot of hot water. Use a meditation chime to usher in a period of silence where circle members are invited to quietly prepare their tea and offer gratitude before drinking it. Participants are then given the freedom to find a quiet place inside or outdoors to reflect on the sensory experience of drinking their tea, giving particular attention to the following:

- How does the tea smell, feel, look, taste? Notice its aroma.
- What type of tea are you drawn to choose?
- Are there any types of memories, feelings, or sensory sensations arising in your body as you sip the tea?
- How do you attentively savor your tea experience?
- How do you embody mindfulness and cultivate presence in your creative practice?
- Breathing in the tea's fragrance, tasting the flavor, observing the color, and feeling the warmth of the tea in your mouth and

throat can nourish and refresh you while carrying you into the present moment.

Check-In: Creative Mindfulness Meditation

Next, the facilitators invite the group to gather closely for a series of brief mindfulness suggestions that bring awareness to sensory experience. The following meditation and mark-making experience is explained and offered as an invitation. Depending on your timeframe, this experience can be modified to accommodate a 15-minute entry into your session, or, if you are offering a longer session, it may be a 30-minute entry into your expressive arts journey.

Before the series of mindfulness meditations begin, each participant chooses paper and various colored pencils and markers for mindful mark making during the experience. Mindful mark making is a process of making any type of spontaneous mark, color, drawing, or writing a word on a piece(s) of paper that comes to mind after a brief meditation. This is a way to nonverbally record experiences and can be used later in the session in a more in-depth expressive arts experience as a visual record of the meditation experience.

The following meditation guides the participants briefly through awareness practice for breath, listening, physical embodiment, sight, sound, touch, and taste. Periodically, the facilitator invites participants to capture their experience with mark making.

Mindful Breath: Breath as Anchor

The following script serves as an example of a guided meditation for the circle facilitator(s). There are also many online options if you conduct a brief internet search. Read the meditation slowly, with pauses between sentences, to encourage everyone to relax. Follow the instructions yourself, as you read, to help you find the best pace for the group.

> Your breath is your life force and brings life into your body. What does it feel like for you to experience your breath? Breathe In. Breathe Out. There is no need to control your breath. Simply notice it. Where do you feel your breath most vividly? Where do you sense it in your body? You may notice your chest or abdomen lift or rise. Observe the rhythm of your breath. See if you can follow just one inhale. And another. Now

shifting, follow one exhale. Now another. Maybe you also notice a pause in between breaths.

If you notice your attention has drifted, this is natural, simply begin again. Follow your breath through a few more cycles. The chime will signal a time to open your eyes and to transition back to the group (*Ring chimes*).

Invite members to take a piece of paper and a marker(s) of their choice to draw their breath. The rhythm of their breath may flow through their body, into their fingers, and onto the paper. This is a spontaneous mark-making process.

Mindful Embodiment

Next, welcome circle members to a brief body scan. This can be focused on simple awareness and relaxation, or you can offer a more in-depth body scan. Circle members can choose to sit, stand, or lie down. Adapt this to your group needs, to physical abilities and preferences.

The following is a brief body scan example to read slowly, with pauses:

> Find a comfortable spot. Notice the places your body touches your chair. Notice how the floor supports your feet. Notice that the earth is holding and supporting you. Notice the air around you. Notice your breath naturally going in and going out. Progressively bring attention to different parts of your body, including your face, ears, nose, mouth, throat, neck, shoulders, chest, heart space, stomach, hips, legs, knees, calves, and feet. Notice sensations as they arise and shift. There may be vibration, warmth, pressure, achy tingling, pulsing, releasing, or relaxing. What sensations do you notice arising in your body?

Invite members to take their marker and paper to make an image or words that represent the flow of energy as they move through the body scan. Did any sensations or messages arise? This can be layered on the first piece of paper, or additional pieces of paper can be used.

Mindful Listening

Next, you are encouraged to listen to the sounds around you.

Listen to the sounds arising in your environment. You may want to name the sounds. You are invited to listen with wide-open awareness. This means that your listening may even extend beyond the room, to the outdoors, or within your body. Let the sounds come to you and touch your eardrums. You may hear birds chirping, children playing, and other neighborhood noises.

Welcome whatever sounds arise. Some, such as the chirping birds, may have a pleasant tone, and some, such as a loud horn, may be unpleasant. Let your awareness travel with all sounds. Can you go inside the sound and notice how sounds arise and then disappear? Open yourself to the sounds, the musical notes of your environment in this moment, in this place.

Invite circle members to make spontaneous marks, colors, and words on their paper(s) that reflect the experience of mindful listening. As previously indicated, this can be layered on the first piece of paper or another piece of paper can be chosen. The mark making can be spontaneous, and, at the same time, circle members can notice and respond to any creative urges that arise.

Mindfulness of the Senses

Continue the meditation with an exploration of different senses. To explore taste, offer a couple of options such as a mint or small chocolate. Encourage participants to touch and smell the mint or chocolate before tasting it. On a table or in the center of the circle, place a variety of sensory objects from nature such as flowers, leaves, lavender, stones, sticks, and different types of fragrances. Invite circle members to select an item from nature and to notice the feel, the texture, and the scent. Set aside a few minutes for exploration of various items using sight, smell, sound, taste, and touch. After a few minutes, invite participants, with eyes closed or open, to draw a mark, color, or symbol that reflects their experience.

Mindful Witness

For this final meditation, encourage participants to draw attention to their mind. Invite them to observe the inner flow of thoughts, emotions, images, and any impulses that arise.

You may notice a stream of thoughts, or the thoughts may arise slowly. It can help to notice if your thoughts emerge as emotions, actions, or images. Now, try to name the thoughts such as planning, comparing, reviewing. Thoughts may have a feeling tone, and these can also be named: pleasant, unpleasant, sad, worried, joyful, tired, content. As you observe and name your thoughts, meet the thought with openness and curiosity and a willingness to accept thoughts as they arrive, without aversion or getting stuck on one thought. After you name a thought, you can let the thought go. You can imagine seeing your thoughts drift by like leaves on a stream or floating on a cloud. Now, we will spend a few minutes in silence, so that you can step into a quiet observer space with your thoughts.

After a couple of minutes, ask your circle members to notice what occurred for them in this mindful-witness experience. Invite them to add some marks that represent what they experienced. As closure for this entire mindfulness experience, ask participants to look at all their mark making and to notice the variety of lines, shapes, colors, marks that they used on their paper in the brief moments of capturing their experiences. Ask if any other words or messages arose that they want to record. The mark-making papers can be used and included in their expressive arts journey later in the circle meeting. The facilitator can invite each person to briefly share their mark making and a few words about the experience.

Lecturette: Cultivating Mindful Presence on the Creative Journey

Mindful awareness cultivates openness, non-attachment, curiosity, non-judgment, and an elevated awareness of one's thoughts, feelings, behaviors, senses, and environment in the present moment. Mindful awareness can be defined as paying attention to present-moment experiences with openness, curiosity, and a willingness to be with what is (Smalley & Winston, 2010).

Mindfulness is the art of awareness with purposeful attention to the present moment, with an intentional stance of non-attached equanimity. Equanimity is a welcoming attitude, a state of conscious awareness, psychological stability, and composure through the moment-to moment changes that arise in daily life (Siegel, 2010).

Other attitudes of mindfulness include non-judgment, loving kindness, compassion, acceptance, non-attachment, non-striving, beginner's mind. Mindfulness practice has scientific support to reduce stress, improve attention, boost the immune system, reduce emotional reactivity, and promote a general sense of health and well-being (Kabat-Zinn, 1994).

Creative Mindfulness

The practice of creative mindfulness combines mindfulness with the creative process. Mindfulness helps us to slow down and move past the stress of daily distractions and can bring us to a place of openness and curiosity that allows the opportunity to access our creativity (Siegel, 2010). Research has shown that mindfulness meditation strengthens and balances neural networks in the brain that increases creativity, divergent thinking, and innovation (Kabat-Zinn, 1994; Smalley & Winston, 2010).

When we bring mindfulness and presence into our creative process, we release patterns of judgment, perfectionism, and attachment, and we enter deeper states of creative flow. When we relax the inner critic through mindful self-compassion, we invite our creative muse, or sources of inspiration, on our journey. This can give us the freedom and courage to take creative risks, innovate, and explore new creative frontiers. Artmaking supports cognitive flexibility and divergent thinking, and opens us to new ideas (Chang, 2014).

Mindfulness practice can be a pathway to unlock creativity (Kaufman & Gregoire, 2015). Likewise, creative practice is a way of knowing and entering more heightened, mindful awareness. Creativity can shift the creator into a meditative state. Like the ocean, creative mindfulness generates a rhythmic flow between the waves of mindfulness and creativity. As one enters the creative flow, creativity becomes a portal to presence, through which the artist can mindfully express feelings on multiple dimensions of consciousness.

Through the creative process, one mindfully observes color, shapes, feeling, textures, as well as layers of light and shadow, which propel us into the present moment. The creative self becomes a teacher and guide, leading us into more mindful awareness, which is our essential nature. Trust the unfolding of your process, as if you are surfing ocean waves; be present with each creative urge. Mindfulness and creativity are ideal companions on the creative journey.

Crossing the Threshold

The facilitators support participants crossing the threshold into an expressive arts journey by offering an embodied, mindful movement experience, such as an outdoor sitting or walking meditation, depending on mobility preferences. The following example offers a walking meditation to help participants experience a felt sense of their artful journey. This can be shared as an example before participants embark on a personal mindful walk, or the facilitator can lead a guided walk.

Movement Meditation

Start walking with a slow, mindful pace and connect to your breath, as though you are walking your artful journey. Notice during the walk when thoughts arise. Notice any sensations in your feet and legs. Slowly observe all sorts of sensations: muscular movements, stretching, pressure, tension, and weight. Keep your attention focused on your body from your hips down, especially your feet.

Be aware of your feet and legs, but also let yourself be present to the environment and to nature if you are outdoors. Take in the sights and sounds of nature with awareness. Stay connected to your moment-to-moment experience of sensing: seeing, hearing, smelling, and feeling emotions. After a few minutes, start walking at your normal pace, maintaining this moment-to-moment awareness. When you notice your mind wandering, bring your attention back to the sensations in your feet and legs as you maintain awareness of the present moment as you walk. Notice your breath and pay attention to your body and to the sounds of nature. As you walk your artful journey, what do you notice and discover in the earth beneath your feet?

Expressive Arts Journey: Sandplay, Soulscapes, and the Artful Journey

Description

Sandplay was the inspiration for this expressive arts process. This therapeutic approach uses a sandtray, water, miniature toys, animal and other figures, or objects from nature to invite the client to create an imaginary world (Homeyer & Sweeney, 2017). Metaphor and archetypal symbols are used to develop a visual representation or story that fosters a sense of balance and wholeness.

The soulscape, a visual depiction of the landscape of your soul/psyche/life force, will be used to mindfully explore your artful journey. Through the experience of sandplay, each participant creates their unique soulscape, a visual representation of the essence of their artful journey. The artistic exploration of your soulscape invites you to connect to your creative passions and feelings, discover novel pathways, and gain deeper insights.

Materials and Supplies

- Extra-large disposable aluminum cooking tins filled with sand
- Items from nature such as feathers, leaves, pinecones, sticks, stones, shells, and mark-making instruments
- Miniature figurines of animals, people, as well as a variety of small household, metaphorical objects
- Various mixed-media art supplies: candles, fiber, old jewelry, art papers
- Water

Guidelines and Process

Invite each person to bring several meaningful items from home or from nature that are symbolic of their artful journey. Provide each participant with their own sandtray, such as an aluminum pan filled with sand. Additionally, offer participants a variety of mixed-media supplies and items, inviting them to select the metaphors and symbols that best represent their unique soulscape and artful journey. Offer each person a seed to plant in their soulscape to serve as a metaphorical representative of their creative life force.

Begin by asking participants to take a mindful minute, close their eyes, and focus on their breathing. Invite each participant to imagine what their soulscape and artful journey would look, feel, and sound like. Suggest they enter mindful play as they create an imaginary world, a soulscape of their artful journey. Figurines and objects can be placed in the sandtray in spontaneous and intuitive ways that reflect each creator's unique experience.

The sandtray becomes a sacred space, a place to play with symbols and metaphors that offer creative possibilities. Encourage participants to engage in their sandbox creations with mindful awareness, self-compassion, non-attachment, non-judgment, beginner's mind, and playful curiosity. What do you notice is embedded and emerging from the sandplay, your visual soulscape, and your artful journey?

Writing Reflection
After completing the sandplay process, invite participants to write and reflect on the following:

- What title, story, poem describes your sandplay and soulscape?
- What creative frontier(s) is mindfulness awakening within you?
- What might the sand be teaching you about the value of impermanence and detachment in your artful journey?
- How will you mindfully nurture and nourish the seeds of your creativity?

Often the hands will solve a mystery that the intellect has struggled with in vain.
— C.G. Jung

Kim: This soulscape, with its center island (Figure 19), represents a Sea of Mind. I chose a tortoise because it symbolizes longevity, ancient longings, and wisdom. This is about my need to accept a new pace in my life and balance the restlessness and the expansiveness of my soul. The ripples represent the interface with our human presence in this lifetime. I experience touch, taste, sound, hearing, and mindsight as ways that we connect. The boat is

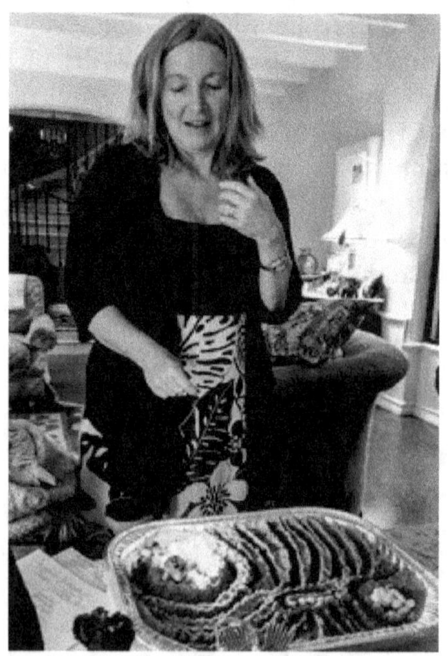

Figure 19: WOW Story: Loving Kindness and Transformation, sandtray, Kim McCallum (2016).

to navigate my mind and consciousness and the materiality of experience. Using senses and embodiment and what I am conscious of to propel it. The fire is my center, my energy. The tortoise moves slowly in between the conscious and unconscious realms.

Conscious Closure and Integration

For conscious closure, gather around each sandtray and invite each person to share their experience of mindfulness and their creative process, writing, and poetry. After everyone has shared their personal experience of their soulscape, the group can discuss any insights, metaphors, symbols, or new awareness that emerged during the mindfulness and artful journey expressive arts session. An inquiry for the group might be: "What was your experience of being a mindful witness for your circle members?"

Close with a Loving Kindness Meditation
This website is a good source:
https://ggia.berkeley.edu/practice/loving_kindness_meditation

> May you be safe.
> May you be happy.
> May you be peaceful.
> May you be healthy.
> May you be strong.
> May you be at ease.
> May you thrive and contribute to
> The wellbeing of Earth and our World Community.
> May you realize that
> You are perfect and whole as you are.

Summary

Mindfulness is central to person-centered expressive arts. The focus is not on the outcome or aesthetic of the art created but on authentic self-expression and exploration through awareness and creative process. Generous creative freedom is provided to let go and enjoy the full experience of the creative process while relinquishing attachment to the result.

Circle members are encouraged to consciously share the challenges and insights that emerge. Ultimately, this is how we bring presence to one another throughout the Creative Spirit Circle process. To hold oneself in a sacred container and to be held there by others can expand our innate creativity.

Creative Weavings

- Create a mindful art journal in which you can practice creative mindfulness and visually express creative ideas and observations.
- Begin a daily mindfulness practice.
- Try a mindfulness meditation app.
- Use rituals to cross a threshold into creative expression, such as a tea ceremony or mindful selection of art supplies.
- Practice a mindful body scan by outlining the shape of your body on a sheet of paper, and then using colored pencils or markers to color sensations, pain, and emotions you are experiencing in your body.
- When you find yourself on autopilot, press the reset button by pausing for mindfulness meditation and expressive arts.

Chapter 9

Dreams and Individuation

A dream which is not interpreted is like a letter which is not read.

— Brachot 55a, Babylonian Torah

Intention and Purpose

How often do you remember your dreams? Those nightly images from your unconscious can help inspire your creativity. Sharing dreams with others may be a pathway for personal growth. This journey explores a theory of adult development and how dreams can be one of the ingredients to help reach your fullest potential. Jill Mellick (2001) said in *The Art of Dreaming* (p. 24): "When we explore our dreams through simple expressive arts, we also strengthen our innate capacity to creatively express our inner worlds, and we widen the path to our souls."

Creative Inquiries

- Can you recall a dream that was meaningful to you? How did you interpret it?
- What is your relationship with your dream life? For example, do you keep a dream diary?
- Have dreams helped you grow? If so, what have you learned from your dream world?
- What does becoming a whole person mean to you at this point in your life? How might dreamwork open doors to your greater potential?

Introduction

This session focuses on what it means to grow as a person and how remembering dreams can support that process. Carl Jung's concept of *individuation* is useful here and means developing into your own unique self. As we mature, we further individuate by striving for *self-actualization*. A term coined by Abraham Maslow (1998), self-actualization refers to a focus on fulfilling your potential. For example, Jung suggested that part of the process of individuating is developing a relationship with your unconscious.

The unconscious is what you are unaware of in yourself and what you defend against remembering because it may be frightening or unacceptable (Ullman & Zimmerman, 1979). Stanley Krippner (1990) pointed out that "Dream activities appear to be metaphors for our waking concerns. And it is often helpful to find a metaphorical image or activity for a personal problem." Personal growth may be enhanced if you become aware of unknown parts of yourself and discover aspects of your life you were avoiding. Your unconscious speaks to you through dreams, daydreams, active imagination, sudden intuitions, synchronistic events, free association, and creative expression.

Circle Member Preparation for Dreamwork
Each circle member brings a dream or dream fragment to work with. Recommend that members record dreams every night starting three to four weeks in advance of the session. Include the following suggestions in your email.

1. Ponder these two quotes:
    a. "People will do anything, no matter how absurd, in order to avoid facing their own souls. One does not become enlightened by imagining figures of light, but by making the darkness conscious" (Jung, 1968, p. 99).
    b. More advanced levels of adult development do not generally occur until around mid-life. Adult development expert Robert Kegan postulates, "What if we are living longer so that we can create more of the order of consciousness that may actually save us from the peril in which we live?" Watch Kegan's (2013) 20-minute video, *The further reaches of adult development* (https://www.youtube.com/watch?v=BoasM4cCHBc), or read an article about Kegan's theory of adult development (Lewin et al., 2019). The article is readily accessible online and has many examples of levels of adult development or "orders of consciousness."

2. Cultivate your dream life. It's normal to not remember your dreams, but you can recall them, or at least fragments of them, if you focus your mind's attention on them regularly. Say to yourself before you go to sleep, "I will remember my dreams." Place a pen and paper close to your bed so you can reach it without much movement. When you awaken during the night or in the morning, write whatever you remember, even if it is just a phrase or a scene. Do this frequently for a few weeks.

3. The following are suggestions from two sources (Lytton, 2020; Mellick, 2001).

    a. Journal about hints that unconscious material is at play as you notice it. This could be dreams, daydreams, slips of the tongue, intuitions, and strong emotional reactions. Notice what you experience. Write down or draw your dreams. Record surprising thoughts, synchronicities, or unexpected emotions.

    b. What do you associate these dream experiences with? Make no judgments; just record the associations or related thoughts or feelings that come to mind. Pay special attention to what is on the edge of your awareness. Breathe, be still, and invite new awareness to come forth.

        i. What feelings do you recall from the dream? What was the "temperature" of the feelings? What do you notice about the feelings in your waking life?

        ii. What images from your waking life such as people, places, or events have appeared in your dream(s)?

        iii. You might ask for others' thoughts; this may spur your memory or associations.

    c. Interpret and integrate the meaning of your dream experience.

        i. Is there something new that has entered your consciousness? What does this dream experience mean to you?

        ii. Welcome this insight non-judgmentally. Accept this formerly unknown, secret, or rejected wish, fear, or memory.

iii. Explore how it relates to other parts of you. Play with it, practice thinking or acting on it, let it come out to play with others.

iv. Sometimes dreams can be disturbing. Anyone can have a disturbing dream from time to time. They can refer to a stressful time, food that doesn't agree with you, or personal problems of one kind or another. If you continue to have disturbing dreams, consider seeking a therapist for consultation.

This process will help integrate experiences from your dreams into your conscious awareness.

Opening Ritual

In the middle of your circle, set up a large bowl of water and float a small candle for each circle member. Invite each participant to light a candle to represent illuminating the nighttime of dreams and the shadowy edges of the unconscious. Jung defined archetypes as images and themes that arise from the collective unconscious and tend to have universal meanings across cultures. Introduce the water archetype as imagery for the unconscious and an alchemic catalyst for individuation. In dreams, water often represents the unconscious, a key source of your individuality (Jung, 1969). Water has been associated with birth, death, and rebirth by many Indigenous Peoples and often represents going inward, into the unconscious and the dream world.

One facilitator may read the following or something else that suits your session:

> Prepare for deep inner reflection and personal sharing. We honor life and welcome our personal and collective renewal and transformation by lighting floating candles. Candles signal light in the darkness and the illumination of truth. Both flame and water symbolize impermanence and transformation. Dreamwork sheds light on internal darkness. What messages are you discovering from your dreams?

Check-In

Invite each person to share something meaningful about their past months' experience with their dreams, intuitions, and synchronicities. Allow about 5–7 minutes for each person.

Lecturette

Certain aspects of personal growth seem to happen automatically. Infants naturally want to explore and learn about the world. Children want control over their lives and to get their needs met. Most parents in the world learn how to help their children move from a focus on their own needs to fitting into a family and community. Beyond that level, however, a person must actively work toward further psychological growth. Human understanding of dreams is still fragmented, but dreams are, among other things, a biological tool to help integrate daily events within the context of our lives and introduce possibilities for growth (Wamsley, 2022). This discussion focuses first on how adults can grow in maturity and consciousness. It also discusses how dreams can aid that process.

Individuation: Further Reaches of Adult Development

Carl Jung (1967) stated that individuation means becoming an "individual," and insofar as "'individuality' embraces our innermost, last, and incomparable uniqueness, it also implies becoming one's own self" (p. 173).

Research indicates that people can move through specific stages of human development (Joiner & Josephs, 2006; Lewin et al., 2019) to individuate. In each of these stages, a person takes on a new mindset, a transformation and enhancement of the way they know and experience the world. Current studies suggest that dream life reflects the needs and tasks of an individual's life within the mindset of their current stage of development (Maggiolini et al., 2020). So, having a map of developmental stages enables a person to understand their current mindset and explore hopes and concerns that arise in dreams.

The rest of this section briefly describes this map of adult development (Joiner & Josephs, 2006). Most people move from childhood to the first stage of adulthood when they understand the difference between imagination and reality and begin to regulate impulses. First, they learn how to get what they need and want—"It's all about me." Fortunately, most people integrate this and move on to the second level of adulthood by learning how to fit in and follow the rules of their own culture. Priorities shift from *me* to *us* and identifying with the relationships one has. Joiner and Joseph (2006) call this the "conformer" stage. It is the most common stage of adulthood; only a minority of people in the world move beyond it.

When individuals integrate and transcend this "tribal" orientation, problem-solving and analytical skills develop. It becomes important to stand out from the crowd in some way, to improve and accomplish things. This stage is called the "expert" level because it happens when people develop some sort of expertise, whether it is cooking or carpentry, poetry, or physics. At this level, individuals begin to notice internal moods and develop a strong self-image. Thinking is still mostly black and white; ideas and things are good or bad, without much nuance.

The next stage, the "achiever" level (Joiner & Josephs, 2006), involves a desire to achieve a goal bigger than the individual. It is here that insight into and acceptance of the many nuances, contradictions, and paradoxes of life begins. More attention is paid to why people behave the way they do. Achievers begin to cultivate their own values, choose their belief systems from the many available, and make independent choices.

The stages mentioned so far have a heroic component to them. People are driven first by a desire to be valuable and belong, next by standing out in some way, and then by setting and achieving goals. A person must build self-confidence and a strong ego to hold their own as part of a larger world.

At the post-heroic levels of human existence, growth is focused on harnessing those earlier drives for the sake of personal and collective well-being. At what Joiner and Josephs (2006) call the "catalyst" level, a person begins to understand that everyone on Earth is interdependent. Thinking begins to shift from dualistic to unitive thinking, from "either/or" to "both/and." Seeing more connections, patterns, and the systems of which they are a part leads to more visions of what is possible. At this level, inner thoughts and feelings become more visible to the person. At this stage and beyond, developing creative expression becomes particularly important. Accessing imagination and using all of one's senses heightens self-awareness and openness to change.

It takes courage to examine inner life and to become aware of prejudice and shadow behavior (Jung, 1967). In the earlier stages of individuation, behavior is driven by genetics and socialization more than active, personal choice. The catalyst level, however, brings the ability to notice and examine emotions and thoughts that emerge in daily life and in dreams. Dreamwork is another way to explore inner life and expand consciousness by connecting to inner selves.

At the catalyst level, shadow and other disparate aspects of self are being actively integrated. This leads to the next level, the "co-creator" stage, and the quest for self-actualization, fully living a person's deepest values and purpose. A person at the co-creator level recognizes that life is mutually created by everyone (consciously or unconsciously), so they actively seek to better everyone's lives using all the collaborative skills they have learned.

Dreamwork is central to yielding a clearer view of the self and suggests greater choices regarding how to think and act. Over time, dreams may also lead to the advancement of spiritual intelligence. A dreamer can consciously incubate dreams to co-create and envision greater possibilities for self and others (Deslauriers, 2020).

At the highest level described by Joiner and Josephs (2006), the "synergist" stage, it becomes possible to transcend the ego and become more and more present to what's happening in the world outside of oneself and respond with wisdom, inclusivity, and compassion *in the moment as it unfolds*. The individual is no longer tied to a particular identity and is constantly re-creating themselves through exploring the many ways of understanding and interacting with other people and with the cosmos. The highest level has been reached only rarely—by a few who are called famous, such as Nelson Mandela and Eleanor Roosevelt, and by small numbers of everyday persons who increase the well-being of all of us by, in Gandhi's words, "being the change" they desire to see in the world, day by day.

Individuals develop unevenly and may behave on a few levels on any given day, while being at a stage that is typical of them for that period of life. To evolve to higher levels, a person must be willing to tune out the norms of society and listen to their inner voice. More of a person's essence emerges, resulting in expanded unique contributions to the world. It takes sustained energy to think for oneself and courage to take a different path from loved ones. As James Hollis (1993) wrote: "We may become strangers to those who thought they knew us, but at least we are no longer strangers to ourselves" (p. 116). Everyone is a work in progress. The key is whether you consider *developing yourself* to be part of your life's work.

The Value of Dream Work to Further Individuation
Dreams offer invaluable assistance from the unconscious that can further individuation. Dreaming is an artistic consciousness and does not conform to the principles of waking life. Dreams speak in a poetic language of primary process, which is imaginal, non-linear, and uses archetypes. Oftentimes, wishes and fears are central to the story within a dream. The residue of the day influences a dream. People, places, and emotions are the artistic tools repurposed to create the dream's message.

While your day mind is busy solving logically, your night mind is following its own agenda in service of what is possible. Dreams counterbalance the linear conscious mind by introducing metaphors, symbols, and imagery, balancing logic with intuition and linearity with circularity. Dreams weave and dance rather than walk a straight line.

No one remembers all their dreams, and many people remember few. Recent research indicates, though, that people probably have several dreams each night, which help to process what's happened to them and guide them in addressing their problems and opportunities. Dreams are another way of knowing and invite you to consider novel ways of being in the world (Taylor, 2009). While you may block out what seem to be negative experiences and feelings during the day, your brain experiences life neutrally and in dreams presents you with symbols and metaphors to heal and integrate life's experiences.

In 2009, Stanley Krippner discussed how dreams are altered states of consciousness and offer ways to work with inner wounds and conflicts. Krippner pointed out that when people deny their pain and behave in a childish way in an intimate relationship, "Dreams will often prod us into embarking on a more rewarding relationship that we need to have with ourselves."

How Does Dreamwork Serve Individuation and the Journey to Wholeness?
As discussed earlier, advanced stages of individuation usually begin in mid-life (Kegan, 2013). The psychological crises in mid-life cannot be worked through with the same tools used to resolve logical problems. Dreamwork is well suited for self-inquiry that leads to individuation and spiritual actualization. A commitment to harvesting dreams leads to developing multiple skills that transcend the rational mind. This includes:

1. Improved metaphoric and imagistic thinking
2. Increased appreciation of the nuances of dream life and variety of dreams
3. Increased openness to the creative potential of the mind and development of intentional work with dreams
4. Better understanding of the fluid boundaries between body and mind
5. Increased ability to apply guidance from dream
6. Increased empathy towards others (Deslauriers, 2000, p. 4)

Jung proposed that in middle age there can be a deeper connection to the unconscious. Dreams often deal with life's big challenges and universal human problems. Dreamwork nudges overlooked issues into awareness and enables a dialogue between parts of oneself that may be suppressed or less developed. Symbols embedded in dreams can open dimensions of experience that were previously concealed. This exploration can lead to acceptance and integration for the dreamer. Sharing dreams is a different type of self-disclosure and leads to greater intimacy in the group.

Dreams serve as a pathway, a threshold, and a gateway to higher levels of consciousness. The authors of this book are collectively using expressive arts and dreamwork to advance our quest for wholeness.

The remainder of this expressive arts journey provides tools for working with dreams to elevate your level of consciousness.

Crossing the Threshold

To deepen your understanding of the dream you brought to this session, partner with one other person and take turns sharing your dreams. It can be valuable for you to hear other people's ideas about what your dream might mean as a springboard for your understanding. Practice your PCL skills. The following dream-sharing process is adapted from the work of dream expert Montague Ullman (1996).

1. Dream Speaker: Share a dream, preferably one that was very meaningful to you or one you do not completely understand.
2. Wisdom Listener: This is a process of deep listening. Ask the dreamer to repeat sections of the dream that are not clear to you. Ask clarifying questions to get a more fulsome image of the dream. Examples include: Who are the characters in your

dream and how do you interact with them? What colors are in your dream? What else comes to mind?

3. Dream Speaker: Once the listener has a clear picture of your dream, you might share reflections on some symbols in your dream and how you interpret the dream thus far.

4. Wisdom Listener: Ask interpretive questions, such as: "What does this part mean to you? What parts of you do the various characters and elements represent? What does your dream remind you of?" When you are ready, respond to the dream by saying "If this were my dream..." This process respects the dreamer's experience while allowing listeners to share their experience of the dream. It is not intended to be an interpretation; only the dreamer can do that. It does offer further ideas about the possible meaning for the dreamer. In this way, the dreamer can feel deeply "heard." For example, you might say something like, "If this were my dream, I would feel excited and yet strangely scared."

5. Dream Speaker: You are free to accept what resonates with you and to reject what doesn't. Dreams are highly personal because they reflect how your mind experiences your life. You may want to articulate to the wisdom listener what is useful about their comments. The whole experience is also enriching for them.

WOW Story
Pam Caraffa shared a dream (2014)

I went to a lush garden with a pond and house. People were lounging and talking. Some knew each other well and others didn't. Freeman Patterson (a famous photographer) said to me, "Settle in and relax." Everything was happening very slowly; I felt I needed to be present in every moment. The colors were shimmering, and the trees were lush and colorful. I was surprised how relaxed and happy everyone was.

Freeman wanted me to talk first, which surprised me. There was a large closet of clothing, and some women, laughing and chatting, helped me pick out a long maxi skirt and a hefty blazer—bright pink with lace in various places. I was very nervous about speaking and didn't understand why I needed to speak. I seemed to be the only one who didn't know what was going on. They were very mature. I was spellbound.

Freeman suggested I share about my leadership and psychology: "You have a lot to offer the group." He wanted me to get the group off to a deeper start, but I felt like I was the one going to the well of wisdom.

A group member's interpretation, "If this were my dream":
It feels good even though I am a bit afraid. They are nice and kind and I picked out a new outfit. The clothes are my persona, and I am putting on a different persona. This feels freeing and the leader of the group is a "free man" in a garden that suggests a new beginning. I keep thinking everyone is grown up. Maybe I will grow up, too, in this beautiful place. The men and women are on separate sides. I have been asked to talk about my "lead-her ship." I get to play dress up! Everything is relaxed and welcoming and I am invited in.

There is integration in the soul and self. Free-Man Patterson is a messenger and has something to say to me. He is saying that I have something from my depths to offer and bring to this circle of creativity that I really want to be a part of. I thought it was going to be work but I am really here to play and create. I am not sure it feels like me, but it is time to put on these new clothes. It feels like the feminine skirt and masculine jacket are parts of me being integrated. I will integrate this lace and pink, and I will flow and be in the moment and not have to produce. They are all mature. This is my tribe. Which side do I sit on: the masculine or the feminine? How do I integrate this? This is where I want to be. He wants me to start. This is my time, and my voice needs to be heard.

The "If this were my dream..." scenario and other questions from the group helped the dreamer connect firmly with the dream. She felt a part of her (a "free male" part) was inviting her to be relaxed despite being a beginner at photography and that she had a lot to bring to this art from her psychological and leadership work. She wants to "lead her ship" and bring her whole self and essence to photography, while also trying on some new parts of herself that haven't emerged in her work life.

Expressive Arts Journey: Art of Dreaming

Description

Dreams frequently have an inherent art form to them. As Jill Mellick (2001) said in *The Art of Dreaming*, "find your dream's organic artform" (p. 12). Words are two-dimensional, but dreams are as three-dimensional as life. What art form suits the dream you want to explore today? It might be drawing, painting, collage, sculpture, weaving, poetry, movement, or music. Choose an art form as a further way to experience and express your dream. These messages from your unconscious have many layers. Using expressive arts to illustrate them in some way often brings additional depths of meaning to light.

Guidelines and Process

Prepare a separate space for each person. Invite everyone to reflect on and creatively express their dream. What color is your dream? What shape and form does it have? How does your dream feel? How do the characters in your dream relate to one another? What does your dream remind you of? How is your dream best expressed? If your dream is best expressed in movement or music, you may practice what you created. Take a few notes so you can share the movement or music with your group during conscious closure.

Materials and Supplies

- Paper for creative expression and for writing
- Pastels, colored pencils, watercolors, acrylic paint, and brushes
- Magazines for collage material
- Clay for sculpting and objects such as beads, old keys, hearts, etc.
- Yarn, cords, hoops for making a dreamcatcher, and other weaving material
- Drums, wooden flutes, a child's xylophone, or other simple musical instruments

Writing Reflection

Step back from your artmaking experience and write about the impact of the experience on you.

- What was it like to creatively express your dream?
- What does your creation tell you about your dream?

- How is your dream assisting your development?
- What has this session and the prework meant to you? Example: Key messages?

(Note: Although this photo [Figure 20] is in black and white, Ginger is describing the artwork as it appears to her in color. Colors may serve as symbols in dreamwork.)

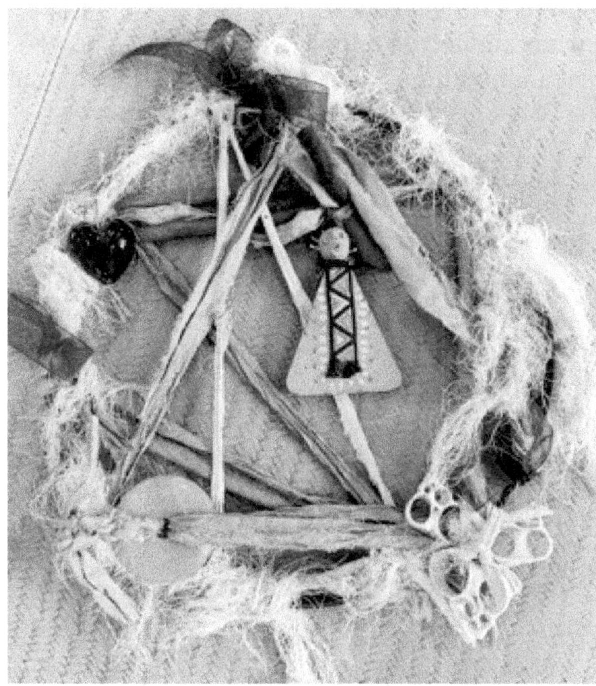

Figure 20: WOW Story, A Dream of Wholeness, mixed media, Ginger Reinert (2014).

Ginger: This image represents a dream I had of a mandala floating in space. An iron hoop from an old Chinese bucket represents the circle of life. The colorful yarn and ribbons connect the many facets of my life chart. Blue symbolizes emerging order and stability, orange wisdom and mindfulness. The fuzzy white yarn depicts the soft edges of chaos, from which order and meaning evolve. Within the mandala are four tokens: a glass heart representing love, a wooden shaman embodying the mystic, shells representing growth, and a Chinese bi (a circular piece of jade) representing spirituality. The two key messages for me from this dream are (a) learning that my subconscious speaks to me in symbols and encourages my self-actualization and (b) that it was important for me to focus more on being and less on doing.

Conscious Closure and Integration

When you come together in a circle again, share your artwork, its impact on your thinking about your dream, and any reflections on the session's meaning for you. If you have been attending to your dreams, share insights on how dreams inform your life journey. Allow 10 minutes per group member.

To close this journey, consider reading the poem "Dreams" by Langston Hughes (2002) or a written piece of your own choosing about the positive value of exploring dreams. You may follow that with a "Drinking Our Intentions" ritual. Pour everyone a small glass of water in honor of the water archetype and its transformative powers. Invite each person to set an intention for the next steps in their dream work and individuation. Drink your water together.

Summary

This expressive arts journey introduced dreamwork as an artistic language that fosters individuation. Dreams play an important role in the journey toward self-actualization because they offer privileged wisdom and spark insights. There are many examples of dreamwork resulting in impactful or creative actions in daily life.

For instance, Mahatma Gandhi had the idea of a hunger strike from a dream, which eventually resulted in the practice of nonviolent resistance and the freeing of India from British rule. The Beatles' John Lennon once said about his music, "The good stuff comes in the middle of the night, out of a creative space, and you have to get up and write it down" (Klerk, 2022, p. 12). Stanley Krippner (2009) counseled that this torn world needs direction from both the realm of dreams and the realm of nature. We need intuition and reason, common sense, and imagination.

Creative Weavings

- Try "dream incubation" (Klerk, 2022): Before you go to sleep, ask for a dream that will help you. For instance, you could ask, "How can I be more creative?"
- Use a dream journal to capture your dreams and other unconscious material as it emerges. Use collage, images, words, titles, and identify key insights.
- Make a drawing, a finger-painting, clay object, or other art about your dreams.
- Pay attention to your thoughts and behaviors. Where do you think you are in your individuation process? How would you like to develop?

- Ask your dreams to show you how to grow.

Chapter 10

Air:
Breathing Creative Spirit into Life

As we sit together, may the cadence of our collective breath connect our souls.
—Nancy Williger

Intention and Purpose

Air is invisible and omnipresent. As such, it is easy to forget that it is there at all. As one of the four elements, air is required for survival, yet it is easy to take air for granted. Part of transforming to a higher level of being is becoming more present to and in a compassionate relationship with everything in life, from the most mundane, such as breathing, to the most complex and challenging. In this expressive arts journey, the meanings of air and breath will be explored.

Creative Inquiries

- What parts of your creative breath (inspiration) do you want to breathe life into?
- What ancient rhythm might be asleep in your soul?
- Where might you need a "clearance"? What clutter needs to be removed to allow the air (your life) to flow?
- Just as air is invisible, so are energy, connection, love, thought, pain, and sound. What invisible parts of your life may need to be explored and expressed?

Introduction

How many times a day do you think about the air you are breathing? Perhaps when the air quality is bad, when there is an odor to the normally odorless element. Perhaps if you are ill or have trouble breathing. Of all the elements, air is likely to be the one you take most for granted. In an airless environment, underwater or in space, you become very aware of how close you are to death if your air supply is compromised. Without air, the leaves would not rustle in the trees; you would not hear the sound of bells in the distance or any sound at all. We would not have discovered the warmth of fire. Air is the basis for all that is beautiful on our planet.

By itself air is invisible; we move through it, and it moves through us. As we breathe, we take in what is outside of us. As we breathe out, we exhale what has been inside of us. The action of breathing helps us become one with our surroundings. We are together in needing and breathing the same air. When you pollute the air of others, you pollute your own as well. What better way to remind us that we are interconnected?

What other invisible things cross your path that you may take for granted? Take a moment to marvel at the curious and beautiful symbiosis of plants and animals when it comes to air. We breathe in oxygen and breathe out carbon dioxide, which the plants then absorb and put into our soil as they send precious oxygen into the air. Nature has created a balanced ecosystem to sustain life.

Think about all the words that come from the Latin root, "spirare" (to breathe). It will take you on a fun journey with inspire, conspire, spirit, spiral, expire, respiration. Perhaps you will think of more words that reflect air and breath.

Opening Ritual and Invitation

Think about the invisible artist who lives within and celebrate the inspiration received from your breath.

Air is all around us when we are inside and outside, though some feel the need for "fresh air" from the outside. Setting the stage for this expressive arts journey might include candles, balloons, flags, fans (paper or otherwise), feathers, wind chimes, tin whistles, and bubble solution with wands or any item that makes you more aware of air. Play soft music as the group gathers and settles into the moment.

One choice is to stand in a circle and, one at a time, have each person fan the air around the person next to them. Another choice is to wave burning sage and watch how the smoke moves in the air. You might have a small altar with one candle per participant that is lit at this stage and blown out at the end. Invite your group to hold their breath for 30 seconds (or less) to experience being without air. Your group may think of many more ideas. The goal is to have the group members become more aware of how important air is in our lives, and how breath serves as daily inspiration.

> *Music is the ultimate elegant encounter of sound and*
> *silence in the invisibility of air.*
> — John O'Donohue (2010, p. 37)

Check-In

With a background of calming music, the facilitator invites group members to talk about what "air" means to each of them, either incorporating answers to some of the above questions or expressing personal awareness, experiences, and ideas about the topic.

Lecturette: Air as Creative Spirit

We all have familiarity with air. Here are some thoughts that could spark new associations with the concept. It is important to read slowly so the group has a moment to contemplate each thought. This also slows the pace in preparation for the gradual turning inward that follows.

- It is our first breath that brings us into the physical/material world and our last breath that takes us into eternity. Watch Samuel Beckett's one-minute play *Breathe* (Wingcom, 2007).
- We can move and dance through air and move the air as we go. With movement, things can stay aloft or make designs, as with dancing scarves.
- Some things are lighter than air and can be suspended in air, holding the space in the moment. Think about helium balloons or kites.
- Fans move air. Windmills are moved by air. Magicians wave a wand to symbolize magic.
- Air sustains life. Without air, death occurs within minutes. Humanity is acutely dependent upon air; yet air is taken for granted, viewed as plentiful, and assumed to endure through eternity. Would cultivating gratitude for air be a good place to begin a gratitude exercise?

- Focus on your breath. Follow your breath on its inward and outward journey.
- Sit on a beach or listen to a recording of ocean waves crashing over and over. Sit outside and feel the air blow against your skin; have you ever thought you may be listening to the Earth's breath?

Inspiration has to do with the creative breath, spontaneity, and the unexpected idea or image that might arrive in the mind (O'Donohue, 2010). As you move into the next phase of the workshop, may your AIR—your "Artist in Residence"—be stirred. Let your breath become inspiration.

Crossing the Threshold

To further the focus on air, the facilitator may read a poem such as "In Praise of Air" (O'Donohue, 2010, p. xxv). Use singing bowls, a gong, or flutes to begin the meditation with soothing sounds or play some music. Cross the threshold with a meditation to help participants go inward in preparation for their expressive arts journey. This is one example of a meditation that includes sitting and movement to explore breath and air as a form of creative energy, or you may want to develop a special meditation for your circle.

Breathing Meditation

As you breathe, slowly, notice how you take in the air outside of you and give back the air from inside of you. Pay attention to the air entering you and the air you release and give back. Thank your body for knowing how to do this even when you are not conscious of breathing.

Without breath, there is no life. Take a moment to give thanks for the air we breathe. Take another moment to commit to become a guardian of the air we breathe. Now, just take another moment to be aware of being alive. As you exhale, let your own breath expand to merge with wind, the clouds, with the atmosphere of the earth.

Take a few moments to focus on the ebb and flow of your breath. It is through breathing that we can come into a rhythm with ourselves. Become aware of where your breath goes as it leaves your body. What images come to mind? Imagine you are lighter than air and can follow the air slowly, up, and up and up. What do you see? What do you feel? (*Be silent for a minute or so to let people experience this moment*). Now, gently, and slowly, notice that your body gets heavier and heavier until you are back in this room. Slowly, open your eyes.

Movement Meditation

Next, invite circle members to shift into a movement meditation. A movement meditation can be enhanced with scarves or fans and music. The facilitator offers an invitation to become aware of how breath moves through your body. Invite circle members to move their hands and bodies and flow with their internal rhythm while simultaneously being aware of the air that touches and surrounds them. This can be indoors or outdoors based on space availability. The movement meditation is an opportunity for circle members to experience the air in their physical environment and to consider how the Earth's atmosphere offers sustenance and is a source of creative inspiration.

Another option is to have musical instruments available to use during the movement. When the movement meditation is over after approximately 5–10 minutes, the facilitator invites the group to gather art materials and move to a previously designated quiet spot to create.

Expressive Arts Journey: Artist in Residence (AIR)

Description

Explore air as an element that sustains life and is a source of creative inspiration. In this part of the circle, each person is free to follow their inner voice and ideas and to create spontaneously. It is helpful for the meeting facilitators to let the group know the topic a couple of weeks ahead of time and offer inquiries that may inspire new ideas about air. Circle members and facilitators also begin gathering art supplies for the artmaking journey.

Materials and Supplies

- Napkins, ribbons, sticks, leaves, streamers, old wind chimes, flags, string, old jewelry
- Glue, paper, paints, collage material
- Scarves
- Drums, whistles, recorders, or other instruments to express the creative connection of air and sound

Guidelines and Process

Collect materials for flags, streamers, wind chimes, hand fans, or anything that moves in the air. These can be materials that are found in your home or yard. Facilitators set up an art table with items such as paper, paints, and collage materials.

After the exploration of air in the breathing and movement meditations, each participant creates a unique metaphorical expression of their personal exploration of air as creative spirit. For example, one participant may select the creative inquiry, "What clutter needs to be removed to allow the air and creative spirit (in my life) to flow?" and another member might be inspired by the recent movement meditation and want to create prayer flags.

After approximately 45–60 minutes of artmaking, the facilitator(s) guide the group to shift into reflecting on key learnings or new awareness through a writing process.

Writing Reflection

Participants are invited to write some reflections during or after completing their project. They are free to respond to a prompt, to write a poem, or to use free writing.

- What did you discover about air and your creative energy during your meditation and artmaking?
- You are the interpreter for the air/creative spirit and the winds of change in your life. What messages are you receiving?
- Write a poem that describes how the air flows through you and infuses your creative spirit using the phrase "I am…"

WOW Stories

Ginger: I thought I'd do something with a magic carpet, but they became prayers flags (Figure 21). I noticed feelings of frustration. I have become accustomed to this feeling when we make art, so I noticed it, acknowledged it, and let it go.

I wrote: "My magic carpet prayer flags dance in the wind, sending my intentions to heaven. Listen, Patience, Dance, and Resonance. I am inspired to be with myself through open curiosity and gentle awareness. I am awakening to the ancient rhythm and its call to soulful spontaneity. The flag is a woven tapestry of beauty, color, texture, and pattern... an inspiration for my life. I will ride my magic carpets against the wind on the journey."

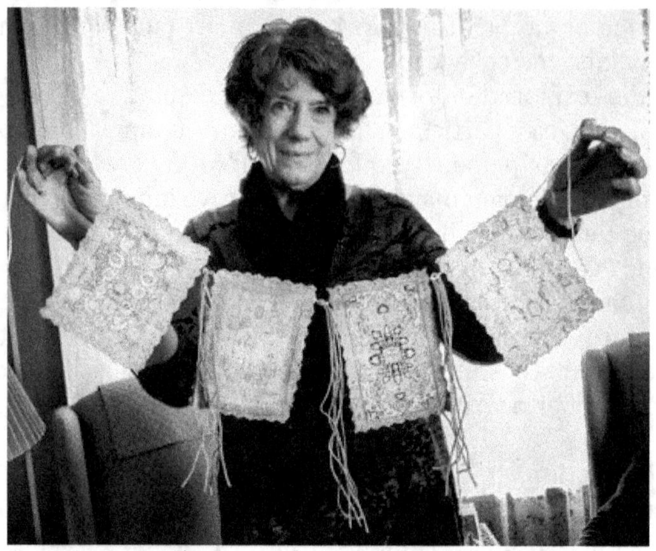

Figure 21: Prayer Flags, paper & string, Ginger Reinert (2016).

I am intrigued by prayer flags. I like the idea of a ritual of prayer closer to God—sending it off. And I've always loved oriental carpets. I added cords to blow in the wind and to reflect color in the rugs. They remind me of snakes, ropes, and interconnection. I recalled one time when the wind came and blew my expressive arts project right out of my car when I was driving home from our circle session.

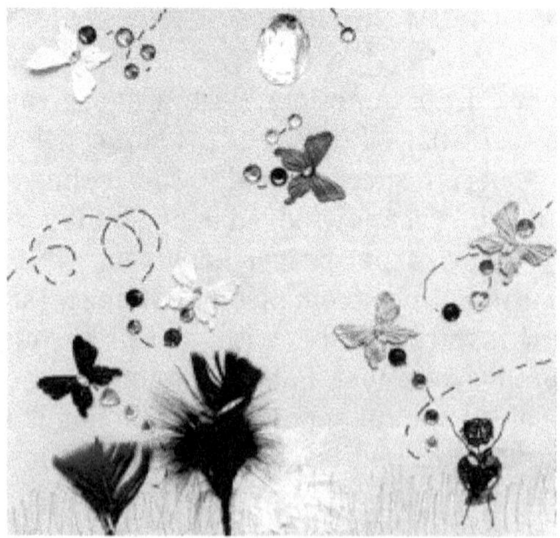

Pam: The butterflies are images of me (Figure 22). They are streaming gems ... letting myself play. Loop-the-loop. Dive bomber butterfly. One in left field. I wrote: "Experience a call to soulful spontaneity, joyful, childlike, a tad irresponsible, most

Figure 22: Play, mixed media, Pam Caraffa (2016).

definitely not planned. The lightness of being. Space as a gift, a big room, a big opening for… whatever. I'm breathing life into whimsy, allowing whimsy to breathe and have a life in me. Rhythm—ancient rhythm of the wind—changing, changeable, a jazz rhythm. Clearance of the clutter; too much structure, just let go. Playfulness. It has been missing in my life. My angel words are balance, forgiveness of myself, self-acceptance, and PLAY."

Terri: I think of my breath as AIR and Wind as the breath of the universe. AIR is gentle and powerful. I made a mobile to hang in my garden (Figure 23). I used a stick from my yard—part of a Hackberry tree. The circle is the universe. The triangle layered on top is symbolic of my mind, body, and spirit. My mobile reflects many cultures and the essence of Nature with different textures, colors, and flags. The yarn represents all the crisscross paths of my Creative Living Web. Life is woven together day by day. These are meaningful symbols to me. Air and breath are spirit. Creative expression is transformed into wisdom which comes from my spirit—my artist in residence. Wisdom is symbolized in the pearls and the mandorla that hangs on my mobile.

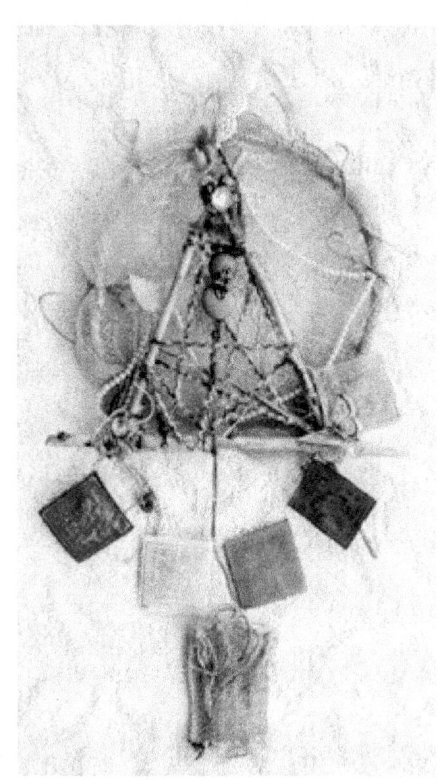

Figure 23: AIR, wind mobile, Terri Goslin-Jones (2016).

Terri wrote the following poem inspired by the element of air.

Artist in Residence (AIR)
Breathe in Life.
Breathe out Peace.
Awaken the ancient rhythm
that dwells within me.
Take flight in the wind.
Explore and create.
Resurrect wisdom secrets.

Conscious Closure and Integration

Each person in the group has an opportunity to share how AIR and creative spirit has been experienced during their journey. Sometimes just talking about the expressive arts experience and process brings new awareness to the topic. Each person has about ten minutes to share their expressive arts process and project.

After the sharing is complete, suggest a closing ritual to integrate the experiences and bring the group together before separating for the day. An idea for this ritual is to go outside and fly kites or release helium balloons. Another is to join hands and give homage to all the elements, noting the importance of each one in our lives and ending with a deep breath in and out.

There are several versions of ways to pay homage to the elements and the direction of the compass with which they are associated (Starhawk, 1989). If you lit candles during the opening section, make a private intention and use your breath to blow out the candles to close the meeting.

Summary

Focusing on air is a way of enhancing our connection to the creative energy that is available inside of ourselves and within the world around us. One possible outcome is that we are less likely to take this amazing world for granted and assume responsibility to maintain its survival. Looking at breath as a creative element can help us to embody and express our creative potential and take better care of our precious selves.

Creative Weavings

- Take five minutes a day to consciously breathe creative spirit in and out of your body.
- Adopt AIR as an acronym that reflects the artist that resides in your body.
- Your group can choose any of the elements to focus on (air, fire, wind, earth) and offer a series of sessions on each element. You may be attracted to one of the elements or have one that is underdeveloped that is calling for residence within your life.
- Take a walk and listen to the AIR as a creative messenger. What do you hear and feel? Record insights in your expressive arts journal.

Chapter 11

Wonderment: Awakening the Magical Child

Always be on the lookout for the presence of wonder.
— E.B. White

Intention and Purpose

The purpose of this expressive arts journey is to awaken wonder, your creative superpower, by exploring the captivating archetype of the magical child. Your inner child is a powerful muse because it has retained some of the innocence, curiosity, and sense of an enchanted world from your early childhood. Wonder is not just child's play. Have you ever experienced that place of creative flow where inspiration mysteriously flowed through you? If so, you were probably in the realm of the magical child and wonder.

Creative Inquiries

- Who is the magical child within and where do they play and frolic in your life?
- How does wonder nourish your creativity through the messy and magical process of artmaking?
- In what way might you reclaim and cultivate your relationship with wonder and your magical child?
- What obstacles keep you from embracing wonder and your magical child self?
- What everyday moments fill you with wonder and dazzle your heart?

Introduction

Wonder is the feeling of awe and joy experienced when you stumble across delightful and unexpected surprises. It is the ability to fine tune your attention to the awe of the present moment and follow the curiosity that tugs at your heart. It is the sacred pause that allows you to take in the mystery of nature and gaze up at the luminous night sky.

Wonder and the magical child are natural companions. If you have spent any amount of time around little children, you have likely experienced the joyful energy of seeing the world through their innocent eyes of curiosity and wonder. Children's developing brains are neurologically wired for wonder. It is a big part of how they learn and how you learn, too. These little ones compel you to re-awaken wonder and remember the child you once were, seeing your world afresh with renewed reverence and creative possibility. All you need is an open heart and a bit of child-like curiosity to stand in wonder. Life is more beautiful, exciting, and wondrous when you see your world through the eyes of the magical child.

Opening Ritual and Invitation

Welcome to the Wonder Circle: Inviting Your Magical Child to Come Out and Play

Open this journey in a playful way that invites everyone into a circle of wonder and the heart of the magical child. One suggestion is to start off by having everyone stand in a circle facing one another, blowing bubbles into the circle center, symbolic of each person's unique magic. The rule for the day is, no acting like a grown-up! Consider handing out "permission slips" to allow everyone's inner child to come out and play for the day.

The magical child is active and likes to move. It is not surprising that along with delighting the mind and spirit, wonder also inhabits our bodies, releasing dopamine and activating the brain's natural reward centers. Wonder is an embodied experience and communicates through bodily movements. Think about how you might incorporate movement or spontaneous dance into the opening ritual of this circle to help participants embody the wonder of their magical child. Building with blocks, or playing hopscotch, catch with a group ball, or dress up, as well as doing the hokey pokey are all great options for fun movement and opening activities.

Preparing Your Space

The set-up of your hosting space provides an environment that will help your participants transition into an atmosphere that is playful.

Customize the play area for your circle members. Some suggestions are:

- Set out various toys and stuffed animals along with fairy lights, balloons, and child party and art supplies. Write affirming words of wonder on the balloons.
- As participants arrive, give each a superhero cape, symbolic of the superpower of wonder.
- Put together a "wonder playlist" of music for the day and invite participants to submit their favorite "wonder" and childhood songs.
- Display some children's books such as *Alice in Wonderland, Happy in our Skin, The Monster Truck, Be Bold, Be Brave, Charlotte's Web, What Do You Do With An Idea, Where the Wild Things Are, The Giving Tree, I Am Whole,* and *The Wizard of Oz.*
- Utilize fun lighting like a starlight globe or disco/projector.
- Assemble party bags filled with child art supplies, glitter, magic wands, and magical messages about wonder.
- Provide fun and funky sunglasses to represent seeing with the eyes of wonder.
- Set up a "wonder altar"—a wonderscape with symbols, and items that reflect wonder and the magical child of each participant. Have each circle member bring a framed photo of themselves as a child to place on the altar.

The possibilities to decorate your hosting space are endless and will set the mood for a day of fun and wonder.

Check-In
Introduce Your Magical Child and Your Relationship with Wonder

For check-in, invite each member to introduce their magical child by sharing a photo of themselves as a child, the nickname they were called if they had one, and their first memory of wonder from childhood. What was their favorite childhood toy, fairytale, song, and/or bedtime story? This is an important time to hold space for one another as you remember, bear witness, and share these vulnerable parts of the child self. This activity can trigger and activate a range of feelings, sensations, and emotional memories for group members. Be especially mindful of how you create safety and witness one another through active listening and the power of presence. The circle becomes a big hug, holding the sacred childhood memories and stories of wonder for each member.

Lecturette
**Wonderment: Awakening Wonder and Embracing
the Magical Child**

In her inspiring book, *Help, Thanks, Wow*, Anne Lamott (2012) described "Wow" as the natural prayer of wonder. Wonder is a heightened state of consciousness and expanded mindful attention (Davis, 2021). It is a mindset of curiosity and awe that opens us to the magic of the world around us. Wonder has captivated humanity since the beginning of time and may be the virtue that will continue to carry humankind forward in our challenging evolution.

We are born into awe, wonder, and mystery. Wonder greets you when you are born and transforms your experience and perception of life throughout adulthood. Wonder fuels creativity and stimulates learning, innovation, and resilience. It opens us to new, expansive ways of perceiving our complex world that create meaning and dissolve bias (Andreasen, 2005). Unfortunately, the responsibilities of adulthood and the demands of our modern lives can diminish our sense of wonder and playfulness.

Wonder and the Magical Child

Wonder is the favorite playmate and the superpower of the magical child, an incredible catalyst for cultivating everyday creativity and joy. We all have the capacity for wonder, and one of the ways to reclaim and cultivate it is to reacquaint yourself with your magical child.

Who is the Magical Child?

Your magical child is your creative muse, inspirational collaborator, a willing adventurer, and wonder seeker. It is your most authentic voice, a free spirit who knows how to play and encounter everyday magic. Your magical child is a creative genius who holds the keys to your creative energy, imagination, enthusiasm, and playfulness. It inhabits your ability to perceive the mystery of the numinous world around you with awe and reverence. It sees the extraordinary in the ordinary. Your magical child is your daydreamer and night dreamer who believes that anything is possible. It is the creative muse that takes you into the imaginal realm of intuitive creativity, allowing you to create from a place of flow and non-censoring.

Your magical child brings the spirit of play into your life, which releases endorphins, improves cognitive functioning, uplifts your mood, and stimulates creativity. Play welcomes joy and meaningful connection to others and the world around you in dynamic ways (Elkind, 2007). To awaken your sense of wonder, invite a playful collaboration with your magical child, who holds within it the sacred mysteries of creativity and enchantment.

The magical child and wonder are relational archetypes of transformation and alchemy. They are creators of sacred space and creative potential. They bridge the worlds of inner imagination and possibility. Through the power of play and curious exploration, these archetypes bring healing and joy to themselves and others.

Vulnerability is the portal through which these archetypes find their full creative expression. It is hard to experience life deeply and put your creative magic out into the world if you are not willing to take risks and be vulnerable. To continue to be open to the presence of wonder, keep your heart humble, open, and receptive. Vulnerability is a doorway to deeper magic, wonder, and creativity. Learning to be completely vulnerable and embrace wonder is the journey of the magical child. This journey may inspire deeply moving soul work. Learn to embrace your magical child, and it will always love you back with pockets full of wonder, hope, and inspiration.

Crossing the Threshold

Before moving into this expressive arts journey, facilitate an activity that fosters a deeper connection with each person's magical child. Moving, sounding, meditating, and reading a short children's book like *Oh the Places You'll Go* or *Where the Wild Things Are* may be options. The following poem and meditation provide an engaging segue into this expressive arts journey and the wonderscape of the magical child.

Meditation: Remembering Little You

Before beginning this meditation, offer each participant playdough scented with an essential oil to hold during the meditation. The playdough is multi-sensory, transporting you back to a sensory, non-verbal place where the magical child resides in present moment awareness.

Take a slow, deep breath. Let yourself settle down and sink inward. Gently close your eyes, soften your gaze, and let yourself be in this moment as you gather your little magical self. There is no comparison to the feeling of coming together with magical playmates; it is like spirit breathing on the embers of your soul.

Take a deep, slow breath for a count of five. Hold your breath for a count of five. Release your breath slowly to a count of five, gently letting go of any stress or tension you may have brought here with you today. Continue to attune to your breath. Let it calm you, quiet you, center you. Let it take you all the way down to your luminous heart space. Feel the warmth here in the heart of wonder. Feel the magical love within and all around you.

This heart is the home of your magical child, the place where you uncover the magic and wonder that has been there all along. It is time to remember now, dear ones, deep within your being. When was the last time you arrived in this sacred place? Breathe deeply here and remember. Feel your heartbeat. Remember the jewels of wonder that are sewn into the magnificent gift that is you. Remember and see the outstretched hand of your magical child taking your hand and leading you into the magic and wonder of your being. Let it guide you into its creative and playful world today: a playground and wonderscape of exploration, magical memories, and creative possibility. Pause. Look. Listen.

As you look into the face and eyes of your inner child, what do you see? What does it look like? How old is your child? How would you describe its traits? What do you want to say to one another? How do you both move and interact with one another? What do you sense in your childlike body? What emotions do you both feel? What do you see and hear? Take some time to enjoy this interlude of wonder with your magical child.

When you are ready to leave the wonderscape of your magical child, give your child a warm embrace and thank them for sharing its playful wisdom with you. As you are ready, slowly return to the room. Listen to the sounds in the room around you, and slowly open your eyes, keeping a soft gaze.

Poetry Reading: "A Bouquet of Possibility" (Quibell, 2020)

Expressive Arts Journey: The Wonder-ful House
of the Magical Child

Description

Using various mixed media, participants create and construct their "Wonder House of the Magical Child," a container and wonderscape that holds various images, symbols, words, and reciprocal dialogue with their magical child. This expressive arts journey invites participants to awaken wonder and embrace their magical child through creative expression and dialogue, vacillating between their dominant (adult) and non-dominant (child) hands.

Materials and Supplies

Shop the children's aisle at your local art store and select a variety of supplies. Gather items from nature, such as sticks, stones, and dried leaves. Some supplies to consider include:

- Acrylic and watercolor paints, crayons and markers, finger paints
- Boxes of various sizes
- Collage images/words and glue sticks
- Glitter, ribbons, papers
- Stamps, stencils, stickers
- Watercolor paper

Supplies of any size can be used to shape the magic house, including shoe boxes. In this exercise, a large sheet of 130 lb. watercolor paper (2 x 3 feet), cut into the shape of a house, was used.

Guidelines and Process

Offer each participant a large piece of watercolor paper cut into the shape of a house. It can be folded so there is a flap to portray the "outside" which, when opened, shows the "inside" of the house. This substrate, or another of their choosing, represents the magic house and wonderscape of the magical child. Invite participants to use and explore a vast array of child art supplies to depict, explore, and dialogue with their magical child throughout their creative process. Encourage them to enter an imaginary realm, inviting a sense of wonder as they scribble, paint with their hands, and dialogue (directly on the substrate) with their magical child, alternating between their dominant (adult) and non-dominant hand (magical child).

What is your magical child's name? How does your child feel and what do they want to express to you? How does it feel to interact with your child? Encourage participants to co-create with their magical child, intentionally inviting it into their creative process and letting it draw itself and write with its non-dominant hand. What symbols, colors, shapes, "wild things" emerge in the wonderscape? Are there windows and doors? What does the inside versus the outside look like? If participants are hesitant about where to begin, have them close their eyes and begin with crayon drawing or loose lyrical scribbles, intuitively using images that came up for them during the meditation.

Because this exercise invokes the inner child, it is especially important to remind participants that the expressive arts journey is not about the final product but about the process of creating itself and who you become through the creative process. Children do not draw perfect adult paintings or creations. They are messy, playful, and carefree in their creative process, which unlocks the magic of creativity.

Invite participants to use both their non-dominant and dominant hands during their creative process. The magical child comes to us bearing its gifts and many lessons on the magic of wonder. One of these invaluable lessons is to let go of perfectionism, have fun, and be more spontaneous and intuitive with the creative process. Invite your circle participants to fold the wings of their intellect, descend into the heart of the magical child, and bring the eyes of wonder into their creative process. Give them lots of permission to be messy, have fun, and let their magical child come out to play.

Writing Reflection

When members are done creating the magic house, hand out colorful paper, and invite them to write a handwritten love letter or a poem to their magical child. Invite participants to reflect on and to use messages from the wonderment creative inquiries, the check-in, the meditation and from their magic house. Each part of the wonderment circle session offers symbols, words, and inspiration for their writing.

Provide private areas at the hosting venue to give participants quiet spaces to write, to journal, and to dialogue with their magical child. When we did this activity, we set up a teepee with twinkle lights as a play and writing space. Remember to have participants thank their magical child for this playful engagement during their expressive arts journey.

WOW Stories

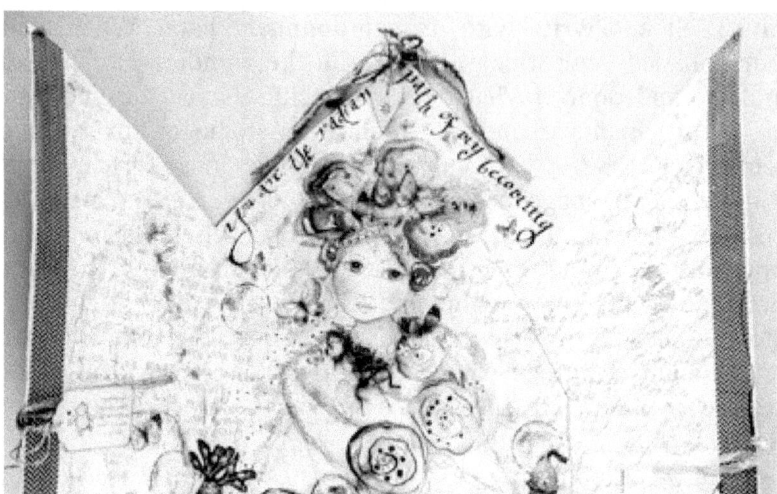

Figure 24: Magical Child, mixed media, Holly Carson (2019).

Holly: My magical child is my daydreamer (Figure 24). She loves to get lost in the creative worlds of wonder, imagination, and creative ideas. She is happiest in the deep woods, painting on the beach, or artmaking. She is my little mystic. She shows me that creative living and loving are where the big magic show up in my life. She lives in the house of my soul, deep in the heart of awareness.

The front doors of her magic house are my heart (Figure 25). I access her through opening my heart, letting myself feel all my emotions and vulnerability. Vulnerability is her doorway to wonder and creativity.

I started out thinking I needed to rescue her and discovered that it was the reverse. She is rescuing me! I need to bring her energy, wonder, joy, and playfulness back into my life. In collaborating with her, I embrace the messy, mystical, and magical gifts of art and life. She is the key to loving more deeply and daring greatly in my artmaking. Her re-wilding energy is transforming me and giving me the creative courage to brave the wilderness of my artistry in new and exciting ways. She is inviting me to be more intuitive and curious with my creative process. Part of how I have compartmentalized her and tamed her has been through my perfectionism and what I have come to call creative co-dependency. I feel like I am releasing her from this and welcoming her home. On a deeper level it feels like a reclaiming of my untamed, free-spirited, wild-hearted self, a type of soul retrieval. It continues to amaze me how art has the restorative capacity to heal us and bring us home to ourselves.

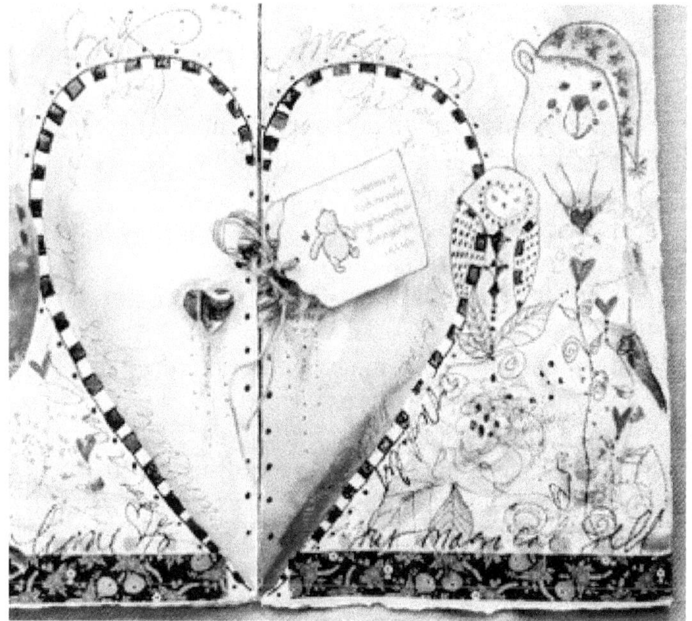

Figure 25: Magical Heart: Doorway to Wonder, mixed media, Holly Carson (2019).

Ginger: During my expressive arts journey, I chose not to create a Wonder House. I was inspired by the opening ritual when I was anointed with rose oil. The rose oil reminded me of my grandmother, who used rose water and glycerin for moisturizer. The fragrance sparked and flooded me with memories of my grandmother and how I played in her closet as a child.

I was so inspired by this memory that was unlocked during our expressive arts journey that I had to capture this experience in writing, and a poem emerged. Later, I shared this poem with my siblings and cousins. My whole family identified strongly with my poem and the memories of being a child with our grandmother.

My Grandmother's Closet
She let me play in her closet
opening boxes of photographs
among her patterned house dresses
and practical shoes.
She smelled of rose water and glycerin
and made me wash my feet with Ivory Soap
before I slept on her ironed sheets. Each night
east bound trains serenaded us with mournful songs.
She laughed and hugged, and said "Howdy" like Minnie Pearl
and made dresses for me out of flour sacks.
Her favorite pastimes were going to prayer meeting
and taking a drive to see the fall color.
She fried chicken, mashed potatoes, and simmered black eyed
     peas.
We ate at her dining room table off of pictured plates
while Jesus looked over us as we dined
on homemade biscuits and sipped sweet tea.
White crisscross curtains fluttered at the windows
and fans droned a monotonous chorus
while a block of ice melted in a wash tub
on the red linoleum countertop.
I was told that she never wore makeup
and her husband left her for her best friend
because she didn't like to dance.
Yet she greeted him with a hug each time he dropped by.
She rocked and sang hymns on the screened-in back porch
and churned homemade ice cream in an old wooden bucket.
She toted a rifle and wrung chickens by the neck,
and hung clothes on the line in the stickered back yard.
Ada wore her long hair in a bun, offered complete acceptance,
and lived a life of abundance—more than enough—

opening a portal of love, God, and family
into her enchanted world of simplicity. The greatest treasures
   on earth.

Conscious Closure and Integration

Invite each participant to share their expressive art process and their experience of wonder and their magical child. This can include what was most meaningful or challenging, along with how they might experience wonder as a creative superpower. What three adjectives describe each participant's magical child? What surprised you? What messages did your magical child have for you?

Additionally, ask each member to share what commitment they are now willing to make to awaken wonder and embrace their magical child going forward. Wonder is meant to be shared. For your closing, have each participant stand in the circle facing outward and collectively blow bubbles, symbolic of sharing your creative magic and wonder with the world.

Summary

It is surprising that it took nine years of meeting in our Creative Spirit Circle before we formally invited our magical child into our expressive arts journey. Looking back, it was there all along, and probably the archetype and muse that brought us together as a circle from the beginning. We encourage you not to wait so long to consciously engage wonder and intentionally court your magical child as a muse in your creative endeavors. This inspiring duo will infuse your circle and group process with lots of playful energy and keep you humbly open to the surprises that will emerge in your group. The creative connection of the circle is deepened when the fire of wonder is tended together.

Through the Creative Spirit Circle process, where we dare to be vulnerable with our creativity and evolving relationships, we open one another to wonder. This collective experience of wonder is akin to what French sociologist Emile Durkheim (1976) called collective effervescence: the bliss, synchronicity, and potent connection a group experiences when they come together around shared purpose and meaning. In a sense, we gift the joy of wonder to one another by sharing our expressive arts experience. Wonder is a big part of how we weave ourselves whole in the Creative Spirit Circle.

Creative Weavings

Cultivating wonder is an intentional practice. Following are some creative practices to accompany you along the path of wonder.

- What commitment can you make to awaken wonder and nurture the archetype of the magical child in your life? Write down this commitment as a letter to your magical child with action steps and review them on a regular basis.
- Create a "wonder list" of adventures to explore with your magical child.
- Start a dream journal to interact with child images that emerge in your dreams.
- Create a "wonder art journal" to dialogue and create art with your magical child.
- Schedule "wonder quests" with your magical child. Bring along a camera to capture moments of wonder. Let yourself wander and get lost in wonder.
- Go on "wonder walks" and bring along a curiosity basket to gather treasures with your magical child.
- Write a gratitude poem to your magical child, thanking them for the gift of wonder.

Note: As discussed earlier in this chapter, topics that focus on the "inner child" have the potential to trigger memories for people that can be traumatic in nature. Even though this journey focus is not on the "wounded child," it can potentially trigger "wounded child" memories. Circle members who have had traumatic childhoods may want to give more attention to grounding themselves and creating safety throughout this expressive arts journey. For example, they may want to give extra attention to how they create safety for their magical child as they create their "wonderscape." Circle facilitators should check on participants throughout this journey to monitor how they are doing as they process the material. As always, offer alternative options to circle members on how they might want to explore the topic of wonder. Refer to the guidelines in Chapter 1 for more information on how to support circle members.

Chapter 12

Wisdom of the Body

Intention and Purpose

The intention of this journey is to explore how our bodies contain wisdom that reflects our life experience and serves as a living vessel for our creative potential. Our bodies vibrate with our life story. The language of the body provides insights into our physical, emotional, and spiritual nature. Authentic Movement (Halprin, 2003) will be a central focus to explore the wisdom of the body. Drumming, sounding, artmaking, and writing will be integrated into this expressive arts experience.

Creative Inquiries

- How have I related to my body and its wisdom during different phases of my life?
- How does my body carry my life story?
- What nourishes me? What depletes me?
- What is happening in my body right now—sensations, body parts, posture?
- Where and how are emotions such as fear, dread, sadness, anger, joy, awe, contentment, inspiration felt in the body?
- How does my body manifest the cycles of nature?

Introduction

How closely do you pay attention to your body's signals and impulses? Do you neglect your body by sitting too long in appointments and then moving unconsciously from one meeting to the next? Or do you take breaks throughout the day and ensure that you choose activities to build physical strength? Do you take care of your physical and emotional needs throughout the day, or do you find yourself feeling overwhelmed and irritable at the end of the day?

Our body is constantly sensing the environment through changing pressures in touch, the sense of vibration in our joints and organs, visual and auditory stimuli, scents, and tastes. Our body also sends messages about internal stimuli through movement impulses or the changing rhythm of our heart or breath. With so much stimulation in today's modern world, we pay little attention to our own sensory experience or to messages that are sent by our body. We do not take the time to pay attention to movements of our tongue when chewing, the sensations in our toes when sitting, or how certain scents affect our moods.

Sadly, most of us don't take much time to play with physical movement or appreciate what our bodies experience, moment to moment.   Nonetheless, it is through our bodies that creativity emerges. Art, music, dance, painting, sculpting, or writing poetry are all expressed with our bodies. Practices can be cultivated to encourage the wisdom of the body to be our creative muse (Paintner, 2017; Rogers, 1993).

Making art and using authentic movement are an opportunity for your circle members to sense and respond to one another in new ways. Dancing, drumming, and singing are practices used to attune to the rhythms of the natural world. Shared movement and meditation can help the body's wisdom reverberate more consciously in your lives. Your Creative Spirit Circle can build on the synergy and synchronization of exploring embodiment together. Consciously working together in an embodied, creative way shifts the energy field in a room as circle members become attuned to a deeper awareness of one another's presence.

This session will explore ways that our bodies create sound, music, and art. Heartbeats set a rhythm. The heartbeat is our inner drum, one that we all carry with us. The drum resonates with and sends out messages to the different systems of the body. For example, happiness or fear changes the way the heart beats. The existence of our inner drums may explain the emergence of drumming as a key form of music making across cultures. We know that drumming is an ancient practice that uses the twin realities of rhythm and sound tones to bring about coherence of the body, mind, and spirit. Drumming circles can bring us into emotional harmony in groups, creating a frequency and synergy that transcends each person.

Opening Ritual & Invitation

As you open your circle, each group member can choose a djembe drum, wood blocks, pan, bucket with spoon, sticks, or any percussion instrument. The djembe drum produces a wide variety of sounds, making it versatile and preferred for drum circles. Members of your group might want to try tapping in different ways (with palms or with flat fingers) to get a sense of variation in sound. If you are using other forms of percussion, have each member practice making beats. Let each person lead while others mirror their beat.

When everyone is ready, you can experiment with playing in unison. Play four beats, and a new member joins in at each new bar, keeping the same rhythm. When each member has entered and all are playing in unison, new rhythms can be introduced. Your group can experiment with the drum sounds and try to play three or four different rhythms in unison. Notice what happens to your energy and your heartbeat as you play together. You can close the drumming circle with a minute of playing the same rhythm. Take a few minutes to record thoughts and words that describe how you feel physically and emotionally. You can also use colors, marks, or symbols.

Check-In

Ask each member about their experience. How did the opening ritual affect your energy and attention? What did you notice related to your body making sounds and playing music?

Lecturette: Making Art through Authentic Movement

This Creative Spirit Circle journey uses movement-based expressive arts, which are rooted in the field of dance and movement therapy to foster cognitive, emotional, social, and physical integration to enhance overall health and well-being. Our body is a miraculous vessel that is capable of manifesting and activating our life force. Our human body holds the entire repertoire of our life experience and communicates messages moment by moment.

Seasons of Life

You can pair this journey with an intention to explore how your body interacts with the cycles of nature. Nature is a creative muse. For example, you might connect this journey to the summer/winter solstice, low tide/high tide, a full moon, or another celestial event. Using Authentic Movement can be an opportunity to explore and celebrate the cycles of nature in your body. Our bodies are the vessel and nature teaches us about birth, growth, loss, and renewal. The movement becomes the artwork and composition.

Language of the Body

The language of the body is constantly expressed through physical movement, feelings, sensations, images, and thoughts (Halprin, 2003). It is common to live in a world of thoughts while suppressing messages from the body. Paying attention to emotions and physical sensation is associated with well-being and personal growth. Authentic movement is an expressive arts process that allows the body to guide and provide insights into our physical, emotional, and spiritual nature. You may find that you must retrain yourself to listen and respond to messages from your body. There are four levels of awareness that can cultivate a deeper attunement that dwells within the body (Halprin, 2003, pp. 104–105).

Physical Body (breath, body posture, feelings)
The first level of awareness is physical, which includes sensations, breath, body posture, and the feelings we experience in different parts of our body. For example, when you begin an authentic movement experience, notice the pace and depth of each breath. How does your stomach feel? Where might there be tightness in your muscles?

Emotional Body (stages and levels of feeling while moving)
The second level of internal awareness is the emotional body. Halprin (2003) recommends that the mover notice the feelings being experienced. Slowing down and feeling emotions such as anticipation, nervousness, anxiety, or joy connects the body to what is happening in the given moment.

Mental Body (looping, ascending/descending mental awareness)
The third level of internal awareness is the mental body. Intellectual thought creates distance from the body and closes the door to emotion and sensation. During an authentic movement process, thinking processes can be observed with a goal of mindfully noting thoughts and then moving into the physical and emotional body.

Spiritual Body (or transcendent body)
The fourth level of body awareness is a type of flow. Creative energy becomes embodied, and the mover feels as if the body directs its own movements without words or thoughts. When a person becomes experienced with this process, one level of awareness informs the next level. Halprin (2003) indicated there may be an "ascending/descending awareness," a looping or interplay between the physical, emotional, and mental with transcendent experiences.

Crossing the Threshold

Body Meditation
Begin by focusing on your physical body. How is your body feeling? Where are the places of tightness or ease? The places of pain or fatigue, pleasure, or release? Then shift your awareness to your energetic body, which can be observed with the breath. Without trying to change your breathing, notice if it is fast or slow, shallow or deep. How is your energy level? What kind of energy are you experiencing? What is the quality of this vital force?

Shift your focus to your emotional body, also known as the heart-mind, so it includes your thoughts as well. What are you feeling right now? Can you make space for that? What is the quality of your thoughts? Are they feeling scattered? Speedy? Slow? Spacey? Just notice and be present without judgment.

Now bring focus to your spirit body, which is your connection to the transcendent. Does this layer feel open or blocked in some way? What is that experience like? What do you notice when you bring your attention to the part of you that is rooted in something much bigger than you? This is inviting space for your "being/spirit body."

Finally, bring your attention to your witness body, that wise, compassionate presence within you that is observing all of this. Honor this spaciousness that can hold all these dimensions of yourself. What is it like to witness these different parts of yourself and realize that any one dimension doesn't make up the whole of your experience?

After the meditation, begin the Authentic Movement process. Each person will have 10–15 minutes as the mover and 10–15 minutes as the witness. This can be adjusted to longer periods depending on the available time.

Authentic Movement Process

The Authentic Movement process includes a designated mover and witness. Invitations for the mover encourage contact with sensation, imagination, emotion, and spiritual realms of being. The person moving listens to messages being sent by the body before moving, while the witness observes close by.

Honor all feelings that arise. There can be discomfort and vulnerability with movement. This is an opportunity to notice your thoughts and to consider the relationship you have with your body. If a circle member has any hesitation to be a mover, they can either choose to be the witness, or they can reflect their hesitation in their movement.

Authentic Movement encompasses all feelings. Lying down, sitting still, lifting a finger, rocking, running, jumping, dancing, and stretching are all forms of Authentic Movement, a form of embodied creativity. Trust, nonjudgment, and quiet attention create safety and freedom for the mover.

Mover

In Authentic Movement, the mover usually begins with closed eyes, listening inwardly, and seeking to embody and express impulses, sensations, feelings, and images that arise in the body in the presence of the witness(es).

Witness

The witness (or witnesses) supports the mover with a clear presence and a sense of compassionate attention. Being a witness is a practice in observation and listening. Strong emotions and images frequently arise in the witness as they, in their body, respond to the artful expression of the mover.

Mover and Witness Dialogue

After the mover feels complete or has moved for the agreed-upon time, for example 10–15 minutes, the mover and witness come together for dialogue. The mover talks first about their experience moving and being witnessed. The mover is invited to speak, without initial reflections from the witness. Next, the witness talks about their experience witnessing the mover. This is the time the witness might share feelings of joy, awe, reverence, memories, or images that arose during the movement.

Group members can work in pairs. If there is an uneven number, then the mover and witnesses can be in groups of three. The mover starts in a space safe where they can move freely. Movers begin with their eyes closed and listen to their inner guidance. Some movers want to dance or have grand movements. Other movers may choose small, micro movements or even lie on the ground. Another mover may focus on touch or using their arms, fingers, legs, and feet.

The intention is to let your moment-to-moment impulses lead your movement, while the witness also focuses their attention on the movements that arise. The mover is guided by emotion, sensation, imagery, and curiosity. Sometimes the mover will notice an internal or external focus. The movement may follow a consistent thread, exploring a theme from the day or shift from one thing to another. All movement is welcome.

Movement Guidelines
Note: The following guidelines are read and reviewed by the circle members prior to the meditation. Their space has been chosen and prepared.

Mover

- Do you need any help preparing the space?
- Do you prefer silence or music?
- This is your special time to discover messages and the wisdom within your body. It is not a performance. Your witness is here to provide a safe space and a protective container for what will emerge.
- When you feel that your movement is complete, you can take the time you need to transition.
- After your movement feels complete, you will be invited to share your experience with your witness.
- If you choose, you can invite your witness(es) to share their personal experience of the movement.
- Thank the mover and express appreciation.

Witness

- Being a witness for another person's expressive arts process is an honor and a sacred experience.

- You can ask the mover if they want you to take a few notes that will offer feedback on the experience. It is most important that you are emotionally present.
- You are providing the space for your partner to be seen and then to hear of their experience for the first time.
- Witnessing is a non-judgmental, receptive process where you listen and observe your partner's experience. If the mover invites feedback, you should share it from your personal experience, "When you moved, I felt...."

The witness is close by and ensures that the mover is in a safe space, especially if the mover's eyes are closed. Each witness observes their partner and observes their thoughts and emotions in relation to this experience. What images arise? What emotions arise? As a witness, you may imagine that your partner is feeling a certain way, exploring a certain theme or assuming a certain role. You may find that your mind is drawn to a memory. You may notice a sense of appreciation or awe arise in response to the mover.

When the mover and witness have experienced both roles and shared their experiences, then they transition to an independent space for artmaking.

Expressive Arts Journey: Body as Messenger

Description

Authentic Movement is the inspiration for this expressive arts journey. After the Authentic Movement is completed, group members can capture aspects of the experience in artmaking such as finger painting and then words. This intermodal expressive arts process encourages the wisdom within the body to emerge and the artmaking produces a visible image of the experience.

The artmaking process is physical. Using your fingers to create is a direct and tactile form of art. Sensations and feelings can be transported from your body and made visible. The artmaking process can be abstract or a type of self-portrait. Grappling with the art expression through finger painting is a way to capture your movement experience. Use conscious, authentic movements to paint your emotions and sensory experience. Authentic Movement and artmaking become a metaphor for daily life.

Materials and Supplies

- Easel, board, pavement, or tables
- Finger paint; watercolor; or water-soluble, non-toxic acrylic or oil
- Paper or canvas: different sizes of paper. Rolls of large paper offer flexibility
- Paper towels, painters' tape
- Water

Guidelines and Process

Facilitators set up art supplies on a table for easy access. Circle members select the materials to paint aspects of the embodied Authentic Movement process. Artmaking is a visual exploration that integrates the wisdom of the body by offering colors, images, pictures, and words. This imagery can be expressed in one painting with a specific focus such as a self-portrait, or there could be a painting series to express different aspects of the embodied experience.

What messages are arising from your body? Possibilities include (a) the physical nature of the body, (b) the emotional self, (c) mental reactions, and (d) spiritual feelings. Layer words, phrases, or descriptions on the painting, or write them on the back. Another artform is to use images and paint to dialogue with body parts. Paint and communicate with your heart, your eyes, your hands, your feet, your throat, or any body part. (Note: See Halprin, 2003 pp. 102–143 for a variety of options.)

Writing Reflection

After completing the artmaking, invite participants to write about their expressive arts journey. Some options include:

- Write a letter to your body and or write a letter from your body.
- Choose a body part and ask for a message specifically from that body part. Example, heart, brain, feet, hands, mouth, eyes.
- Is there a title for your Authentic Movement and artwork? What is the affect/feelings? Write about your creative process and key learnings.

- Is there a dialogue or story that emerged from your Authentic Movement? Artwork? What is the title? A key message? Is this experience part of a larger story?

WOW Story
Kim McCallum, *Coming Home,* Authentic Movement

Percussion Meditation

I listened to the fountains, cicadas, birdsong, and winds and wanted to sing along, gently tapping the djembe drum with the water sounds, moving the rain stick to the cicada's cadence, adding a beat to the bird song. Appreciating the sounds of nature, and wanting to join in.

Experience as the Witness

The mover (Terri) began by lying down on the ground outdoors. Her gentle, graceful movements were like a ballet. She explored her garden with both a child's eye and a wise stewardship, moving through gateways and quiet contemplative garden rooms. I imagined that knowing her garden was like knowing parts of herself. I imagined the garden was her body, her soul. I felt both reverence and awe in my experience witnessing her movement.

Experience as the Mover

In my body meditation, I noticed the quality of my energy was calm yet expansive. The warmth of the sun on my skin intensified; my breathing was gentle. I asked myself, "How does my body carry my life story? How do I remember who I am through my body? How has my relationship with my body evolved?"

My movement session began. In my movement, I explored my life story, from childhood through adulthood. In the beginning, I had the impulse to swing, pumping my legs, feet toward the cotton clouds, eyes toward the sky, then head down, moving back, I looked toward the earth. I moved my body in space as if I was flying.

Next, I remembered moving as a school-aged child. I moved through the woods, toward a creek, finding my special ancient tree, stretching my arms around its vast strong trunk, looking up toward the canopy of leaves, abundant shade, a gift to all. I played out this story as I traveled through the garden and hugged a tree.

I then had an impulse to run, stretch, and explore. I wanted to be seen, known, and I wanted to connect with others. But when I became an adolescent, my body changed; integration and freedom were more difficult. As I moved through the garden, I remembered that as a teenager my body was objectified. I lost my emotional and spiritual connection to my body. I felt divided.

In my authentic movement experience, I returned to a sitting position with a desire to reconnect with my body. My heart and emotions were seeking integration within my body. As I sat on the ground, I went inward and imagined my body as a vessel for creation and birth. I remembered my children being born and I experienced an outpouring of love and emotion.

Next, I verbally shared my experience with my witness. An insight that emerged through my Authentic Movement experience was that I recognized the importance of my senses as a means and a way to return home, to myself, my body, my soul.

Then, I transitioned to express my movement through visual art. In my art I was drawn to using watercolors to embody the image of the ancient trees of my childhood. I expressed my body through hugging and swinging.

Key Message: There is joy in knowing one's place/one's home, and returning to this essential part of myself, to my child body, to nature, to my soul. I titled my Authentic Movement experience *Coming Home*. I concluded my expressive arts process with a letter to my body.

> Dear Body,
> My favorite gift you gave me was my children—four beautiful souls. You nourished them and held them and made me feel the miracle of my animal nature. There is so much pleasure you have provided. The sensation of a breeze and skin smiling, the ripe juicy sweet and sour of fruits we have tasted, the thrill of flying on a swing (Figure 26), listening to Yo-Yo Ma, seeing the sunset of the desert and the ocean… so much beauty.
> Sometimes you revolt, shake with heights, bloat with certain foods, cough, and itch with allergy. You remind me time has passed. We bear the marks of that knee surgery, there remain events inside unknown to me; there is sun damage from my greedy sun worship. I have sometimes wanted you to be different, less sensitive, more agile, to have better veins. But now and forever forward, I want you to know that I hold you in the highest regard and promise to only love you and listen to you while we dance this last dance together.
> With great gratitude, your partner in life, Kim

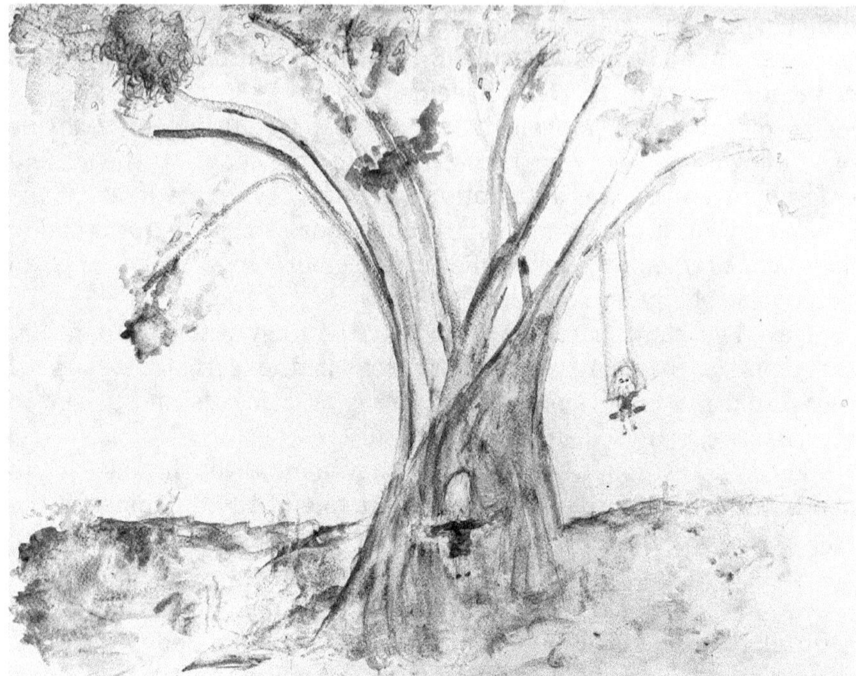

Figure 26: Coming Home, Authentic Movement, Watercolor, Kim McCallum (2022).

Conscious Closure and Integration

Invite circle members to share partial or completed artwork and written notes, letters, or poems about their Authentic Movement experience. Other circle members listen non-judgmentally and bear witness as each member speaks. When everyone has shared, the leader can close the session with group sounding and a meditation or blessing.

Group Sounding

Invite circle members to close their eyes and spontaneously make sounds such as chants, claps, foot stomps, hums, finger snaps, laughter, shouts. These are all ways to make music with their body. The sounding usually starts out with one individual and soon there will be simultaneous group music being made. There will come a natural time when the group sounding is complete, and everyone is silent. After a minute of silence, the facilitator closes with a mediation or blessing about the wisdom of the body.

Closing Meditation
Ask the group to settle into their breath, while the facilitator says:

> May I be healthy, may I be aware.
> May I feel at home in my body, may I live with ease,
> May I honor the wisdom in my body.
> Let's repeat together: May I be healthy, may I be aware, may I feel at home in my body, may I live with ease, may I honor the wisdom in my body.

Creative Weavings

- Create seasonal rituals to connect your body to the changing seasons.
- Dance indoors or outdoors with wild abandonment.
- Include Authentic Movement in a regular expressive arts practice.
- Develop a special celebration for each of your senses.
    - *Taste/smell*: Cook a favorite childhood dish. Savor a piece of chocolate.
    - *Touch*: Take a bath, swim. Receive or give a massage. Wrap yourself in a special blanket. Walk in nature and touch the flowers, trees, and experience the Earth's body. Cuddle with a pet.
    - *Sight*: Feast on a favorite vision by walking in a garden, go to an art museum, view treasured photographs. Use flowers and plants to beautify your home. Hang crystal suncatchers by windows.
    - *Sound*: Attend a concert, sound/gong session, play favorite music, listen to sounds in nature. Have fountains, chimes and nature sounds in your environment.
    - *Smell*: Use aromatherapy, plants, candles.
- Engage in a form of movement meditation: yoga, tai chi, Qigong, walking meditation.
- Read poetry about the body such as "Earth Your Dancing Place" by May Swenson or "For Calling the Spirit Back from Wandering the Earth in Its Human Feet" by Joy Harjo.
- Take deep breaths, sending your breath to your heart and throughout your entire body. What wildness resides in your body that wants to be expressed? Use movement, sounds,

and art to give voice to the wild parts of yourself that want to be expressed.

Chapter 13

Sacred Portals and Inner Knowing

Remember the entrance door to the sanctuary is inside you.

— Rumi

Intention and Purpose

Portals are thresholds, passageways. When we access a portal, we facilitate a shift in consciousness by opening sensory channels and transporting ourselves to other realms and ways of knowing. Any ritual or experience that shifts your understanding, such as artmaking, chanting, dancing, drumming, immersing yourself in nature's landscape, meditating, writing poetry, visiting sacred buildings, or sounding can be considered a portal. This expressive arts journey is an invitation for your circle to explore portals.

Creative Inquiries

- Have you experienced creative expression and artistic forms as a doorway or threshold that offers you a shift into another realm? Examples include art, dance, poetry, movies, music, theater, writing.
- Is there a place, a building, or a landscape where you experienced a felt sense of sacred energy?
- Have you experienced a spiritual practice as a portal into another realm? For example, chanting, drumming, ecstatic dance, meditation, prayer, tai chi, singing, sounding, or yoga.
- If you could access a portal experience for personal transformation, what would you most like to explore? What questions would you ask?

Introduction

Some of the ways portals will be explored in this circle session include human connection, a mirror meditation, visiting sacred sites, and artmaking. A portal is a threshold to access new ways of thinking, seeing, hearing, or feeling.

These new realms or portals move us inward, inspiring us, shifting our mindset, and revealing the unconscious. Portals may connect us to a spiritual or mystical realm and offer shortcuts to other dimensions and a way to experience an alternative reality. The notion of a portal is archetypal. Portals can move us out of linear time and allow us to see backward, forward, and even catch glimpses of the parts of self that may reside in the shadow. Prayer and meditation practices assist in maintaining an openness to spiritual potential that open pathways to transcendental experience (Cuckson, 2020).

Opening Ritual

This opening ritual explores "human connection" by using sensory experience as a portal. Sensory stimulation or deprivation may increase awareness and receptivity. Humans connect through a gaze, shaking hands, an embrace, a caress, listening, and looking into each other's eyes with an intention for connection and understanding. The practice of touch and personal connection may increase our energy coherence. Human connection and present-minded awareness offer a state of well-being. When introducing this opening ritual, you can offer a multitude of ways for circle members to connect.

For example, if people are sensitive about personal space or connecting through touch, you may choose to acknowledge one another with a bow or offer an opening ritual using mindful listening or a group mindful walk as human connection. If your circle has been together for an extended period, mindful breathing and sharing physical space such as a hugging meditation may expand your connections. You can adapt the following hugging meditation for a connection that works best for your Creative Spirit Circle.

Hugging Meditation

Stand facing each other as you follow your breathing and establish your true presence. First bow, opening yourselves to the vital presence of one another. Then open your arms and offer your companion to the left a hug. During the first in-breath and out-breath, become aware that you and your partner are both alive. With the second in-breath and out-breath, think of where you will both be one hundred years from now. Finally, with the third in-breath and out-breath, be aware of how precious it is that you both are alive and on this creative journey together.

Enjoy three more deep conscious breaths to bring yourself fully present. With the fourth breath, be aware of your presence in this very moment and extend an invitation to yourself for happiness. With the fifth breath, be aware that the other circle members are present in this moment and extend an invitation for their happiness. With the sixth breath, be aware that we are here together, right now on this Earth, and extend an invitation for gratitude and happiness for our Creative Spirit Circle. Then release your hug and bow to each other to express your gratitude.

For the purposes of this meditation, hugging has the intention to connect with another person through the soothing and caring gesture of a hug (Thich Nhat Hanh, 2021). There are six science-based health benefits of human touch. This type of touch may:

- Release oxytocin and activate feelings of contentment and relaxation.
- Relax the body and relieve stress; with a hug, bodies slightly fall into each other, muscles relax, which has the therapeutic effect of lowering cortisol levels.
- Relieve pain by releasing endorphins that can block pain pathways in the brain and soothe aching by increasing circulation to soft tissues.
- Relieve depression, reduce worry, and elevate your mood; increased dopamine and serotonin levels are an instant mood booster.
- Increase understanding; a hug can cause an exchange of feelings between two people and produce feelings of understanding and empathy thanks to the release of oxytocin, often referred to as the "love hormone."
- Boost the immune system and improve heart health (Carson, 2012).

Lecturette: Portals as a Threshold to Other Ways of Knowing

The word "threshold" comes from "threshing," to separate the grain from the husk. To cross a threshold is to move into a new realm. When we cross a threshold, we shift our mindset. We move from ordinary awareness to other ways of knowing.

Entering a portal is an opportunity to experience your life in a new way. A portal can serve as a place for transformation and offer insights into other realms. Crossing a threshold through a portal is a numinous experience and presents a place of change and new horizons (Gregoire, 2021). A door, chute, or ladder is an archetypal image that moves or connects one's experience and being to another place in thought or space. We can also imagine portals as moving us inward, shifting our mindset, revealing the unconscious. Dreams and imagination link us to our unconscious and serve as a portal that broadens our experience and worldview. Portals are common in film and literature such as *Alice in Wonderland, Harry Potter, Outlander, The Lion the Witch and the Wardrobe,* and *The Wizard of Oz.*

Sometimes only one of the senses may be used when exploring portals, such as listening to a drum or Tibetan gong with eyes closed. Another example is using visual concentration on an object such as a candle, mandala, or mirror. Sensory focus and exploration can transport one from ordinary to alternate realities. At other times a combination of sensory experiences are stimulated. Spiritual ritual, chanting, and prayer can serve as connections to the mystical realm (Francis, 2020).

Life events may affect our perceptions and open our thinking, such as a near-death experience, the birth of a child, a marriage, or the death of a loved one. The inner language of the subconscious provides vivid symbolism. Our creativity, intuition, relationships, and enlightenment thrive when we are released from only using the logical mind. Archetypes are an important element of the collective unconscious. Pictures, images, and archetypal energy serve as portals to inner knowing. When we think in images instead of words, we encounter limitless possibilities (Brenner, 2013).

Landscapes and buildings can serve as a portal. Scientists describe the existence of electromagnetic fields surrounding living beings and the Earth. When scientists speak of portals, they are often referring to portals located many thousands of miles above Earth in the upper atmosphere. Particles surge back and forth through these openings, which are doorways between Earth's magnetic fields and the sun's.

This interchange can have dramatic effects. The existence of a portal can rely on a vortex of energy to sustain it. This is an area of mass energy in a high concentration, usually originating from magnetic, spiritual, or other unknown sources (Lowth, 2016).

For example, some think of ley lines as a web of energy that connects sacred sites around the world. The energy feels more electric than magnetic and is said to boost spiritual skills and expand consciousness. This type of portal might bridge inter-dimensional divides and enable interaction and experience between different planes of existence. There are places that may increase openness to other realms and other ways of knowing. These include areas in nature where there is beauty, sound, water, and earth elements that open sensory experiences. There are places in nature that are sought out because people experience the Earth's energy as stronger and more focused. Examples include Cairo, Egypt; Carnac, France; Machu Picchu, Peru; Sedona, Arizona; and Stonehenge, England (Radford, 2013).

Stepping through a portal may activate intuition and initiate a felt body sense where you have a shift of consciousness and "know in your bones" that you have crossed a threshold into a new way of being. The wisdom and support of your Creative Spirit Circle can encourage crossing gateways that were previously closed. Exploring your portal experiences with expressive arts offers an opportunity to learn from one another's stories, discoveries, and expanded states of consciousness.

Crossing the Threshold

Choose a sacred space in your community or create an altar in your circle meeting space to focus this practice. You might consider entering a monastery, mosque, synagogue, or walking through a significant gate, a hidden path, or another doorway. Nature provides many opportunities to explore portals. A local beach, forest, garden, or park offers portals of transcendence. After choosing the place for your Creative Spirit Circle's portal exploration, develop prompts to help group members enter and explore this threshold.

As an example, the Cathedral Basilica of St. Louis, built in 1914, was used as a sacred place for the authors' portal exploration. Before entering the building, prompts were offered for circle members: explore the altar, choose a pew to pray or meditate, visit the smaller chapels, gaze through the stained-glass windows, or contemplate the magnificent mosaics that adorn the building. A small mirror was given to each circle member for a personal mirror meditation before entering the cathedral, along with written meditation guidelines. Upon entering the magnificent structure, each person explored the space in silence and then found a place to sit for the mirror meditation.

Mirror Meditation Practice

The Maya of Mexico used mirrors to contact the spirit world. Painted on their pottery are numerous examples of images of people gazing into a mirror (J. Rogers, 2019). We will use this mirror meditation practice today.

Find a quiet spot and sit comfortably with a small pocket mirror propped up in front of you. Offer a specific intention. Start by bowing to yourself. Allow yourself to become aware of your breath. During this mirror meditation, try to notice what emerges moment to moment, with openness, curiosity, kindness, and acceptance. Look into the mirror as if you are greeting your past, present, and future self. If you notice you are beginning to criticize or evaluate your face, let go of judgment and refocus your gaze on your eyes. Observe yourself for about ten minutes. Where do you go when you look in the mirror? Your gaze becomes the focus of your practice. The mirror creates a focal point and a tool for you to track your attention. Notice your emotions, notice the changes in your face. Who is behind the face? What happens when you really look into the eyes in the mirror? Your gaze can help you come back to your center (Kaufman, 2022; Well, 2022).

Experience your aliveness, and the miracle of your life. Take a few minutes to jot down some notes, questions, or insights that emerged from your mirror meditation. This can serve as inspirational material as you continue your expressive arts journey.

Expressive Arts Journey: Discovering Portals

Description

After leaving your sacred portal space in silence, reassemble at your circle meeting location. This expressive arts journey offers an opportunity to capture and further explore your portal experience. This may include the embracing meditation, the mirror meditation, visiting a sacred place, and/or the exploration of your portal inquiries.

Invite each member to submit favorite music that carries them to another place or time. Examples might include classical music, Celtic music, chants, *Phantom of the Opera, Anthem* by Leonard Cohen, cello works played by Yo-Yo Ma, drumming, or singing bowls. Include inspirational music playing in the background

All these experiences may create openings to a new threshold. Your portal can be depicted in a variety of art media. This could be clay, collage, watercolor, collecting natural elements from nature to show a visual image of your travels, and exploration of other realms. Through this artmaking each person creates a representation of their portal experience.

Materials and Supplies

- Journal or paper and pencil or pen
- Mirror (small, pocket)
- Watercolor paints and paper, magazines, glue for visual art collage
- Vibration and sound can be a portal. Use your voices for chanting.

Guidelines and Process

Once you have chosen your creative medium, allow your subconscious feelings and thoughts to direct your creation rather than pre-planning an outcome for your artwork and or writing. Allow about 40 minutes for personal reflection and artmaking. Explore what emerged for you during your sacred portal exploration and mirror time. How would you like to express your thoughts and feelings about your portal experience? Circle members are invited to follow artmaking with written expression, such as a poem or prose piece about their experience.

Writing Reflection

- Describe your observations or feelings about your art creation, your portal inquiries, and/or your mirror meditation.
- What messages does your artwork embody about your portal experience?
- What shapes, colors, or words create a portal of reflection for you?
- Write a story or poem about the portal carrying you to a new threshold in your life.

WOW Story

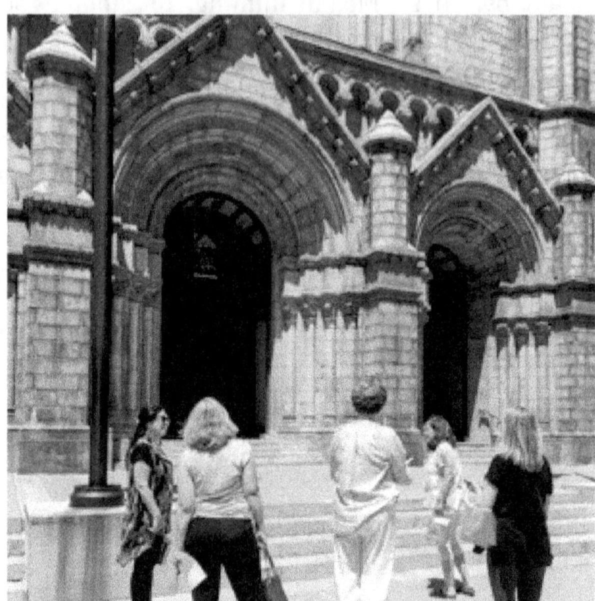

Figure 27: Our Creative Spirit Circle visits the Cathedral Basilica of St. Louis.

Kim McCallum wrote in 2018: The Basilica activated my senses (Figure 27). The light shining through the stained glass windows reminded me of ancient times. The grandeur of the architecture and the art on the high ceilings built a sense of joy and connection inside of me. Building a cathedral is a weaving of many artisans over generations. I experienced the vast ancestry of my humanity and my spiritual heritage. I was aware of the large cathedral doorway, the mosaics, and I experienced a connection with the artwork and the lives of the artisans. I noticed the portrait of Mary and Jesus. One of his sandals had come off his foot. The artwork provoked an opening to my emotional realm. I felt the helplessness and exposure of maternal love. Mary could not protect her son. Motherhood holds so much pain and vulnerability. I recalled painful times I had experienced as a mother of four children. There were so many times that there was so little I could do to take away my children's suffering. In that moment in the Basilica, I had a profound awareness that I was not alone in my suffering.

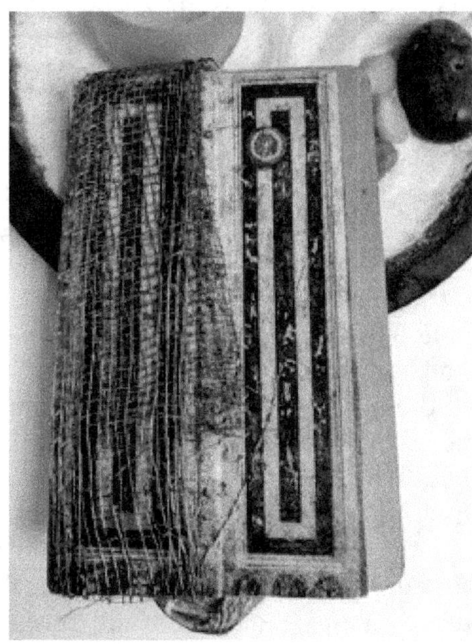

Figure 28: Inside Door, mixed media, Kim McCallum (2018).

I did the mirror exercise for over half an hour. I had never done this before and was amazed. I looked and focused my eyes as I breathed and noticed my aging face as content. Then, I thought of my face over time and saw an image of my face as a child. I was flooded with memories. I recalled poignant moments in my life and felt intense joy. This was powerful. I went to a place that transcends time and experienced a different type of energy. I felt grateful.

When I returned to our circle meeting space, my art came together slowly. I created a book (Figure 28) that pulled me into the imaginary portal of monks chanting. It feels coherent and magical.

Conscious Closure and Integration

For conscious closure, gather in a seated circle and invite each person to share their portal experience and their creative process of writing or artmaking. After each person has described their personal portal and artmaking experience, the group can discuss any insights, metaphors, symbols, or new awareness that emerged during their time together. An inquiry for the group may be, "Have there been earlier times in your life when you had a significant portal experience but perhaps did not realize it at the time?" During our conscious closure experience, Ginger described a portal experience in Tara, Ireland in 2018:

I once unexpectedly crossed an energetic portal on the Hill of Tara in County Meath, Ireland. This was the ancient ceremonial and burial site for 11th century royalty. It was the official seat of the High Kings of Ireland. As I wandered the wind-blown landscape, I came upon a grave bearing one of the Irish Mother Goddess symbols, Sheela na Gig. She is a symbol of birth and fertility. As I walked away, I felt a shocking rush of energy from the ground through my body, from my feet all the way to my crown. It almost knocked me down. Never having experienced anything like this before, I stood dazed, trying to understand what had happened.

When I entered the gift shop at the bottom of the hill, the curator said to me, "You felt it, didn't you?" I asked what he meant. He responded, "The energy. I can see it in your face." He told me that the Irish believe there are "ley" lines connecting sacred sites around the world. They are portals to another world. I had just stumbled upon one of them. This one encounter opened me to the exploration and receptivity to similar experiences in my life.

Close with a poem or blessing about the new beginning created by walking through a portal.

Thresholds
Ginger Reinert, 2000

Stand on the threshold of this life and see beyond the known.
Pause and acknowledge paradox before the time has flown.
Enter a place where choice becomes a ritual of change.
In ceremony there create a blessing that remains.
The liminal includes a space of creativity.
Improvisation offers grace of non-duality.
Convergence of the unseen world within the ebb and flow.
A contemplative cloister where the pace of time is slow.
Be held by something larger now; a Sacred pulse is near.
Experience Divinity. The Way to Peace is here.

Summary

There is power in using a group ritual to open pathways into the unconscious and into spiritual realms. An example is the poem "On the Pulse of Morning" (Angelou, 1993). Layering experiences with meditations, a visit to a sacred place, poetry, artmaking, and journaling may amplify the effects. These esoteric doorways provide entry into a realm of discovery and mystery. When we open ourselves to the possibilities of transcendence, worlds of wonder are disclosed. We can move between levels of consciousness toward more authentic fullness. You may want to consciously commit to practices that you feel support the opening of portals for you, on your own and with your group.

Creative Weavings

- Notice the thresholds you cross and the portals you enter on a daily, weekly, monthly, and yearly basis.
- Keep a journal of the messages, feelings, insights you receive from these experiences.
- Develop your intuition through meditation, sounding, and body practices such as chanting, yoga, or tai chi.
- Take photographs of beautiful doors, windows, and other portals in your community. Journal about the experience.
- If another expressive art journey comes to mind that you now realize was a portal for you, how so? What impact did it have on you?

Chapter 14

Honoring Our Ancestors

It is in the roots, not the branches, that a tree's greatest strength lies.
—Matshona Dhliwayo

Intention and Purpose

Our ancestral lineage provides a rich heritage from which to draw creative energy, wisdom, and inspiration. The stories of our family history live deep in our DNA, providing an important backdrop that includes cultural ancestry, artistic traditions, and trauma. There is value in learning how our ancestors used their creative energy and honoring the impact they have had on our lives. In this session, the focus is on how our ancestors influence our creativity.

This expressive arts journey uses weaving to understand how our ancestors' stories and myths are dynamic threads woven into life's tapestry. For those who are adopted, ancestors include the family members and community you grew up with. Ways to honor, connect, and nurture our relationships with our ancestors are also presented.

Creative Inquiries

- What stories were you told about your ancestors?
- What rituals have you learned from your ancestors?
- How are you similar and different from your ancestors?
- Where are your ancestors located in your imagination? How do you communicate with them (or not) at the present time?
- What would you like to ask your ancestors?
- What would you like to share with them?
- How did your ancestors express their creative spirit?

Introduction

The death of loved ones can have an intense impact on our spiritual journey. Honoring the dead can help with that process. Many world cultures honor their ancestors in elaborate ways. Some countries such as India, China, Cambodia, Korea, and Japan worship their ancestors and believe that they can intercede in real world activities. This practice is an important element in their cultural identity (One World Nations Online, n.d.).

In the United States, elaborate funerals or memorial celebrations are often planned for those who have died. Soldiers who have fallen are honored on Memorial Day. Each day, ceremonies take place at the Tomb of the Unknown Soldier at Arlington National Cemetery. Flags are flown at half-mast when an important national figure dies. The dead are honored and remembered. Why?

It seems the living believe it is important to remember the dead, the sacrifices and contributions they made, and the lessons we learned from their lives. Perhaps the most colorful remembrance of the dead happens in Oaxaca, Mexico on *Dia de los Muertos*, the Day of the Dead, on November 1 of each year. This is a sacred tradition.

In October of 2018, three members of our Creative Spirit Circle journeyed to Oaxaca to experience the week-long celebration with our guide, Wendy Phillips, PhD, co-founder of *El Colectivo Macondo*, an expressive arts and Indigenous worldview training program based in Oaxaca.

In Mexico, art and craft traditions are ancient practices passed down to each generation. As an educator and expressive arts practitioner, Dr. Phillips connected artisans from Oaxaca with students and faculty who traveled from the United States and wanted to study with local families who were devoted for generations to art practices such as ceramics, mask making, sculpting, and weaving. This session, Honoring our Ancestors, emerged from the experience of visiting and working with local artisans in Oaxaca during *Dia de los Muertos*.

Opening Ritual and Invitation

Create an Altar or Shrine to Honor the Ancestors

Assemble an altar or shrine on a table. Invite your circle members to bring family photographs, memorabilia, candles, and/or other symbols of water, air, fire, and earth. Choose photos, symbols and mementos that hold special meaning for your family. Many people add favorite foods, beverages, and keepsakes of their loved ones. Flowers add beauty and life. In Mexico, marigolds are found everywhere as their scent is believed to attract the dead to the altars. These items weave the ancestors into the present moment.

Create a sacred space and focus your ritual on greeting your ancestors and thanking them for being a part of your life, thus creating a bond between the generations. Read the following blessing or one written by a group member:

> May we honor the ancestors in our family constellation.
> May we honor the ancestors of the land where we live.
> May we honor our ancestors' heart and spirit.
> May we recognize that in every family system there is generational trauma.
> May we have compassion for ourselves and each other during challenging times.
> May we acknowledge the pain, sadness, and grief living within us and within the world.
> May we express our gratitude and honor our ancestors' creative spirit.

Dance of the Four Directions

After each circle member lights a candle, invite the group to engage in a traditional or new dance and a prayer or meditation. The purpose of this is to engage our whole body, mind, and heart while contemplating personal history. Our bodies come from our ancestors. When we join in sacred dance and prayer or meditation, our physical engagement can bring new awareness by activating the wisdom within the body.

Many indigenous traditions believe their ancestors participate from their realm with those currently "in life." You may choose to imagine your ancestors dancing with you. Offer your members drums, rattles, bells, and music. Then, invite your circle members to:

- Turn to the east in a line with palms facing up.
- Take three steps to the left. Stop and clap.
- Take three steps to the right. Stop and clap.
- Repeat the movement as you turn facing north, west, and south.

The facilitator may write or select an online resource to guide the group in an extensive dance and meditation to the four directions—for instance, the Prayer to the Four Directions attributed to Chief Seattle: http://www.starstuffs.com/prayers/fourdirections.html. A dance to the four directions connects our awareness to the Earth, to the changing seasons of our life, and to knowing that we are part of a universal family. Ultimately, whatever we do to the Earth and to one another, we do to ourselves.

Check-In

Invite the group to share stories of the ancestors whose photographs are on the altar. Participants may use the creative inquiries above to tell their story and explain why these particular people were chosen out of many family members. After sharing, participants may talk about how they would like to be remembered after they are gone.

Lecturette

How long is a person remembered after death? Do memories of loved ones last a generation or two? One would hope so. Some cultures work at remembrance more intensely than others. In the cosmology of the Indigenous Peoples of Central Southern Mexico, it is believed that on one day of the year the ancestors return to celebrate life with the living.

Day of the Dead is a ritual that has been practiced for hundreds of years. On *Dia de los Muertos*, it is believed that dead relatives come from the underworld and ancestors come from the heavens to reunite in the middle on the earthly plane with the living. It is a happy time when people build elaborate altars in their homes and businesses and spend the night in cemeteries remembering those who are not lost but are always with us (Figure 29).

There is a connection of past and present that unites the community (Haley & Fukuda, 2004). The Indigenous Peoples believe ancestors enjoy the relational and sensory experiences at this time as they did when they were in the cycle of life. (This is not to be confused with Halloween, which evolved from the Celtic Samhain holiday.)

Many Mexicans still express their spirituality through dance, clay, and weaving while respecting and building on ancestral traditions, and in doing so believe that the universe evolves. The Day of the Dead celebration in Oaxaca is one of connection to the past, to the ancestors, to the community, and to the universe through spirituality and art. If you do not believe in an afterlife, you may simply think of their practices as an example of a way to make needed connections with your history and how it has shaped and is still shaping you in ways you don't recognize and can't work with if you don't pay attention.

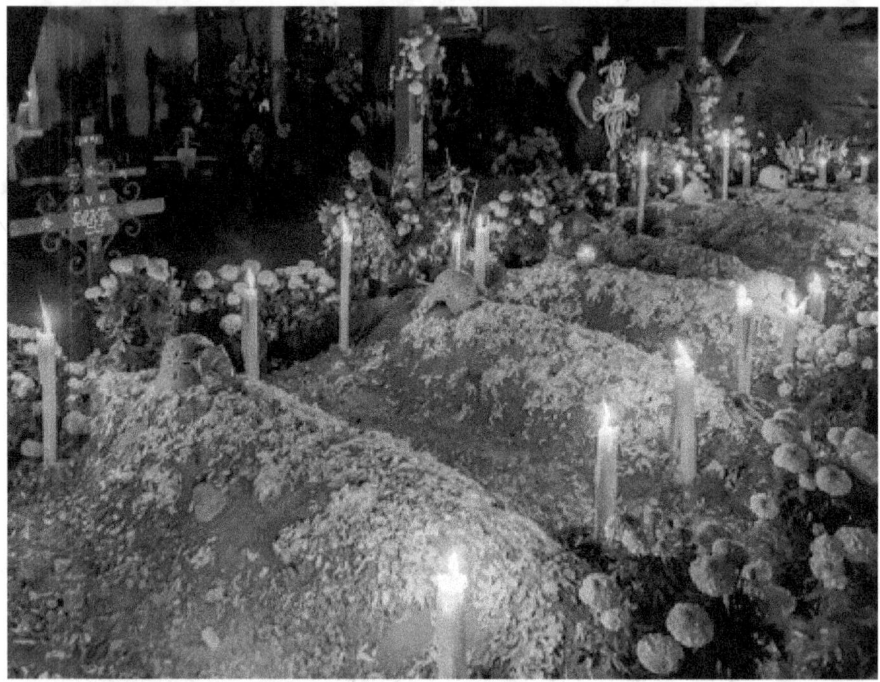

Figure 29: Graves Covered in Marigolds, Oaxaca (2018).

Why is this important? The few studies that have been done on the impact of connecting with and seeking to understand the histories of our ancestors, even just our parents, indicate that this increases self-esteem, decreases anxiety, and increases resilience, among other things. (For a short article about one of these studies, see Chandler, 2013.) The concept of *emotional genealogy*, coined by Fein (2014), describes how connecting with our ancestors lends stability and meaning to our lives by helping us understand who we are in a way not accomplished by only drawing a family tree.

You may use intermodal expressive arts specifically suggested by Day of the Dead practices or another method of creativity. Below is a description of several forms of art that you might choose.

Clay

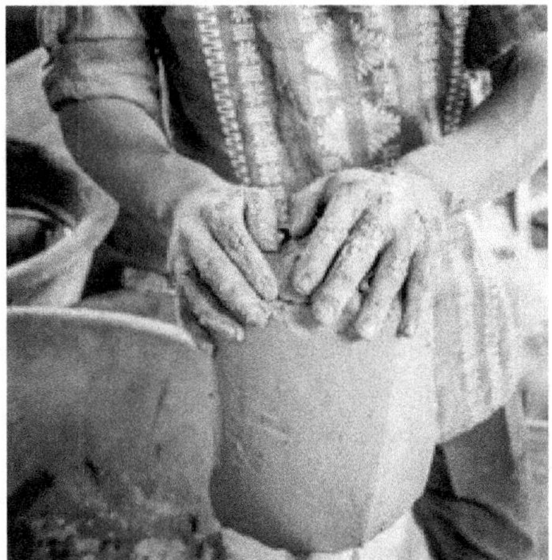

Figure 30: Oaxacan artist rests his hands on a newly kneaded block of clay.

The potters of Oaxaca have used the ancient clay mines outside of town for over one thousand years to create beautiful pots and figures. Creating with clay (Figure 30) is a spiritual process using the dark clay of the area with the white clay of another. The tension of opposites is always present in the creations. We come from the earth and Mother Earth meets all our needs. Working in clay brings us to our beginnings and grounds us in our bodies.

Dance

Sacred dance serves as the embodiment of connection and energy. Art is not just about itself; it is about, among other things, connections between people and the Earth. The family and community are sacred in Oaxaca. In dance, they greet others with love through energetic movements of the hands and face in the four directions to experience the elements of wind, air, fire, and water. Involving your entire body in your creative endeavors awakens all your senses, including intuition and body memories, and enhances inner awareness and creative expression.

Dreaming

Many people are visited in their dreams by departed loved ones. Honor this encounter by recording the dream in written form. Look for symbols and messages. You may invite a visit by verbalizing the intention of dreaming of lost relatives before you go to sleep at night. Jeremy Taylor (1983) pointed out the intention can trigger the experience (see Chapter 9 on Dreams and Individuation for more tips on working with dreams). Do not be afraid. Ancestors may have much to teach you. Even if you cannot consciously imagine an ancestor speaking to you, your unconscious mind may recall stories your family told or memories from your childhood that are relevant to your current life and place them in your dreams.

Music and Feasting

Other ways of connecting with ancestors are through music and feasting. As Dr. Marina Aguirre de Samanego (2020), a Mexican historian, noted, singing the old songs that were sacred or important to your departed loved ones brings back an essence of that person through the sense of hearing and the vibrations created by the act of singing. It can be sacred music or more popular songs. In the graveyards of Oaxaca on October 31, mariachis play traditional music throughout the night. This takes place as family members and friends bring food and beverages as offerings. The vigil lasts all night when it is said that the veil between the living and dead is the thinnest.

Weaving

Weaving tells a story and provides a tangible portal to the numinous world. The intricate designs and numerous threads of a tapestry create a synergy of spirit. Most traditional weavers, including the Oaxacan, include symbolism and meaning (Fischgrund, 1999). You may weave to share what is important in your life at this time. Use color, texture, lines, and symbols to convey your message (Figure 31).

In indigenous weaving patterns, the universe at the center is surrounded by four quarters. Color is important and it is created

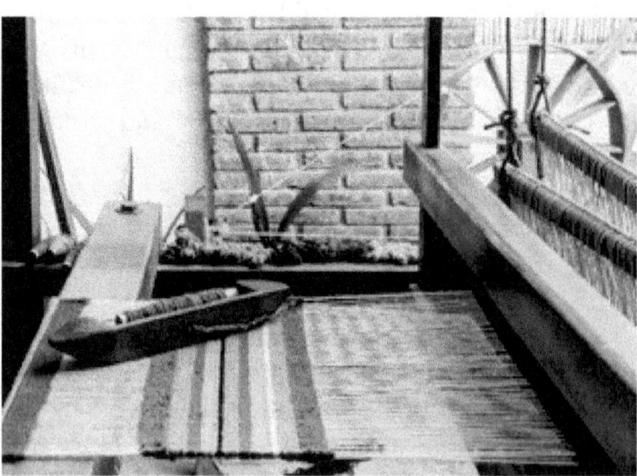

Figure 31: Weaving in Oaxaca (2018).

through natural dyes made from pecans, marigolds, fuchsia, cochineal, indigo, and other natural sources. Symbolic geometric patterns include pyramids, lightning, corn, butterflies, spirals and snakes, mountains. The diamond-shaped God's Eye symbol at the center of most weaving is a portal to the spirit world. The four sides are the boundaries of space and time (Aguirre, 2020).

Crossing the Threshold
Gather your members around the altar. Your circle facilitator may present the following poem and meditation or one you have created.

WOW Story
Ode to Oaxaca on Dia de los Muertos
Ginger Reinert (2018)

In the Valley of Oaxaca
on the towering White Mountain
lived a spiritual people
who brought meaning to this land.

Praise the beauty of the landscape
praise the blessings of abundance
and invoke the four directions
to unite the many gods.

As they worship by creating
dancing, weaving, and clay sculpting
they become the fifth dimension
thus completing nature's plan.

Praise the beauty of creation
praise the grace with which they offer
and invite the loved ancestors
to return and be at one.

As they worship at the altars
and parade throughout the village
offering joy and consolation
so they honor those who died.

Praise with marigolds and cockscomb
praise with candles, food, and fireworks
and create a grand fiesta
Guelaguetza to us all.

Now to celebrate the old ways
and acknowledge where they came from
to preserve an ancient culture
where the sacred leads the way.

Praise with incense as it rises
smoking, healing prayer ascending
also praise with song and drumming
and invoke the heavens home.

Praise the cemetery vigil
praise a living room remembering
welcome all who will attend there
on the journey of return.

Meditating with our Ancestors

We are all part of the human family. We recognize that some relationships have nurtured us while others may have been extremely challenging. There is something to learn from each of these experiences.

Make yourself comfortable. Stretch your body and take a few deep breaths. You may want to close your eyes. After each meditation stanza is read, pause for a few seconds to reconnect with your breath.

- Feel supported by nature's abundance. Connect to the energy of life as you inhale and exhale.
- Be aware of your presence in the moment. Picture a weaving that includes the threads of your ancestors. Their triumphs, failures, and emotions run through this fabric of time.
- Choose beloved family or friends to join you in this meditation. Breathe in their wisdom and offer them gratitude.
- What wisdom does your beloved community offer you at this moment?
- As you move into the past, look for other key people who walked your ancestral path. Offer them gratitude for the knowledge, love, and care they offered you.
- When you have greeted your ancestors and community, ask them to sit with you for a while. What messages or images resonate between yourself and these loved ones?

- Again, thank all of them for their wisdom and guidance.
- Relax in the warmth of their loving connection with you. Continue breathing slowly.
- When you are ready, open your eyes slowly.

The leader invites each participant to share their experience of communicating with the ancestors for a few minutes.

Expressive Arts Journey: Ancestors and Life's Tapestry

Description

This expressive arts process explores ways to weave the tapestry of your life with that of your ancestors. Your life's tapestry includes your history and relationship with your ancestors. Let this work of art express the wholeness of your story.

Materials and Supplies

- Gather some of the following: dowels, yarn, embroidery thread and small hoops, beads, papers, shells, and/or charms, tokens, and travel memories.
- Invite circle members to bring materials such as photos, letters, cards, notes, recipes, old tools or jewelry, anything that reflects memories of ancestors and their ancestral land and creative practices.

Guidelines and Process

Weave intuitively. Choose your supplies with different generations and people in mind, representing them with different colors, textures, lengths of yarn, etc. You may think of the threads or yarn as steps in your life or paths you walk.

Think about messages you received from your ancestors in the guided meditation. What have you learned from your ancestors? You may wish to write a description or explanation of your weaving. Other options for a creative arts journey are collage, clay, paint, or poetry. Choose the style of expression that inspires you to explore and integrate what you are learning about your ancestors.

Writing Reflection

After completing your artmaking, select a writing invitation to deepen the group's recollection of ancestors:

- What food might you prepare for your ancestors that they would enjoy?
- Choose an ancestor and prepare a toast or eulogy. Write a prayer or blessing for your ancestors.
- Write a poem that honors your ancestors.

WOW Story

Pam: I dreamt last night of a mixture of architecture, cabinetry, watercolor paintings, various designs, and pastry—

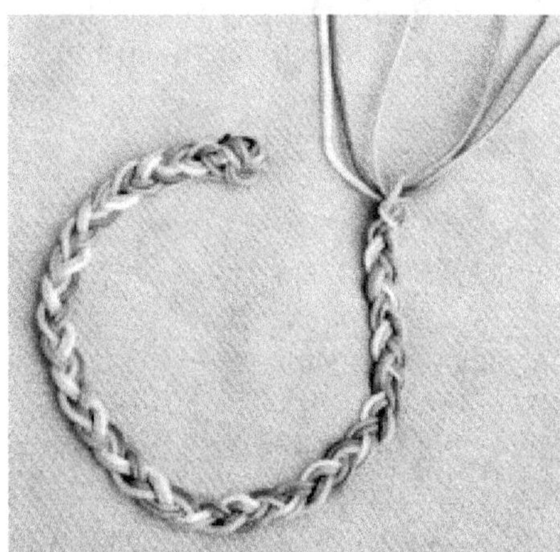

all skills of various ancestors. I think it was their sacred call to me, knowing I would be working with our circle today. I don't think about my ancestors a lot, and when I woke up, I realized that every one of my ancestors was an artist! I have this creative ancestry that I had forgotten.

Figure 32: Ancestor Friendship Bracelet, cording, Pam Caraffa (2019).

One grandfather was a maker of fine cabinets and furniture. The other was an architect who designed several of the oldest skyscrapers in Hartford, CT. Maternal ancestors were ship designers and builders in Denmark, and my grandmother made beautiful lace and creative pastries. My mother was a watercolorist and fiber artist, and my father was a writer.

I want to befriend my ancestors, so I made a friendship bracelet (Figure 32). It's made of earthy and royal threads and represents my ancestral, creative cosmology. I realize now that they gave me this creative and artistic ability to see and work with patterns and designs, as well as for photography, and the creative corporate work I have done over the years.

Conscious Closure and Integration

Invite each participant to bring their artmaking into the circle and to share their experience with one another. The facilitators can ask the group, "Are there any insights that have emerged from your creative exploration with your ancestors as you listened to one another?" In closing, the following poem or one of your choosing may be read by the leader as each participant drops a small pebble into a bowl of water.

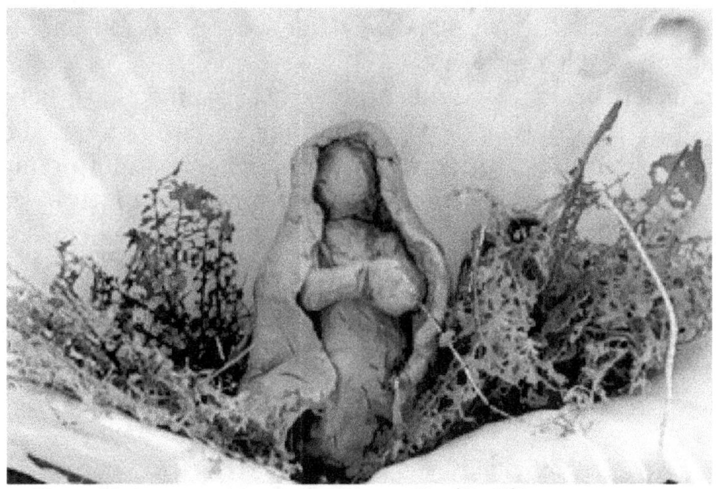

Figure 33: Image and Poem, Wanderer, Clay/Shell/Grasses, Nancy Williger (2019).

So many lives gone before.
I am just one more.
Like raindrops falling into a pond,
leaving ripples before,
merging into the greater whole.
The miracle of life
How quick it is passing.

Summary

Messages from your ancestors can be a path to the soul and a more whole self. Weaving ancestral connections into our lives informs our journey. Every thread strengthens the universe as a whole, as every life adds to the evolution of the world. The fabric of the universe is threaded with life's unique experiences. A map of becoming is like the geometry of weaving, creating a diversity of forms. It all has purpose. To be aware of this truth and to honor it is a vital part of the process of growth.

There are patterns in your relationships that continue to surface in each generation. You inherited your identity and some of your life story from your ancestors; you are the next chapter in that story. By honoring the source of your life, you honor all life, and your perspective enlarges to include and value all who came before. You also can change the story, if needed, to create greater well-being for yourself and future generations. To change the influence of your past, you must consciously explore what happened and choose what to sustain and what to alter.

Ancient people understood the connection between the generations. There is a permeable membrane between life and the soul's connection to everything. Humans are multi-temporal. Ask yourself: How would I like to be remembered by future generations? Each story is a compilation of the stories that came before. The legacy continues to grow through you. You can honor your ancestors not only by remembering them, but also by fulfilling your personal potential and purpose. Through this evolution, you create reality and make peace with life and death.

Creative Weavings

- Interview relatives for stories of loved ones who passed away.
- Research your family's genealogy, including their emotional genealogy.
- Take a DNA test to discover your lineage. Take a pilgrimage to places your ancestors called home.
- Collect recipes from various family members and create a cookbook to honor the importance of sharing food with one another.
- Take a picnic to the grave of a loved one. Pack their favorite food and beverage and share it with them in celebration of the life they lived and enjoyed.
- Make a family tree collage. Draw or paint a tree on a large piece of paper and place symbols of different family members beneath it. Around the tree write messages to yourself about the meaning of your ancestors to you.

Chapter 15

The Art of Transition

One must have chaos to give birth to a dancing star.
— Friedrich Nietzsche

Intention and Purpose

The intention of this expressive arts journey is to develop innovative ways to navigate changing events that inevitably emerge during different stages of life. Transitions are turning points and even when positive can cause upheaval. In this chapter, the challenges and invitations of transition, uncertainty, and facing the unknown are examined and explored through collective weaving, movement, and the art of mask making. These three modalities offer symbolic portals that open participants to mystery and creative pathways that support transformation through life transitions.

Creative Inquiries

- What changes and transitions are you experiencing in your life?
- How is transition reshaping your life?
- What fears do you have of change? If you released your fears, what would transform?
- What meaning are you discovering through change and transition?
- What are you longing for?

Introduction

Transitions may compel you to re-examine your present way of being in the world. They challenge you to shed old roles, rethink priorities, and be more intentional with living your life. Transitory periods usher in profound opportunities for growth and transformation and can break you open to the depths of the human heart and spirit. Change is a springboard for growth. This expressive arts journey espouses the use of arts to understand and express various aspects of the self in transition, and to remember your larger belonging to yourself, the world, and mystery.

Opening Ritual and Invitation

Rituals are an intentional practice that fuel your creative process with presence, depth, and meaning. They can be a symbolic way to acknowledge and navigate changes throughout life. The ceremony of a ritual is an artful way to cross crucial thresholds of change and can be a connection to the collective unconscious. The beautiful diversity of rituals that honor and mark change can be seen across world cultures and religions. At the same time, the tradition of rituals transcends cultural differences and establishes a sense of unity (Beck & Metrick, 2003).

Rituals tap into the archetypal realm, encourage embodiment, observe the seasonal cycles and patterns of change, and transport you into deeper levels of consciousness. They serve as an outward reflection of your inner transformations and provide a tangible expression of the changes you are experiencing.

For the opening ritual of this expressive arts journey, offer each participant a sheet of paper and have them tear, fold, and shape their paper in a way that reflects a change they are experiencing in their life. This ritual is symbolic of the malleable nature of change. Open your circle by having everyone light a candle. Then each person will place their paper on the circle altar and name a change or transition they are currently experiencing. Awaken the senses and clear energy by burning sage. Close the opening ritual by reading a poem such as "Journey" by Mary Oliver (1992, p. 114).

Check-In: Mandala, Weaving Ourselves Whole

Consider reading a poem such as "The Way It Is" by William Stafford (1999, p. 7), to begin your check-in.

Preparation
Obtain a circular loom, 2–3 feet in diameter, and prepare it for threading and weaving prior to the group meeting. Have various yarns, fibers, and ribbons available for the check-in activity.

Through the art of transition, creative ways emerge to weave ourselves whole. We do not journey alone through transition but are deeply connected through the web of life. Transition enables us to continually weave, unravel, and reweave our personal and collective lives. We need each unique color, cultural strand, and societal perspective to weave our world whole.

Imagine your life and creative spirit circle as a mandala tapestry and ponder these questions as you look at the challenges of the past year. Invite each participant to check in and take turns weaving on the circular loom as they share their experience of collective change and transition. The following questions are a helpful guide for your discussion and check-in.

- How have the collective threads of change impacted the weaving of your life?
- What has been the consistent thread you have held throughout the seasons of your life?
- What new threads are you welcoming into your life?

Lecturette: The Art of Transition

Transition is generally understood as a transformation from one state of being to another (Bridges, 1999). Like a butterfly's metamorphosis in leaving the comfort of its cocoon, it is the internal and external processes of change that give birth to a period of transition, during which you may transform in profound ways. These internal transformations are often both psychological and spiritual in nature. Periods of transition often become initiatory passages that ripen the soul, paving the way for the birth of a new sense of self. They make possible an emergent way of being, awakening consciousness and acting as a catalyst that can redefine your identity and how you make meaning in your world. Transition, challenge, and change can frequently be difficult. A natural tendency is to resist life's changes and cling to familiar comfort zones. However, much like the heroic journey, the psyche will nudge you until you encircle the profound transitions of life and the gifts of change take root in your soul and transform you.

Change and transition are complex and multi-layered. In his book, *Life is in the Transition*, Bruce Feiler (2020) pointed out that transitions are a vital period of creativity and rebirth that help one to re-evaluate and find meaning in life. Change is inevitable. Numerous voluntary and involuntary transitions and shifts occur over the course of a lifetime. Sometimes multiple transitions and changes are experienced simultaneously. Each developmental stage of life comes packed with its own initiations and transitions, inviting growth, expansion, and transformation.

William Bridges (1999), one of the first authorities to do ground-breaking research on the topic of transition, influenced how we conceptualize change and transition both personally and organizationally. In his book *Transitions*, he identified three main stages of transition: (a) the ending, (b) a middle stage of confusion and chaos, and (c) a final stage of new beginnings. He described transition as a bridge that connects different periods of your life and the inner reinventions and redefinitions one goes through to incorporate change into one's life.

Transitions do not emerge in a linear path; they arise in a progressive spiral through multiple internal deaths and rebirths, moving you along the path of becoming. Transitions grant an opportunity to find the gift and lessons in each life stage with presence and conscious awareness. The ego's tendency is to grasp old familiar ways and resist the *new* normal. But the soul has a way of loosening your grasp on life and teaching ways of non-grasping. If you allow it, transition becomes a potent teacher.

In her book *Emerging Woman: A Decade of Midlife Transitions*, Natalie Rogers (1980) described six stages of transition: (a) making a decision, (b) creating a bridge, (c) saying farewell, (d) letting go, (e) limbo, and (f) re-rooting. She encouraged us to be conscious changemakers, mindful of the imagery, intuitions, and messages that arise amidst transition. Her trailblazing work in person-centered expressive arts (1993, 2011) is an inspiration to utilize creativity as a catalyst for change and integration. When we engage our creativity, it becomes a transformative agent of change and a path to wholeness.

Imagination thrives in the liminal times of unknowing and uncertainty and can serve as a crucible of emergence during periods of transition. The chaos of change creates new brushstrokes of meaning on the canvas of life. We all need creativity to flourish through seasons of uncertainty. Artmaking is all about changing and transforming. As you engage your creative wellspring, you journey along the path of becoming. You make the art, and the art makes you. You are not just writing poetry; you are becoming the poem.

Crossing the Threshold

Embodied Movement: The Dance of Transition

Oftentimes, your body knows the path forward through transition before your mind does. For this segment of the expressive arts journey, create a playlist of music that goes with the theme of change and invite participants to move freely for five to ten minutes, welcoming the winds of change while attuning to the new rhythms that are emerging through their bodies. Movement engages the physicality of transition, engaging all the senses and activating the imagination.

Sometimes you just have to move and join the dance of change. Notice how you embody the natural rhythm of change as you move through life. Drop into a feeling state and try to locate somatic markers, those intuitive sensations in the body that help guide you. Become aware of how you experience and sense change in your body. Notice what wisdom your body is relaying to you about change.

Explore ways to welcome change with compassion rather than resistance. What imagery arises? Where are you holding polarities of emotion in your body? Allow your body to dance the feelings of change. What metaphors emerge in the dance of transition? What sounds express this new way of being?

When the dance of transition is complete, make a few notes in your journal about your experience and any messages your dance conveyed.

Expressive Arts Journey
Facing Change: Connecting the Mask and the Soul

Description

This expressive arts journey explores the art of mask making. The Mask is a powerful archetypal symbol that re-emerged globally during the transition and upheaval of the COVID-19 pandemic. For centuries, masks have been created around the world in every culture.

Masks are a means of creative expression that allow the wearer to transcend their egoic self and explore other personas, roles, and timeless dramas. They are a container for one's feelings and reflect various archetypes within the psyche of the self. For example, a mask may be symbolic of your persona (persona in Greek means "stage mask"), higher self, shadow, future self, and dream self. Mask making is an evocative way to explore multiplicity, stories of change, and parts of the self that have been exiled. They use your creative process to examine life stage transitions, shadow material, and identify pathways of change. The whole self has many parts. The art of transition is a call to wholeness amidst the winds of change.

This expressive arts journey offers participants an opportunity to explore the masks they wear as they "face change," experience transition, and open to transformation in creative ways. Who are you through the drama of life's transitions?

Materials and Supplies

- Acrylic paints, spray paint, and paint brushes
- Collage papers and words
- Ephemera such as jewels, rhinestones, ribbons
- Glue sticks and glue gun
- Items from nature such as sticks, moss, leaves, shells, feathers, or flowers
- Markers for writing on the mask, if desired
- Paper or plastic face masks

Guidelines and Process

Invite participants to select a mask and embellish it using a variety of mixed media supplies. Ask everyone to freely express themselves, creating on both the inside and outside of the mask, utilizing writing, painting, collage, drawing, etc.

Writing Reflection

- Title: What is the mask title/name asking to be known?
- Affect: What is the primary mask emotion asking to be felt?
- Question: What is the primary mask inquiry asking to be heard?
- Affirmation: What is the mask affirmation?

WOW Stories

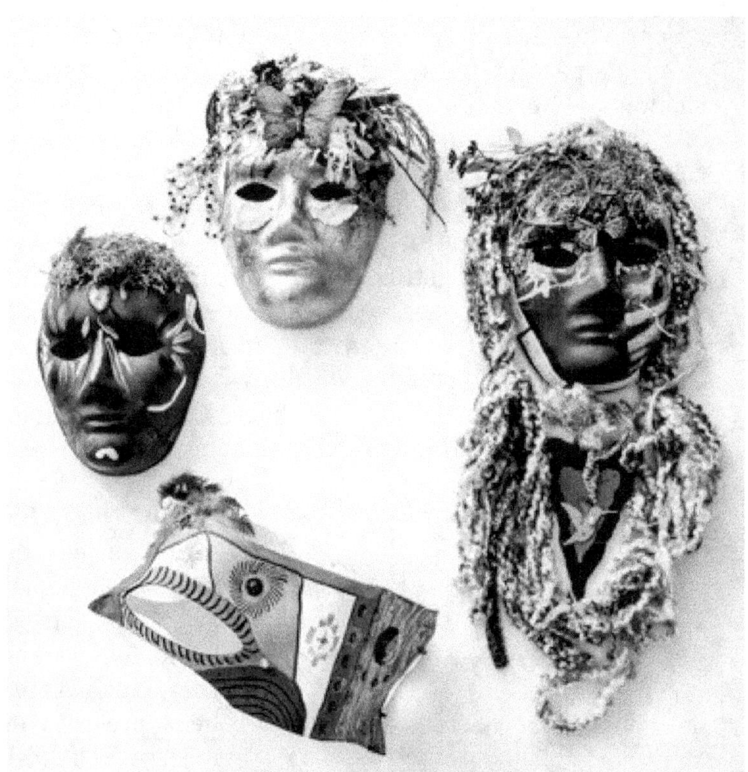

Figure 34: Masks of Four Authors, starting at the far left & moving clockwise - Pam Caraffa, Holly Carson, Terri Goslin Jones, Nancy Williger, (2021).

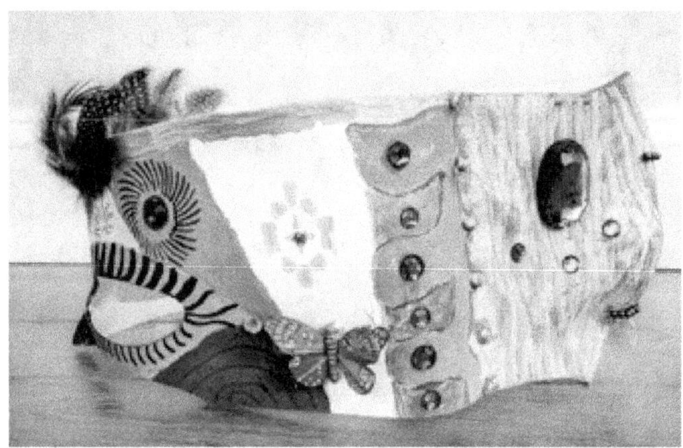

Figure 35: Bejeweled Warrior, mixed media, Nancy Williger (2020).

Nancy: Masks literally determine how we "face" the world. Sometimes our true face can make us vulnerable and show too much. A mask can help us be anonymous and allow us to reveal a part of ourselves that we normally keep in the shadows. My mask is the mask of a bejeweled warrior (Figure 35). She is brave and connected to the earth. She is of many colors and sees all. She is soft and hard, glitzy, and down to earth at the same time. She is who I would like to be.

My mask is made of a face covering I was given at the hospital when I was getting a CAT scan. For this procedure, it was molded to my face, and when the scan was over, the attendants asked if I wanted to keep it. At the time, I felt I could do something creative with it. When our Creative Spirit Circle decided to make masks, I knew the perfect time had come to bring life to this intriguing object.

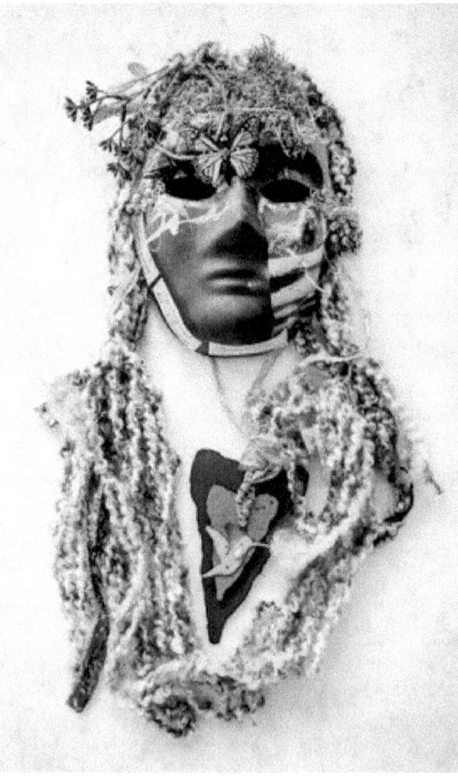

Figure 36: Earth Dancer, Mixed Media, Terri-Goslin-Jones (2020).

Terri: *Affect*: Earthy, gritty, ancient, divine, mystical, enchanted. *Fear*: Not letting my "Wild One" out and at the same time not being present with my monastic self. *Message:* Messy moments create treasures. I have roots and wings and sweet honey resides in my life's cracks.

Affirmation: I live moment to moment in an ancient process of riding/surfing the tides of my life. My *Earth Dancer* is ancient, divine, enchanted and creates treasures. The intention cards that I selected at the start of our Art of Transition circle included Sacred space, Grace, Create, and Gratitude. My Earth Dancer represents the transformation of divine energy. I am in a state of grace. I gratefully view each day as bursting with creative moments. I reflect deeply on both sides of everything, yes/and...

I trust Divine timing and grasp that I am immersed in mystery. I cut my poems into stanzas and the verses are a halo around my Earth Dancer's head. My Earth Dancer is and lives poetry: moss, grass, earth, gallops on my archetypal horse, my wild one. Who are you? Why are you here? There are secrets in everybody. Every "body" on this Earth holds divine secrets.

I want to jump on my wild horse and gallop through consciousness. This is my last chance for freedom as I move out of full-time overflowing work and shift into my creative cosmos. I was raised on stormy waves. As a small kid, I learned to surf the breakers of life. I am resilient. I am learning to receive peace even in chaos. I imagine the universal energy resides in me. My desire is to dwell in the miraculous, to embody and to *realize* the "miracles at play."

Conscious Closure and Integration

For the conscious closure of this expressive arts journey, invite participants to share how they are experiencing change and transition in their lives, their experience of mask making, movement, and their reflective journaling. Explore what insights and wisdom emerged for each participant through mask making and the various exercises in this journey. Close this journey with a poem or blessing. You may find something in Julia Cameron's (1999) book *Transitions: Prayers and Declarations for a Changing Life.*

Summary

We live in times of great change, challenge, and possibility. Periods of uncertainty can inspire incredible creativity, and help you reimagine new and effective ways of living, working, relating, and existing in the world. This expressive arts journey has looked at transition on the micro (individual) and macro (collective) levels using a variety of creative modalities. To engage in the art of transition is to be an artist of being alive. Life is the art medium. Change ignites creativity and liberates the inner artist to express the inexpressible and navigate deeper pathways of becoming and knowing. Trust and have reverence for your life journey. Transition is an art.

Creative Weavings

- Incorporate into your art journal ways that you are becoming an artist of being alive through seasons of change.
- Make a vision collage to visualize and explore possibilities about the changes you are seeking, dreaming of, and imagining.
- Write a letter from your wise elder to your current self. (Where are you struggling? What might you want to give up or quit? What love and wisdom might your wise elder have for you?)
- What vow or commitment might you make to support growth and expansion? If inspired, write a personal manifesto for yourself.
- Write a self-care plan, selecting key areas from the Creative Living Web (Chapter 4) to thrive during life's transitions. Incorporate exercise, meditation, prayer, self-compassion, and creative self-care practices.

Chapter 16

Conscious Closure:
Weaving Wisdom and the Art of Circling

The vessel for personal and planetary evolution is the circle with a spiritual center.
— Jean Shinoda Bolen

Intention and Purpose

Conscious closure, which is at the end of each expressive arts journey, is a time to digest each person's experience and weave insights into collective wisdom. This chapter uses the conscious closure process to reflect upon the arc of expressive arts journeys for one or many years of circle work. Contemplation and dialogue are a way to digest experiences and integrate the energy that feeds our creativity.

In this journey, circle members explore personal growth, identify elements of the circle that have impacted the group, and assess how relational creativity has emerged as the group grows in cohesiveness and depth. Reflection brings learning to life. Artmaking and conversation about multiple circle journeys enable insights to emerge about the growth and well-being of each circle member and the group as a whole. A thriving circle is a spiral. Rather than cycling around to the starting point, a focus on imaginative learning from collective experiences enables each member and the group to evolve to a new beginning with expanded layers of growth.

Creative Inquiries: Reflecting on the Journey

The following inquiries form the basis for your discussion during this session.

- What themes, circle topics and group experiences have impacted or inspired you over the past year(s)?

- How have you changed as a circle member over the past year(s)? For example, describe your challenges, growth, and expansion during this period.
- Where have you experienced creative tension? Consider areas such as artmaking, co-facilitation, group process, and risk taking. How have you worked with the tension?
- As you reflect on this timeframe, what wisdom might you share with your circle?
- What desires or intentions do you have for future circle sessions?

Introduction

This journey is a catalyst to *reflect on* experiences throughout the year(s), *dialogue* about key learnings, and then *re-envision* your group's future direction. In this meeting, you will have an opportunity to hold up a mirror and observe yourselves, individually and collectively, discuss growth, and mark how circle processes have catalyzed changes. Through the expressive arts experience, you will share an image that is symbolic of the collective wisdom that is being woven together.

Distribute your group survey before the circle meeting (Appendix E) to support a dialogue about personal and group experiences. The facilitators will compile and share the survey results. The survey will give you a sense of the pattern of thoughts, feelings, and lessons learned across your circle of individuals. The combination of conversation about the survey results and multi-modal engagement in creative artmaking provides a rich source of exploration for circle growth. The conscious closure process at the end of this journey facilitates developing a specific plan for the next phase of weaving your tapestry together.

Opening Ritual and Invitation

A key part of reflecting upon your circle's experience is sharing with each circle member the gifts they brought to you during your time together. To open this ritual, invite each member to light a candle symbolic of the creative energy brought to the group experience. Take a moment to consider how each person's presence contributes to synergy in the whole circle. People cannot always see their strengths or understand how their unique presence contributes to the community experience. This is a chance for each of you to understand how your presence and creativity contribute to the overall group process.

Next, tape a large sheet of paper on the back of each person in the group. Provide each participant with a marker. Take turns writing on one another's paper what you have learned from them, words that describe them, what they bring to the group, and what you appreciate. Take turns reading out loud the written comments for each person.

Check-In

Have the facilitators choose a poem that speaks to your group's creativity. An example is "Initiation Song from the Finder's Lodge" by Ursula LeGuin (2019). Then, discuss what you have learned about one another. Circle members can claim their unique contribution to the group by sharing a word from the feedback. Examples might be, "I bring courage, I bring a sense of adventure, I bring candor," or "I bring a poetic voice."

Lecturette: Weaving Wisdom: The Art of Circling

Expressing yourself through art provides a powerful mirror for self-reflection. This is magnified in a close-knit circle and yields innumerable threads for weaving wisdom individually and collectively. Wisdom offers keys to surpass and transcend daily life. In his compelling book *Transcend, The New Science of Self-Actualization,* Scott Kaufman (2020) described the process of becoming whole as a continuous voyage through life akin to sailing. He suggests sailing because the key to a good life is not the hierarchical level you reach but the degree of integration you have within yourself and with the world. Sailing is a wide-open journey, necessitating many subtle changes inside you (the boat) and your interaction with your surroundings (water, wind, landscape). The better you know and the more comfortable you are with your boat and your surroundings, the easier it is to go on a purposeful journey and feel the occasional joy of transcending your previous existence. Kaufman (2020) confirmed our premise that creative companions on this continuous journey increase the potential for growth, transformation, and, ultimately, transcendence.

Jean Houston (1982) also emphasized that creativity thrives in the shelter of others. It can be argued that you cannot fully know yourself without coupling the experience of yourself in community with your experience in solitude. We thrive in the company of family and friends who stretch, witness, and support us. Like braiding sweet grass or weaving a basket, there is a reciprocity in the art of relational creativity. This enables you to weave a Creative Spirit Circle that becomes a container to hold your group's collaborative medicine.

Houston (2009, 2022) asked each person to consider what the world would be like if you tapped into your full potential and released yourself from the smaller story you've been living. She noted that great creatives are guided by a power either deep within them or beyond them. This "spiritual" power is called an inner voice, muse, or spirit. Whether it is reported as a religious belief, a wise guide, or a voice within, creatives pay close attention to this power and allow it to motivate and guide them with great courage.

Creativity requires attending to inner voices, being attentive and responsive to the reality in which you live, and discovering ways to collaborate with others. A Creative Spirit Circle combines all these elements. Like the enso circle, we are always in the process of "circling," growing, becoming, transcending, and moving toward wholeness. In this circle of belonging, the creative connection and the creative process become a portal for transcendence.

Abraham Maslow and Natalie Rogers viewed creativity as the height of self-actualization and transcendence. Maslow (1976) stated: "Transcendence refers to the very highest and most inclusive or holistic levels of human consciousness, behaving, and relating, as ends rather than means, to oneself, to significant others, to human beings in general, to other species, to nature, and to the cosmos" (p. 269). Kaufman (2020) expanded on this definition, writing that transcendence is "an emergent phenomenon resulting from the harmonious integration of one's whole self in the service of cultivating the good society" (p. 218).

Natalie Rogers advocated that a journey inward through expressive arts is a way to tap into the unconscious and gain insight and empowerment. She affirmed, "As we learn how to be authentic and empowered in a small community, we are then inspired to move to the larger circle. We become co-creative and collaborative, being able to access our higher purpose and powers" (Rogers, 1993, p. 9).

Crossing the Threshold

Meditation: Weaving Memories

The following meditation can be read, accompanied by singing bowls and tongue drum soundings. This meditation is an invitation to access your inner wisdom. It is also an opportunity to scan and consider how you have grown individually and how your group has grown as a Creative Spirit Circle.

> Tune into your breath. Breathe. Let yourself relax. Feel your chest move in and out as you inhale and exhale. Listen to your breath. Relax your face, your eyes, your mouth, your tongue, your cheeks, your jaws. Let your face begin to melt. Take a deep breath. Feel a softening sensation move slowly around your head, down your neck, into your shoulders and across your shoulder blades. Feel your feet firmly planted on the floor and imagine that you have roots growing from your feet through the floor and into the earth. Let your thoughts come and go without judgment.
>
> Take another deep breath. Every exhale can bring you deeper into a state of complete freedom. Let your breath carry this relaxation down your arms, your chest, your stomach and middle back, melting into your pelvis and bottom, and down your legs into your feet. Breathe. Relax. Know that you are safe, right here, right now. Your mind, body, and spirit are fully present and fully grounded.
>
> As you settle into this safe, secure place, continue to notice your breath. With each inhalation, breathe in the fullness of your life. With each exhalation, release what needs to be released, letting go of any tension that remains in your body. Become aware of your imagination and find the path that takes you to the dwelling place of your intuition, your creativity, and your inner guide.
>
> You have an intuitive part of yourself that reflects wisdom and deeper levels of creativity. Find in your mind's eye the night sky as a guiding light that may lead you to your inner guide. You might see your guide as an image, sense your guide as a presence, or simply notice an open, reflective shift in your own thoughts.

Invite the depth of your inner presence, your spirit, to join you. Your inner guide might show you intuitive feelings, words, pictures, sounds and smells. In your imagination, begin to take a walk, a stroll, or a hike to meet your inner guide. Walk on a special, secret path that takes you on your unique journey; reflect on and remember moments when you felt your inner guide's wise presence. Experience appreciation and deep love. Your guide is nearby. Soon you come upon a gate, a door, or an archway that leads into your inner guide's sanctuary. You may hear your guide's voice, smell your guide's scent, and feel the energy. Look around and notice your surroundings again. It feels so good to be here in this sacred place.

Notice your breath. Let yourself relax and feel fully grounded in your body. Your inner guide is with you; their wisdom, their intuition, their creative spirit is perfect for you right now. Observe your surroundings and the experience of being with your inner guide. What do you notice with your senses? Are there any scents or flavors? What sounds do you hear? If your guide appears as an image, what do you notice? What is your inner guide offering you? There may be a question you would like to ask. You can ask anything. As you become aware of any messages, put your hands on your chest and feel your heartbeat. This gesture carries the message into your heart for safekeeping. Know that all is well. Rest here. Breathe here. Be aware of your inner wisdom. (*Pause.*)

Soon you will leave your wise inner guide. Before you leave, your guide will give you a ritual of return, a symbol, or a small gift to help you stay connected. You may hear words, see a movement or images, or you may feel through simple intuition. Receive your gift and message for your return. Listen. Accept this gift with gratitude.

As you look once more at your inner guide, visually take in your surroundings and convey your goodbye, knowing that you can come back here anytime you want. Mindfully begin your return journey, walking back through the gate or archway and onto the familiar path. You realize that your inner guide is a part of you and available to you whenever needed. (*Pause.*)

As you focus on your breath, begin to move your fingers and toes. Slowly move your head from side to side. Breathe deeply and fully, preparing to open your eyes and come back into the present moment. Softly open your eyes and come back to the room. Take a few minutes to jot down the details of this journey.

Give the group about five minutes to do this. Let them know that they can begin their expressive arts journey right away or as soon as they finish writing.

Expressive Arts Journey: Weaving Ourselves Whole

Description
In this expressive arts journey, participants are invited to reflect on how the process of using expressive arts within a Creative Spirit Circle has "woven them whole." From your Creative Spirit Circle archives, select imagery, poetry, and journal writings that you created in your circle meetings over the year(s). Or you may choose to create a new piece of artwork inspired by your group experience. Artwork can be woven together into a collage, or you may be inspired to create something brand new that serves as an inspiration for the future.

Materials and Supplies

- Acrylic and watercolor paints
- Collage and mixed-media ephemera, including ribbons and various fibers
- Glue stick, Mod Podge, or gel medium
- Markers and gel pens

Guidelines and Process
Use symbols from previous artwork and/or develop new creations that represent key learnings and the embodiment of your creative spirit during the past year(s). Select and include string or ribbon to illustrate the process of "weaving" creative spirit into daily life. Some possibilities for artmaking with this journey might include painting, an art journal page, sculpting with clay, collage, or photography.

Writing Reflection
Provide ample time for circle participants to write and reflect on their expressive arts and circle experience. Options might include returning

to creative inquiry questions for reflection, writing a poem, or using journal writing to create a poetry collage.

WOW Stories

Nancy: When I started with this circle, I had no idea what was going to happen. Although I had artistic leanings as a child, as an adult there was no time for creative endeavors. I had some familiarity with art therapy, but no personal experience, and I had never heard the term "expressive arts." Entering the empty-nest stage of life, I looked for ways to further my spiritual development. One of our early group expressive arts journeys focused on beading. I found that putting beads on a string was calming and relaxing, and I opened to the creative process in a new way.

I value lifelong learning. Each topic we covered in our circle meetings sparked my awareness of new areas of creativity. After each session, I continued to expand my creative expression and knowledge about archetypes, female deities, meditation, and an appreciation of the Earth's elements. Our circle has stimulated me intellectually and creatively in ways I could not have imagined, not to mention the benefits derived from being with the other five amazing women. I have never been in a group that is as respectful, accepting, and validating as this one. Our differences are cherished by all and appreciated for the richness they bring to our tapestry.

As I thought about the expressive arts part of this circle meeting, an image came to me of a bubbling cauldron of creativity. The image I created (Figure 37) is a liquid stew of

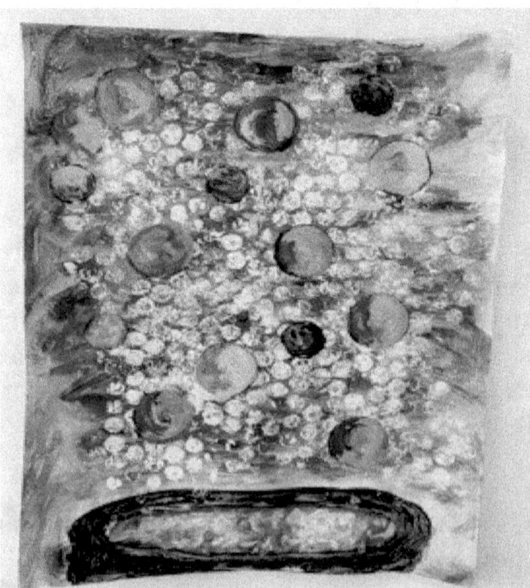

Figure 37: Cauldron of Creativity, mixed media, Nancy Williger (2022).

many ingredients. It is sending bubbles into the air. The bubbles are colorful but last only a short time, a reminder of the transitory nature of experiences and of life. I used acrylic paint on paper (a couple of years ago, I had no idea what acrylic paint was or what kind of paper to use). This group has been my cauldron for creativity and continued growth, and I cannot begin to express how grateful I am.

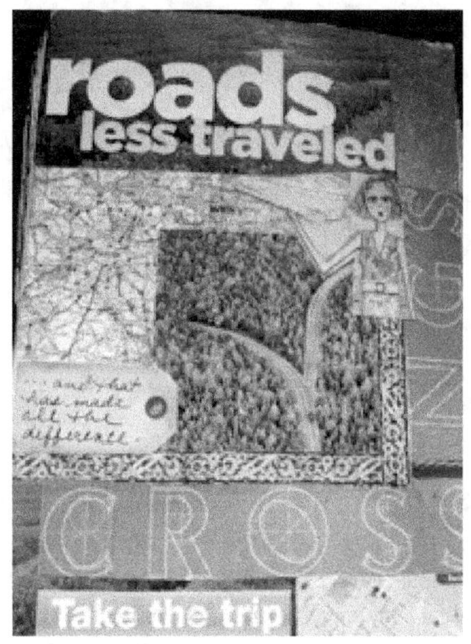

Figure 38: Road Less Traveled, collage, Ginger Reinert (2016).

Ginger: I have never considered myself a creative person, but I have become more comfortable with the creative process after engaging with our circle for the last eleven years. Expressive arts tap into my subconscious and trigger images and words that provide profound messages. The process provides a vehicle that I can use to find meaning and peace in my life. It has made me see the world from a different perspective, helping me to become more mindful. Patience has been a gift of this practice. There is a Zen-like calmness that washes over me when I engage in expressive art projects.

When I am working on my collage journal (Figure 38), I really get into the flow of creativity. When working on my art journal at home, I will go for days and not want to go out. My office looks like it blew up and is the biggest mess. I love it and want to jump in and stay there. There is so much more to be explored. This practice carves out a sacred place and time in which I can explore realms of spirituality. It takes me to a mystical place, and it is easy to get lost. I want to stay there and not come back. I want to discover the road less traveled.

Holly: The Creative Spirit Circle has been an incredible catalyst for growth and expansion, and a dynamic, supportive container of creative as well as spiritual emergence. There is a tender, reverent way we hold one another, our mutual creativity, diverse spirituality, along with life lessons and growth. The creative spirit encouraged a creative generosity,

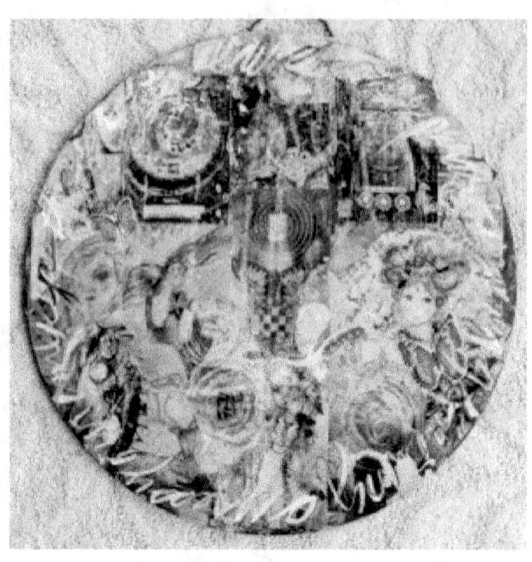

Figure 39: Poiesis, mixed media on wood substrate, Holly Carson (2022).

luminosity, and hospitality that has flowed from and through our circle, enriching my life in deep and meaningful ways (Figure 39). Perhaps the greatest surprise for me has been the power and depth of the collective consciousness that is experienced through creating together.

Each circle theme has been like a sacred pilgrimage to the "center," bringing its own unique experience of needed medicine to each of us. Creativity and spirituality are inextricably linked, and the collective experience of creating together has taken me to spiritual depths and creative heights I might never have discovered and most likely would never have traveled alone. It is like being creatively companioned. Together we have conceived, labored, and given birth to emergent parts of ourselves, claimed our hidden wholeness, and learned what it means to live vulnerable, wild, and holy lives through this magical experience we call the Creative Spirit Circle process. Our Creative Spirit Circle has been one of my life's greatest invitations to participate in an exquisite adventure. It has taken me on creative pathways that have widened my perspectives on life and taught me potent lessons on the art of living and being.

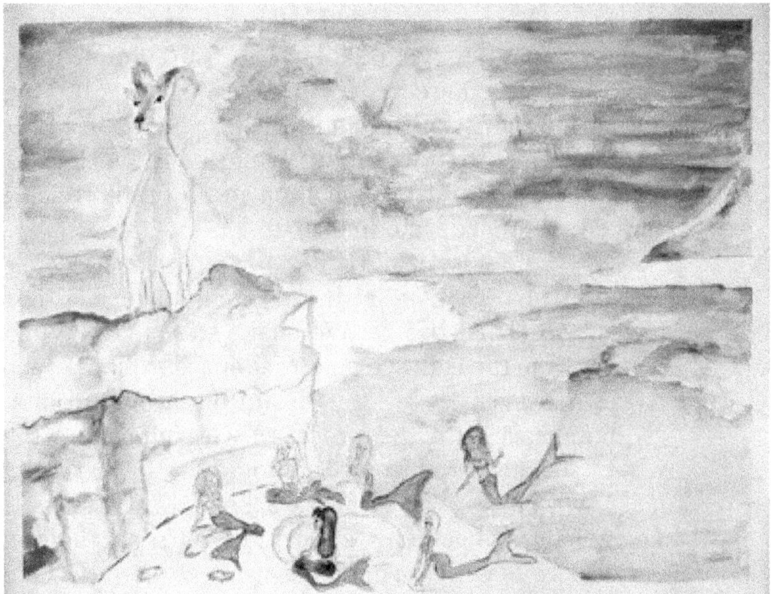

Figure 40: Selkes Circle and Wisdom, watercolor, Kim McCallum (2022).

Kim: I have found our circle experiences to be transformative. We have navigated so much together. In the last two years while writing this book I retired, moved, planned a wedding, and lost a parent. There is a way that creating together opens me up to different types of inspiration. I feel life is full; I feel more present and open to the beauty around me. For much of my life, I have lived in ideas, science, and words; I always loved philosophy. I did not have any experience with the basic artmaking techniques for many of our expressive arts journeys, but this was not important. Being a novice in art allowed me to approach each journey with a child's eyes, although I admit to some hesitance related to a lack of mastery. Having a practice that involved artistic expression woke up a part of me that had lain dormant. I am more appreciative of my creative side and have started to paint with watercolors (Figure 40).

Exploring so many topics—aging, our shadow sides, transition, love, portals to spiritual realms—while leading with my creative musings has been a true pleasure. Artmaking in parallel and together moves me beyond ordinary boundaries. Often what emerges in my artwork are images and ideas that appeared in several of our works, like sharing a dream. These journeys allowed me to experience being part of something bigger, a "greater" whole. I have treasured our openness, the opportunity to share our experiences together. It is a gift to be influenced consciously and unconsciously in a way that inspires. I feel confident that I can use our journeys to deepen my experience and investigation of any topic related to the soul or personal development.

Pam: Our Creative Spirit Circle has taken me to a place I have never been before. We share strong, family-like bonds that give me the courage and freedom to explore my inner self more than ever. Now, I am less in my head and more in my red-hot heart with the process of learning how to express what I see and feel through photography and writing, so hot I feel I will burn up. I feel like the song, "This Girl is On Fire"! The mystics tell us that we must lose ourselves before we find ourselves one with the universe.

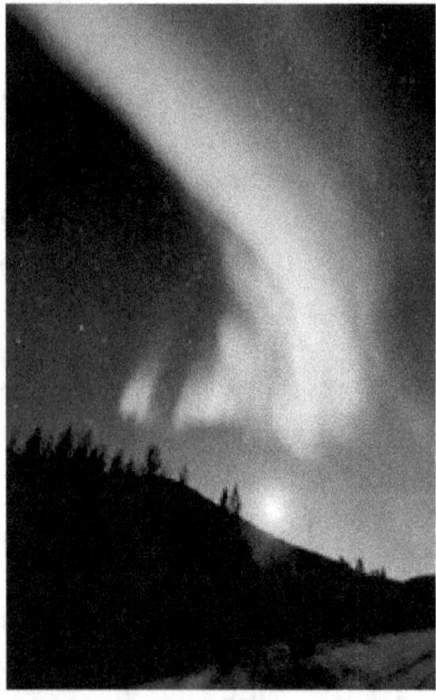

Figure 41: Aurora Meets Moon, photography, Pam Caraffa (2015).

Changes in me are evident in my images, which range from representational (Figure 41) to a focus on metaphor (Figure 42). Although I have always been attuned to philosophy, art, and mysticism and my career called me to engage a higher vision, day-to-day work was frequently more down to earth. Our circle encourages subtle attunements to my inner life. As I listen deeply and increasingly open myself to the way others in my circle and life experience the world, I embrace the world more fully. The mirroring and sharing in our circle help us access more of what consciousness has to offer than is possible as an individual. As I let inner promptings lead my artistic expression, rather than just my intellect or emotions, I feel more than ever our world's losses and rebirths, the heat, the cold, the fear, the excitement. I experience the sheer interconnectedness of us all. And, occasionally, I am one with the cosmos.

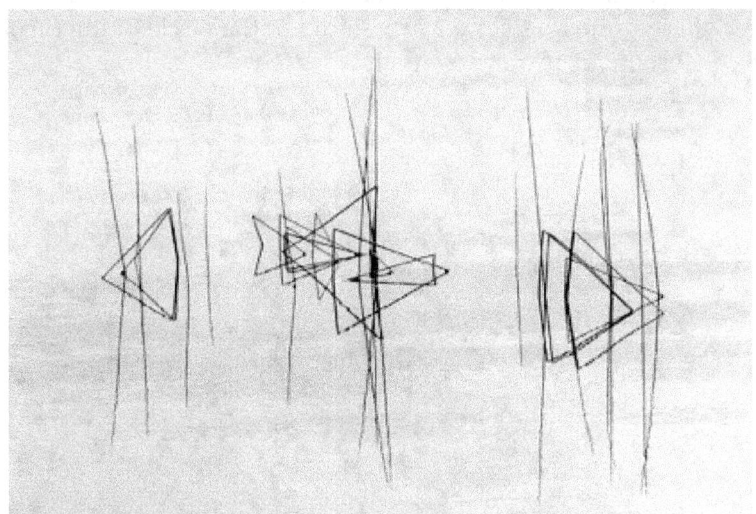

Figure 42: Geometry of Life, photography, Pam Caraffa (2022).

Terri: Our Creative Spirit Circle process balances the structure and creative inspiration I need to stay committed to harvest my creative energy. Our circle is a creative incubator for me, a place to experiment and to pioneer. Expressive arts and circle work touch all parts of my life. After each session, my creative energy overflows and is expressed in art journaling, writing poetry, and designing creative workshops and graduate courses for my professional work.

As we envision our next decade together, an important learning for me is that contemplation and silence are essential for my creativity to emerge. Our circle is a place to imagine and explore emerging changes in my life. My experience in our circle is reflected in my watercolor painting (Figure 43) of an individual in the circle of life next to a mandorla, which is an ancient symbol of wholeness.

My painting reflects our circle as a place for exploration, integration, and expressing creative spirit. Through our process of co-creation, we develop a third and new way of "being and seeing." The intersection in the middle transcends duality and is a place of surprising creation. We are individuals, and yet we are one in a creative community.

Individually and together as circle members, we desire to evolve into our greater creative potential. Our evolution is fueled by our love for each other and by our creative spirit. We free solo and yet we are united in the circle of life through our creative journey together.

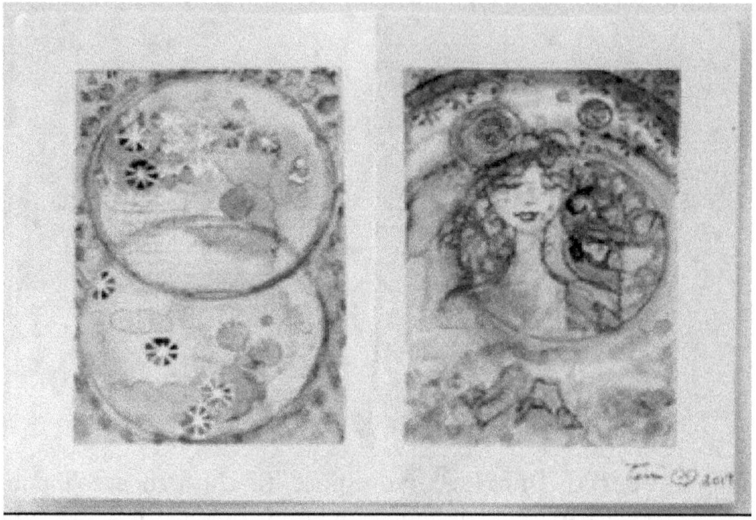

Figure 43: Circle of Life, watercolor, Terri Goslin Jones (2019/2022).

Conscious Closure

The conscious closure journey is a time to review the past year(s) of your circle experience, and to envision new stages of growth together. Begin this review with a ritual to bring your minds and hearts into an open and imaginative space. Create, ahead of time, a circle of stones or items from nature, wide enough to encircle all members. This circle can be formed inside or outdoors.

Each member places a candle in the center. As you sit down, take a moment to pause, breathe deeply, and softly gaze at one another, feeling fully the experience of being held by belonging in your Creative Spirit Circle. Ask each participant to share, as desired, their artmaking, reflections, and experience of this expressive arts journey. Next, invite circle members to share their future vision for the group and any ideas they have for designing the next cycle of your collaboration. After you have heard from all members, each member might share a word or phrase to recap what they want more of in your circle.

Clarify your wishes, creative longings, and goals as you continue this creative path together. Note the commonalities and differences in what is shared. What hopes do you share for your circle's future? Are there places where you have divergent desires?

Articulate and summarize what you agree upon and then discuss any areas where you do not agree. You may come to agreement easily, or you may continue to differ in one or more areas. If you have divergent views, try alternative solutions, review what happened, and continue to seek common ground. There is no one right way to conduct sessions, beyond practicing the PCL guidelines (Appendix B) and following the overall Creative Spirit Circle process.

To close this journey, stand in a circle and blow out the candles, perhaps holding hands as you share gratitude for the time you have spent together. Invite each member to offer a sentence for a group blessing. Or use the blessing at the end of this chapter.

Summary

The intentional process of a conscious closure journey helps Creative Spirit Circle members identify and integrate the many impactful lessons learned through the various expressive arts journeys your group has experienced together. These lessons are the digested experience, the wisdom weaving of your circle. There are different types of learning and growth in consciousness that come from artmaking, silence/meditation, group process, and insights from sharing your individual and collective perspectives. The conscious closure journey also helps clarify your group's vision as you travel forward on creative pathways of continued discovery and transformation.

As we complete our book and this journey of conscious closure, we want to share with you some of the wisdom we have woven from our experience together as a Creative Spirit Circle.

Wisdom Weavings

Be Present and Trust the Process

We have come to appreciate that *witnessing presence* and *creative process* are critical elements of the Creative Spirit Circle. They hold the tension of the interactive threads in your creative connections: relationship with self, one another, and your art. Creativity asks us to be present. Creative life lives in the now. Eberhart and Atkins (2014) defined presence as, "a personal quality as well as an experience of encounter…characterized by multi-level awareness, a multi-fold openness, and an appreciative curiosity" (p. 129). Creative process dynamically brings you into present moment awareness as you interact with your artmaking and one another.

Cultivate the unique presence and witnessing you bring to your circle relationships and artmaking. Allow time to practice presence in your group, as this is the container to nurturing collaboration and authentic relationships. Consciously establish practices, both in and outside of the circle, that support presence and moments of wholeness.

Be Brave and Commit

It takes courage and commitment to pursue the creative path. Stay open to your ongoing personal growth as well as the development of relationships with your circle members. Show up authentically and creatively for yourself and your circle; a transcendent quality emerges in the group that opens doorways to increased awareness, heightened consciousness, and deepened intimacy with life, others, and spirit. The risk of being vulnerable with your creativity is always worth the effort. What you give comes back to you one hundred fold. Let the creative spirit guide you beyond what seems possible.

Be Curious and Open

Curiosity and openness to new experiences are essential aspects of creativity, always inviting you to welcome new experiences and to seek and explore all possibilities. Ruth Richards (2007, 2018) identified openness and bravery as key elements of our everyday creativity. Curiosity is what seeds your inquiries, taking you deeper into your creativity and your experience of the Creative Spirit Circle. Your curiosity ushers you to the threshold of the imaginal realm and radical openness allows you to behold the symbols, images, color, and poetry that the creative spirit will bring to you.

Be Creative as a Way of Living

The expressive arts experience takes you into visceral realms of living in new ways. Engage your senses and the imaginal realm. Art speaks its wisdom directly to you through symbols, color, and images (Richards & Goslin-Jones, 2020). A group offers abundant access to different viewpoints, dimensions of consciousness, and a collective intelligence that grows over time. This is magnified in the Creative

Spirit Circle, where you are invited to cross a threshold into the liminal space of the collective consciousness of the group, an even deeper portal of knowing. Creativity is the language of the soul and opens you to the deep intuitive knowing of the psyche (Rogers, 1993, 2011).

The End is the Beginning

The enzo circle symbolizes that the end is the beginning, and the beginning is the end; we are all in a continuous process of engaged transformation and becoming whole. The Creative Spirit Circle process supports, develops, and sustains these benefits of everyday creativity. Richards (2007b) wisely said:

> From the distance we have traveled, one can see the core of everyday creativity across domains, as a dynamic, conscious, open, and healthy way of encountering life, which hold for us all a means of coping, thriving, growing, seeing more complexly, finding deeper meaning, and working more harmoniously together in a rapidly changing world. (p. 313)

We hope this book and the Creative Spirit Circle process ignites your everyday creativity and your desire for personal growth. May your circle fuel your inspiration to travel creative pathways of discovery and growth.

Creativity is an exquisite gift. May you have the courage to open it, explore it, and let it take you into the flow of your own being, connect you more deeply to others, and bring your unique expression to the world. Tend the fire of your creativity. When things unravel, your creative spirit will find a thread and begin weaving again. Bring your circle's creative energy to the weaving of the world. Trust the process. You have everything you need. Life is your creative loom.

The following blessing was written for you by the authors.

Creative Spirit Circle Blessing

May you discover your deepest longing.
May your longings take you on playful, creative adventures
of discovery, wonder, and joy.
May you find creative companions to love you
and tend the creative fire alongside you.

May you see patterns of meaning in the little things of life
and share your discoveries.
May you nurture the poetry of simplicity
and embrace the silence of spirit.
May you neither push nor block the creative
flow of the river of life.
May you live within the mystery of life
and immerse yourself in wonder.
May you experience joy in being part of this exquisite Earth.
May you thrive and grow wildly.

Appendix A

International Expressive Arts Therapists Association

In 1994, the co-founders—Jack Weller, Anin Utigaard, Stephen Levine, and Phillip Speiser—named this new non-profit the International Expressive Arts Therapy Association (IEATA). The association hosts international conferences and provides professional guidelines, ethical standards, and a professional network to promote expressive arts into the world for "growth, healing, communication, and collaborative learning" (http://www.ieata.org). IEATA offers many Zoom workshops and resources that serve as inspiration for those interested in the field (Goslin-Jones, 2020).

Consider joining the International Expressive Arts Therapists Association (IEATA) for additional inspiration. The organization is open to all who want to use intermodal expressive arts for personal or professional interests.

Definitions

The following definitions establish a framework for expressive arts (Goslin-Jones, 2020, p. 478).

Aesthetic Responses are the physical and mental responses that arise in the presence of a creative act or work of art.

Art as Medicine is a healing process in which the person meditates and engages with the images or materials or sounds, tells stories about the artwork, dialogues with the art, and dramatizes insights through bodily movements.

Authentic Movement is often used as an improvisational physical movement practice to access internal body sensations and feelings. Unconscious impulses that emerge through movement are expressed in the moment.

Collective Unconscious is a key concept within the psychological theory of Carl Jung. It refers to the portion of the unconscious mind that originates in ancestral memory and experience. Jung believed it to be common for all humanity, something we are born with, as opposed to the personal unconscious of an individual. The collective unconscious is expressed through *archetypes*—the signs, symbols, and patterns of thinking we inherit from our ancestors, such as shared assumptions about the sun or moon as a symbol or our valuing of heroes and motherhood. Dream interpretation is one way to access these symbols and patterns to help an individual connect more fully with their inner selves and humanity in general.

Creativity includes four main components: process, person, product, and press of the environment. Creativity may lead to a product, idea, object, or behavior that is both original and meaningful to others. The creative process can be accentuated by expressive arts as they initiate an encounter or intense engagement with one's environment and life experience.

Everyday Creativity is a process and a way of life that increases your capacity to experience the world in original and meaningful ways no matter what you are doing. Work, family life, community involvement, extracurricular activities—all aspects of life can become more creative with conscious engagement and practice.

Expressive Writing, when combined with other forms of expressive arts, is a process of freeform writing about emotions and experiences. It supports the integration of insights that arise from using other expressive art modalities.

Person-Centered Expressive Arts (PCEA) offer an integrative, multi-modal process including mindfulness, movement, sounding, artmaking, and writing for self-exploration, creative expression and integration. It is explored in a safe and supportive environment offering unconditional positive regard, empathy, and congruence. Unconditional positive regard refers to support and acceptance for each group member. Also, the artistic and verbal expression is free from judgement, assessment, or external interpretation. Empathy is the ability to understand and reflect another person's feelings and experience. Congruence is the discernment and awareness of one's internal experience and communicating in an honest and authentic manner.

Registered Expressive Arts Therapists (REAT) use the expressive arts in therapy, social work and counseling and may work in hospitals, private practice, or residential facilities for individuals, or for global organizations.

Registered Expressive Arts Consultant Educators (REACE) use the expressive arts in teaching, coaching, and consulting and across a wide spectrum of disciplines such as education, coaching, workshops, healthcare, hospice, peace building, organization development, cultural change, non-profit work, spiritual development, and conflict resolution.

Relational Creativity utilizes authenticity, empathy, originality, presence, and personal qualities that permit openness, and mutuality with self and others. It includes ways of manifesting interpersonal, intrapersonal, and spiritual potential. Person-centered expressive arts can foster healthier relationships, growth, and transformation by offering a safe and supportive environment for creative and authentic exploration and interactions.

Sounding includes chanting, drumming, music, singing bowls/gongs and vocalization for the purposes of emotional expression, healing, and integration.

Appendix B

Person-Centered Listening (PCL) Guidelines for Sharing Your Expressive Arts Experience

1. Everything is an invitation. There is no right or wrong way to make art. No experience is needed.
2. Be aware of your feelings as a source for creative expression.
3. These experiences can stir up many feelings. Expressing your emotions can be helpful in releasing feelings, heightening self-awareness, and gaining new insights.
4. Be aware of your body and take care of yourself.
5. Be aware of and support the group process.
   a. Pay attention to how frequently you speak or don't speak and balance it so that everyone is contributing. Ask questions of those who are very quiet.
   b. Honor individual differences in members' experience, backgrounds, and views, including seen and unseen diversity.
6. Use Person-Centered Listening:
   a. Focus on yourself first. Most psychological "help" that others experience comes more from your presence, and how you embody your own personal work, and less from what you do or say for others' sake. The purpose of the circle is, first, for you to grow and become more creative and, second, for you to support others doing the same.
   b. Avoid giving unsolicited advice and trying to fix one another. Focus on listening.
      i. You may ask questions for better understanding, or to encourage a person to share more of themselves and their work.
      ii. If a person specifically asks for input, feedback, or suggestions, give your honest opinion in a positive way. For example, "Have you thought about?" rather than "Stop doing..."

    c. Practice congruence: Be the genuine and real person you are. Practice being as honest with yourself as you can about who and how you really are.

    d. Practice empathy: Everyone has a different perception of the world. Try to understand each circle member's thoughts and feelings as *they* (not you) experience them. Walk in their shoes, in the way *they* would walk.

    e. Practice giving unconditional positive regard to yourself and others: To grow and be creative, it is necessary to accept yourself as you are. To be a contributing member of an expressive arts circle, accept each member as they are. You may not approve of some of your own or others' actions, but you genuinely care for yourself and one another.

7. If you choose to observe instead of participating in a specific activity, keep an open mind and heart and honor the process of each member.

8. Everything that happens in the expressive arts circle experience is kept confidential.

If a member repeatedly ignores these guidelines or influences the group with negative behavior, the group holds them accountable quickly, firmly, and kindly. Use positive language that says what might be done rather than what not to do: "Let's listen for a while to what she has to say," or "Remember, we're here to listen to what he is experiencing; we don't need to give him any advice unless he asks for something specific," rather than "Stop interrupting" or "Don't tell someone what they should or could do."

Integrating and Sharing Your Expressive Arts Experience (5–10 min.)

1. After you create an artistic expression, reflect for a few minutes about your experience by writing down a key message, including words that describe your feelings. Or ask the art what it wants you to observe. Notice your feelings and try to stay open. Remind yourself that the person-centered approach embraces unconditional positive regard, openness, and acceptance.

2. Then, share your experience verbally with your partner, "the witness." If for any reason, you are not ready to share your

experience, you can pass. There may be times when you need more personal time with your experience. If this is the case, you can be the witness for your partner.

Being the Witness (5–10 min.)
The purpose of being a PCEA listener/witness is to help your partners see and hear themselves more clearly. It is a discovery process for a person to verbally share their expressive arts experience with a committed and non-judgmental listener.

1. Being a witness for another person's expressive arts process is an honor and a sacred experience.
2. The PCEA listener/witness provides space for your partner to be seen and to verbalize and be heard for the first time.
3. Witnessing and PCEA listening is non-judgmental. It is a receptive process where you listen. You may want to record words or phrases of your partner's experience. It can inhibit the other person's sharing if you shift the dialogue to personal feedback or share comments and interpretation of their artwork.
4. Reflect by verbally summarizing what you heard the person say to you. Notice your thoughts, but do not verbalize them. Redirect your attention to the speaker's experience. Then verbally reflect to the person what you heard and what they said to you. If you jotted down notes, you may simply read a few of the words that were spoken.

Note: This summary is informed by Natalie Rogers (1993), *The Creative Connection Expressive Arts as Healing*.

Appendix C

Creative Spirit Circle Process and Timetable

Roles are Rotated Among Circle Members

Facilitators

For each session two circle members serve as facilitators. The facilitators choose forms of artistic expression that complement the topic of the session and develop the circle plan and general guidelines.

Memory Keeper

The memory keeper will take notes of what is shared by each person in this section and in the conscious closure section. Note taking is another form of witnessing.

Session Framework

Every session uses the same circle framework, and each section of the framework has a specific purpose in forming a rich and creative experience for everyone.

Intention and Purpose (5–10 min.)

At the beginning of the session, the facilitators share the desired outcomes in a way that invites immersion into the subject and circle focus.

Creative Inquiries

Write several questions to engage members in the session topic. Creative inquiry questions may be sent out ahead of time, with the announcement of the session, to stimulate thinking, feeling, and imagination around the theme.

Introduction (5–10 min.)

This part of the session invites your heart, mind, body, and spirit to join in the circle. The facilitators briefly clarify the meaning of the topic using a poem or quote. The facilitators provide an overview of art supplies and logistical considerations.

Opening Ritual & Invitation (5–10 min.)
This section utilizes ritual to welcome circle members to the experience. This is a time to embody the purpose of your session and to create an environment conducive to energetically embrace the topic for a few hours.

Check-In (15–20 min.)
During this time of your circle, invite each person to share thoughts about some aspect of the topic that is relevant to them. Sharing one's thoughts aloud in a group is a significant way to engage with the topic.

Lecturette (15–30 min.)
For some sessions, you and your circle will know the topic fairly well and only need a common framework for your discussion. At other times, the topic may be new to all or some of the group and require more explanation through the preparation and sharing of a brief topic overview.

Crossing the Threshold (10–20 min.)
This portion of the day is to cross over the expressive arts threshold as mindfully and with as much heart and spirit as possible using intermodal processes. Circle members are invited to transition from the group experience to a personal inner journey via a brief mindfulness meditation and or movement or sounding and then use quotes or creative processes that serve as a catalyst for the imagination.

Expressive Arts Journey (60–75 min.)

Description. Give your circle members an explanation of how they might work with the materials and supplies provided.

Materials and Supplies. Each session will have its own needs in terms of materials and supplies. Facilitators provide basic materials and supplies relevant for their session or invite members to bring what they want to work with.

Guidelines and Process. Offer art materials and possible forms of art expression for the expressive arts journey. Even when guidelines are offered, members may choose a different form of creative expression.

Artmaking (45–60 min.) Facilitators prepare a place for each circle member to sit and work, either at a table on their own or with others, or in separate spaces or rooms. Facilitators set up art supplies on a table for easy access and allow each circle member to select the materials they desire.

Writing Reflection (15 min.) Facilitators invite everyone to use the last 10-15 minutes of individual time to reflect and write on their artmaking experience, to mark and digest what has happened so that they remember and integrate it.

Conscious Closure and Integration (60 min.)

During Conscious Closure, circle members are invited to share partial or completed artwork and written notes. Other circle members listen with empathy, nonjudgmentally, and bear witness to each member. At the end, thank each person for sharing. After everyone has shared something, close your meeting with a planned ritual.

Creative Weavings

In the handouts shared during the session, offer suggestions for personal integration of the topic after the session has ended.

After the Meeting

The memory keeper completes the notes, gathers photographs of the artwork and the experience, and combines them into an email sent out after the session. This also serves as a way to maintain a record of your sessions: the topic, who facilitated, the art modalities utilized, notes.

Appendix D

Creative Living Plan

The following pages include:

Part 1: Creative Life Map to identify key experiences that have shaped your life thus far.

Part 2: Creative Living Web, a tool to help you develop your *whole* self.

Allow yourself time for reflection. This process will help you explore where you are in your life now and to identify what you desire for the future. Choose the areas that capture your interest.

Part 1: Creative Life Map: "Let your life speak" (Palmer, 1999)

> *Life isn't about finding yourself; life is about creating yourself.*
> — George Bernard Shaw

Directions: Brainstorm key events that have shaped your life. Capture your first thoughts about major highlights of the categories below. What lessons of wisdom have emerged through these experiences?

	Child 0–10	Teen 11–20	Young Adult 21–30	Adult 31–40	Mid-Life Adult 41–60	Wise Elder 61–80	Sage 81–100+
Family Life							
Spiritual Development							
Education, Lifelong Learning							
Creative Passions							
Role Models, "Best Friends" who nurture and help you grow							
Physical and Emotional Well-Being							
Life work							
Peak Experiences							
Episodes of Misfortune							
Weaving Life Lessons Into Wisdom							
THEMES							

Part 2: Creative Living Web

The Creative Living Web process will help you develop your *whole* self. Each person may choose one or two areas as a priority for their Creative Spirit Circle focus at any given time.

Life Mission/Purpose/Provocative Proposition

- What do you desire in your life over the next 3–5 years?
  Note: You will have an opportunity to explore this further in the circle session *Weaving a Personal Vision for Creative Living.* Your circle meeting will include a guided imagery and expressive arts journey. In preparation for this process, respond to as many of the following questions as beckon your attention.

Life Work
- What are your optimal lifework dreams and goals? What legacy do you want to bring to the world?

Physical/Psychological Well-Being
- What supports your optimal physical and psychological well-being?
- When you notice yourself or your family/friends veering off course, what strategies do you have to come back to your optimal health?
- What new strategies may you want to learn for mindfulness, self-compassion, physical and psychological well-being?

Spiritual Growth
- What practices connect you to your higher self, to a higher power, or to divine energy?

Life Maintenance
- What life priorities will require your energy during the coming months (home repairs, medical care, etc.)?
- How might you creatively address these or ensure they do not drain your creative energy?

Friends/Community
- Which people in your life give you energy and emotional support?
- How can you invest positively in the relationships that are most important to you?
- If you don't have a long-term partner or relationship, do you want to develop one?
- How can you give back and contribute to the community?

Education/Life-Long Learning: Personal and Professional Development
- What are your educational or lifelong learning desires?

Creative Passion
- What part of yourself brings you joy? How can you develop joyful living?

- Is there a new creative endeavor that you would like to explore (travel, music, art, improvisation, gardening, learning another language, pilot lessons, or something else)?
- What are further ways you may express or embody your provocative proposition or a key insight? Examples include: a book title, dance, dream, improvisation, child's play, poem, podcast, song, or speech. (Note: Members could share these expressions with the circle and work on them over time.)

Appendix E

Creative Spirit Circle Survey

Note: Send this survey to each group member before your circle meets. The facilitators will compile the survey results and return a summary for each member to read. This can be revised and administered periodically to your group members.

1. Name of our circle
2. Time of day to meet (length)
3. Number of sessions per year
4. How would you personally like to grow?
5. What topics would you like to explore?
6. What are the two or three things that you value and are most important to you as a member of this circle?
7. What adds depth for you?
8. After your group has met for several sessions, ask: What are one or two things you would like to discuss, change, or shift? Is there anything you would like more of? Less of?
9. What is your desire for the future regarding process?
10. What is your desire for the future regarding content?
11. Are there any novel or unique locations you would like to explore for future sessions? (These might be local or could require travel.)
12. Do you want to have a periodic retreat format (2–3 days)? How much time and cost would you be able to devote?
13. Are there any external facilitators or new members you would like to include? What should the maximum size of our group be? If someone leaves the circle, how do we handle transitions?
14. How does the group want to purchase/store art supplies?
15. How do you want to develop the circle schedule for dates, facilitator partnering, memory keeper, and other roles (e.g., quarterly, annually)?
16. Do you have other suggestions, questions, feedback?

Appendix F

List of Meditations

1. Chap 4 – First inner guide meditation
2. Chap 6 – Short, centering meditation
3. Chap 8 – Teachings about meditation and a movement
    meditation
4. Chap 10 – Breathing and moving meditation
5. Chap 11 – Remembering little you meditation
6. Chap 12 – Body meditation
7. Chap 13 – Mirror meditation
8. Chap 16 – Weaving memories meditation

References

Academy of American Poets. (n.d.). Poets.org. https://poets.org

Aguirre, M. (2020). Mexican folk art: Mythical, magical, and sublime. *Bucket List Mexico*. https://bucketlistmexico.com/product/mexican-folk-art-mythical-magical-and-sublime

Aizenstat, S., & Houston, J. (2022, April). *Embody your creative spirit: Find your own lure of becoming*. Jung Platform.

Andreasen, N. (2005). *The creative brain: The science of genius*. Plume.

Angelou, M. (1993). *On the pulse of morning*. Random House.

Angelou, M. (1982). Creativity: It's the thought that counts. Interview by Mary Ardito. *Bell Telephone Magazine, 61*(1). American Telephone and Telegraph Company.

Archibald, L., & Dewar, J. (2010). Creative arts, culture, and healing: Building an evidence base. *A Journal of Aboriginal and Indigenous Community Health, 8*.

Artress, L. (2006). *The sacred path companion: A guide to walking the labyrinth to heal and transform*. Riverhead Books.

Artress, L. (1995). *Walking a sacred path*. Riverhead Books.

Baumeister, R., & Leary, M. (1995). The need to belong: Desire for interpersonal attachments as a fundamental human motivation. *Psychological Bulletin, 117*(3), 497–529.

Bayles, D., & Orland, T. (2001). *Art and fear: Observations on the perils (and rewards) of artmaking*. Image Continuum Press.

Beck, R., & Metrick, S. B. (2003). *The art of ritual: creating and performing ceremonies for growth and change*. Celestial Arts.

Bethurst, R., & Monin, N. (2016). Shaping leadership for today: Mary Parker Follet's aesthetic. *Leadership, 6*(2), 115–131. https://doi.org/10.1177/1742715010363206

Bolen, J. S. (1999). *The millionth circle: How to change ourselves and the world — the essential guide to women's circles*. Conari Press.

Boyatzis, R. E., Rochford, K., & Taylor, S. N. (2015, May 21). The role of the positive emotional attractor in vision and shared vision: Toward effective leadership, relationships, and engagement. *Frontiers in Psychology, 6*, Article 670. https://doi.org/10.3389/fpsyg.2015.00670

Brenner, A. (2013, January 29). The inner language of the subconscious: A picture is worth a thousand words. *Psychology Today*. https://www.psychologytoday.com/us/blog/in-flux/201301/the-inner-language-the-subconscious

Bridges, W. (1999). *Transitions: Making sense of life's changes*. Lifelong Books.

Buber, M. (1970). *I and thou*. Touchstone.

Burton, T. (Director). (2010). *Alice in wonderland* [Film]. Walt Disney Pictures; Roth Films; The Zanuck Company.

Cameron, J. (1999). *Transitions; Prayers and declarations for a changing life.*
    Jeremy P. Tarcher/Putman.
Campbell, J. (2004). *Pathways to bliss: Mythology and personal transformation.*
    New World Library.
Campbell, J. (1973). *Erotic irony and mythic forms in the art of Thomas Mann*
    (Essays from Sarah Lawrence faculty). Sarah Lawrence College.
Carson, R. (2012). *The brain fix: What's the matter with your gray matter:*
    Improve your memory, moods, and mind. Health Communications.
Carson, R. (1998). *The edge of the sea.* Mariner Books.
Chandler, M. A. (2013). Study: Teen's knowledge of family history a sign of
    social-emotional health. *Washington Post.*
    https://www.washingtonpost.com/local/education/study-teens-
    knowledge-of-family-history-a-sign-of-social-emotional-
    health/2013/12/10/72fb7606-61ce-11e3-bf45-61f69f54fc5f_story.html
Chang, F. (2014). Mindfulness and person-centered expressive arts therapy.
    In L. Rappaport (Ed.), *Mindfulness and the art therapies* (pp. 219–234).
    Jessica Kingsley Publishers.
Cooperrider, D. L. (2017). The gift of new eyes: Personal reflections after 30
    years of appreciative inquiry in organizational life. *Research in*
    Organizational Change and Development, 25, 81–142.
Cooperrider, D. L., & Whitney, D. K. (2005). *Appreciative inquiry: A positive*
    revolution in change. Berrett-Koehler.
Cropley, D., Cropley, A., Kaufman, J., & Runco, M. (2010). *The dark side of*
    creativity. Cambridge University Press.
Cuckson, T. (2020, June 7). Inner knowing is the no 1 powerful way to find
    meaning. *Yoga Journey for Life.*
    https://www.yogajourneyforlife.com/inner-knowing/
Davis, J. (2021). *Tracking wonder, reclaiming a life of meaning and possibility*
    in a world obsessed with productivity. Sounds True.
Deslauriers, D. (2000). Dreams in the light of emotional and spiritual
    intelligence. *Journal of Advanced Development, 9,* 105–122.
Durkeim, E. (1976). *The elementary forms of the religious life.* HarperCollins.
Eberhart, H., & Atkins, S. (2014). *Presence and process in expressive arts work:*
    At the edge of wonder. Jessica Kingsley.
Elkind, D. (2007). *The power of play: Learning what comes naturally.* Da Capo
    Lifelong Books.
Feiler, B. (2020). *Life is in the transitions: Mastering change at any age.*
    Penguin Books.
Fein, J. (2014). What is your emotional genealogy? *Psychology Today.*
    https://www.psychologytoday.com/us/blog/life-is-trip/201401/what-
    is-your-emotional-genealogy
Feinstein, D., & Eden, D. (2008). Six pillars of energy medicine: Clinical
    strengths of a complementary paradigm. *Alternative Therapies, 14*(1),
    44–54.

Fischgrund, A. (1999). *Zapotec weavers of Teotitlan*. Stanton Museum of New Mexico Press.

Fincher, S. (2010). *Creating mandalas for insight healing and self-expression*. Shambhala.

Fox, J. (1997). *Poetic medicine: The healing art of poem-making*. Jeremy P. Tarcher/Putnam.

Francis, L. (2020). *Portals: Opening doorways to other realities through senses*. Routledge.

Freeman, L. (2009). *Mosby's complementary and alternative medicine: A research-based approach*. Mosby/Elsevier.

Goslin-Jones, T. (2020). Expressive arts. In M. Runco & S. Pritzker (Eds.), *Encyclopedia of creativity* (3rd ed., pp. 478–484). Academic Press.

Goslin-Jones, T. (2011). Using expressive arts to transform the workplace. In N. Rogers (Ed.), *The creative connection for groups: Person-centered expressive arts for healing and social change* (pp. 354–357). Science and Behavior Books.

Goslin-Jones, T. (2010). *The perceived effects of person-centered expressive arts on one's work experience* (UMI number: 3418296) [Doctoral dissertation, Saybrook University]. ProQuest Dissertations and Theses.

Goslin-Jones, T. (1999). *Waking up*. Presented at the Cramer Institute, St. Louis, MO.

Goslin-Jones, T., & Herron, S. A. (2016). Cutting edge person-centered expressive arts. In C. Lago & D. Charr (Eds.), *The person-centered counseling and psychotherapy handbook* (pp. 199–211). Open University Press, McGraw-Hill Education.

Goslin-Jones, T., & Richards, R. (2018). Mysteries of creative process: Explorations at work and in daily life. In L. Martin & N. Wilson (Eds.), *The Palgrave handbook of creativity at work* (pp. 71–106). Palgrave Macmillan.

Gregoire, C. (2021, February 3). *10 Things highly intuitive people do differently*. HuffPost. https://www.huffpost.com/entry/the-habits-of-highly-intu_n_4958778

Haley, S., & Fukuda, C. (2004). *Day of the dead: When two worlds meet in Oaxaca*. Barghahan Books.

Halprin, D. (2003). *The expressive body in life, art, and therapy*. Jessica Kingsley.

Holbrook, R. L., & Comer, D. R. (2017). Mandalas: A simple project to explore creativity. *Management Teaching Review, 2*(3), 202–210. https://doi.org/10.1177/2379298117709782

Hollis, J. (1993). *The middle passage: From misery to meaning in midlife*. Inner City Books.

Homeyer, L., & Sweeney, D. S. (2017). *Sandtray therapy: A practical manual*. Routledge.

Hughes, L. (2002) *Dreams*. https://www.poetryfoundation.org/ poems/ 150995/dreams-5d767850da976

Houston, J. (2009). *A passion for the possible: A guide to realizing your true potential.* HarperCollins.

Houston, J. (1982). *The possible human: A course in enhancing your physical, mental and creative abilities.* Jeremy P. Tarcher/Putman.

Joiner, B., & Josephs, S. (2006). *Leadership agility: Five levels of mastery for anticipating and initiating change.* Jossey-Bass.

Jordan, J. (2018). *Relational-cultural therapy* (2nd ed.). American Psychological Association.

Jordan, J., Kaplan, A., Miller, J. B., Stiver, I. P., & Surrey, J. L. (1991). *Women's growth in connection: Writings from the Stone Center.* Guilford.

Jung, C. (1969). *Collected works of C.G. Jung, Volume 9 (Part 1): Archetypes and the collective unconscious* (G. Adler & R. F. C. Hull, Ed. & Trans.). Bollingen Series XX. Princeton University Press.

Jung, C. (1968). *Collected works of C.G. Jung, Volume 12: Psychology and alchemy* (G. Adler & R. F. C. Hull, Ed. & Trans.). Bollingen Series XX. Princeton University Press.

Jung, C. (1967). *Collected works of C.G. Jung, Volume 7: Two essays in analytical psychology, Part 2: Individuation* (G. Adler & R. F. C. Hull, Ed. & Trans.). Bollingen Series XX. Princeton University Press.

Kabat-Zinn, J. (1994). *Wherever you go, there you are: Mindfulness meditation in everyday life.* Hyperion.

Kaufman, S. (2022, September 8). Tara Well, The mirror meditation. In *The psychology podcast.* https://the-psychology-podcast-with-scott-barry-kaufman.simplecast.com/episodes/tara-well-mirror-meditation-nsgdeCg9.

Kaufman, S. B. (2020). *Transcend, The new science of self-actualization.* TarcherPerigee.

Kaufman, S. B., & Gregoire, C. (2015). *Wired to create: Unraveling the mysteries of the creative mind.* TarcherPerigree.

Kegan, R. (2013). *The further reaches of adult development – Robert Kegan* [Video]. Renaissance Society of America. YouTube. https://www.youtube.com/watch?v=BoasM4cCHBc

Kegan, R (1994). *In over our heads: The mental demands of modern life.* Harvard University Press.

Klerk, M. (2022). *Dream guidance: Connecting to the soul through dream incubation.* Hay House, Inc.

Knill, M., & Atkins, S. (2021). *Poetry in expressive arts: Supporting resilience through poetic writing.* Jessica Kingsley.

Knill, P. J., Levine, E. G., & Levine, S. K. (2004). *Principles and practice of expressive arts therapy: Toward a therapeutic aesthetics. Jessica Kingsley.*

Kossack, M. (2021). *Attunement in expressive arts therapy: Toward an understanding of embodied empathy* (2nd edition). Charles C. Thomas Publisher.

Krippner, S. (2009). *Anyone who dreams partakes of shamanism* (Keynote address). International Association for the Study of Dreams Convention. Chicago, IL, United States.

Krippner, S. (1990). *Dreamtime and dreamwork: Decoding the language of the night (A new consciousness reader).* Penguin Publishing Group.

Lamott, A. (2012). *Help, thanks, wow: The three essential prayers.* Riverhead Books.

LeGuin, U. (2019). *Always coming home.* Library of America.

Lewin, L. O., McManamon, A., Stein, M. T. O., & Chen, D. T. (2019). Minding the form that transforms: Using Kegan's model of adult development to understand personal and professional identity formation in medicine. *Academic Medicine, 94*(9), 1299–1304. https://doi.org/10.1097/ACM.0000000000002741

Lord, M. (2015). Group learning capacity: The roles of open-mindedness and shared vision. *Frontiers in Psychology, 6,* Article 150. https://doi.org/10.3389/fpsyg.2015.00150

Lowth, M. (2016, May 20). *Ten ancient sites that might be stargates, portals, and wormholes.* https://listverse.com/2016/05/20/10-ancient-sites-that-might-be-stargates-portals-and-wormholes/

Lyon, G. E. (1999). *Where I'm from* (Writers' & Young Writers' Series #2). Absey and Co.

Lytton, N. (August 7, 2020). *Dissecting our dreams: The divine, angels, sex, guns, snakes and Ayahuasca.* Freedom Hack Radio. https://www.youtube.com/watch?v=Jsl703uJDQ4

Maggiolini, A., Di Lorenzo, M., Falotico, E., Gargioni, D., & Morelli, M. (2020). Typical dreams across the life cycle. *International Journal of Dream Research, 13*(1), 17–28.

Maslow, A. H. (1998). *Toward a psychology of being* (3rd ed.). Wiley.

Maslow, A. H. (1971). *The farther reaches of human nature.* Arkana/Penguin Books.

Maslow, A. H. (1976). *The farther reaches of human nature.* Penguin.

Mellick, J. (2001). *The art of dreaming: Tools for creative dream work.* Conari Press.

Mulcahy, M. (2013). Mandalas as a tool for transformation to enable human flourishing: The influence of Carl Jung. *International Practice Development Journal, 3*(2), 1–4.

O'Donohue, J. (2000). *Eternal echoes: Celtic reflections on our yearning to belong.* Harper Perennial.

Oliver, M. (1992). *New and selected poems.* Beacon Press.

One World Nations Online. (n.d.). *Ancestor worship in Taoism.* https://www.nationsonline.org/oneworld/Chinese_Customs/taoism_ancestor_worship.htm

Paintner, C. (2017). *The wisdom of the body: A contemplative journey to wholeness for women.* Ave Maria Press.

Palmer, P. (1999). *Let your life speak.* Jossey-Bass.

Pargament, K. I. (2011). *Spiritually integrated psychotherapy: Understanding and addressing the sacred*. Guilford.

Pollack, J., & Cabane, O. F. (2017, March 17). Are people more creative alone or together? Trick question. *Fast Company*. https://www.fastcompany.com/3069033/are-people-more-creative-alone-or-together-trick-question.

Quibell, D. (2019). *Soul bird: Poems for flying*. Mandorla Books.

Radford, B. (2013, November 19). The lore and lure of ley lines. *LiveScience*. https://www.livescience.com/41349-ley-lines.html

Richards, R. (2018) *Everyday creativity and the healthy mind: Dynamic new paths for self and society*. Palgrave Macmillan.

Richards, R. (2014). A creative alchemy. In S. Moran, D. Cropley, & J. Kaufman (Eds.), *The ethics of creativity*. Palgrave Macmillan.

Richards, R. (2007a). Introduction. In R. Richards (Ed.), *Everyday creativity* (pp. 3–22). American Psychological Association.

Richards, R. (2007b). Twelve benefits of living more creatively. In R. Richards (Ed.), *Everyday creativity* (pp. 289–319). American Psychological Association.

Richards, R. (2007c). Relational creativity and healing potential: The power of Eastern thought in Western clinical settings. In J. Pappas, W. Smythe, & A. Baydala (Eds.), *Cultural healing and belief systems* (pp. 286–308). Detselig.

Richards, R., & Goslin-Jones, T. (2020). Everyday creativity. In M. Runco & S. Pritzker (Eds.), *Encyclopedia of creativity* (3rd ed., pp. 455–462). Academic Press.

Rilke, R. M. (1993). *Letters to a young poet* (M.D. Herter Norton, Trans.). W.W. Norton & Company.

Rogers, C. (1965). *Client-centered therapy: Its current practice, implications and theory*. Houghton Mifflin Company.

Rogers, J. (2019). *Mirrors as portals: Images of mirrors on ancient Maya ceramics* (Publication No. 6701) [Master's thesis, University of Central Florida]. UCF Electronic Theses and Dissertations. https://stars.library.ucf.edu/etd/6701

Rogers, N. (2011). *The creative connection for groups: Person-centered expressive arts for healing and social change*. Science and Behavior Books.

Rogers, N. (1993). *The creative connection: Expressive arts as healing*. Science & Behavior Books.

Rogers, N. (1980). *Emerging woman: A decade of midlife transitions*. Personal Press.

Runco, M., & Pritzker, S. (2011). *Encyclopedia of creativity* (2nd ed.) Academic Press/Elsevier.

Runco, M., & Richards, R. (1997). *Eminent creativity, everyday creativity, and health*. Ablex Publishing Company.

Seattle, C. (n.d.). *Prayer to the four directions*. Ya-Native: Preserving and Sharing our Culture. https://www.ya-native.com/prayersandblessings/prayertothefourdirections.html

Seo, Y. A. (2007). *Enso: Zen circles of enlightenment*. WeatherHill Inc.

Serlin, I., Krippner, S., & Rockefeller, K. (2019). *Integrated care for the traumatized: A whole-person approach*. Rowman & Littlefield.

Schuldberg, D., Richards, R., & Guisinger, S. (2022). *Chaos and nonlinear psychology: Keys to creativity in mind and life*. Oxford University Press.

Siegel, D. (2018). *Awareness: The science and practice of presence*. TarcherPerigee.

Siegel, D. J. (2010). *Mindsight: The new science of personal transformation*. Bantam Books.

Siegel, D. (2007). *The mindful brain: Reflection and attunement in the cultivation of well-being*. W.W. Norton.

Smalley, S. L., & Winston, D. (2010). *Fully present: The science, art, and practice of mindfulness*. Da Capo Lifelong Books.

Stafford, W. (1999). *The way it is*. Graywolf Press.

Suzuki, S. (2006). *Zen mind, beginner's mind*. Shambala.

Starhawk. (1989). *The spiral dance: A rebirth of the ancient religion of the great goddess*. Harper Collins.

Taylor, J. (1983). *Dream work: Techniques for discovering the creative power in dreams*. Paulist Press.

Taylor, J. (2009). *The wisdom of your dreams: Using dreams to tap into your unconscious and transform your life*. TarcherPerigee.

Thich Nhat Hanh. (2021). *How to practice hugging meditation*. https://www.lionsroar.com/how-to-practice-hugging-meditation/

Ullman, M., & Zimmerman, N. (1979). *Working with dreams*. Delacorte Press.

Ullman, M. (1996). *Appreciating dreams: A group approach*. Sage.

Wamsley, E. J. (2022). Constructive episodic simulation in dreams. *PLOS ONE*, *17*(3), Article e0264574. https://doi.org/10.1371/journal.pone.0264574

Watts, L. (2000) *Mandalas: Spiritual circles for harmony and fulfillment*. Southwater.

Well, T. (2022). *Mirror meditation: The power of neuroscience and self-reflection to overcome self-criticism, gain confidence, and see yourself with compassion*. New Harbinger Publications, Inc.

Whyte, D. (2012). *River flow: New and selected poems*. Many Rivers Press.

Wily, E., & Shannon, M. (2002). *A string and a prayer: How to make and use prayer beads*. Red Wheel/Weiser.

Wingcom. (2007, November 11). *Samuel Becket – Breath* [Video]. https://www.youtube.com /watch?v=io_scJbhCOY

Winston, K. (2016). *Bead one, pray too: A guide to making and using prayer beads*. Moorehouse Publishing.

Zander, R. S., & Zander, B. (2000). *The art of possibility*. Penguin Press.

Index

Author Biographies

Pam Caraffa, PhD

I joined our *Creative Spirit Circle* to expand personal growth within a creative community. Our expressive arts practices nurture my way of being in the world and enrich my life. Professionally, I have been a university professor, consultant, executive coach, and corporate VP of organizational and leadership development to guide personal, cultural, and organizational transformation. I have offered innovative seminars to institutions such as the Center for Creative Leadership, Chief Learning Officer Global Symposium, the International Coaching Federation, IMD Business School, and Cornell and Washington Universities. Supporting nonprofit leadership is a passion, and I've served on several boards, most recently the Keyway Center for Diversion & Reentry and Mitrata Nepal Foundation for Children. I am currently focused on family & friends, board work, photography, physical fitness, travel, and continual growth.
Email: pwcara@sbcglobal.net.

Holly Carson, MA, LPC, LCSW

My search for a creative and spiritual community of women led me to the Creative Spirit Circle. My greatest learning as a participant in this experience has been that every creative endeavor is a new adventure, a sacred path, full of lessons in the art of being. I have led thousands of clients on their healing journey as a psychotherapist for over forty-three years through my private practice in St. Louis, Missouri. I am a licensed professional counselor, licensed clinical social worker, and certified life coach, and received my MA in Counseling Psychology at Lesley University in Boston. My therapy practice is currently focused on work with women across the life spectrum. My life's work has exemplified the power of art and creative expression to heal and transform our brokenness and awaken us to our true self.
Website: http://hollycarsoncounseling.com.

Terri Goslin-Jones, PhD, REACE

I joined the Creative Spirit Circle with a desire to be engaged in a creative community committed to evolving consciousness using

person-centered expressive arts. The immersion in this circle process nourishes my entire "way of being." In my professional life, I serve as Psychology/Creativity Studies faculty at Saybrook University and previously worked as a VP of Human Resources and Organizational Development Consultant. My reason for teaching and serving as an advisor for doctoral research is to support life-long learners in a quest to create change in their life and in their part of the world. Creativity is at the heart of my work. I am an expressive arts practitioner, a poet, mindfulness facilitator and lead poetry circles as a graduate of the Institute for Poetic Medicine. My creative passions include family life, expressive arts, gardening, a love for life-long learning, physical fitness, poetry, spirituality, and international travel.
Website: www.terrigoslin-jones.com. Email: tgoslin-jones@saybrook.edu.

Ginger Reinert, MA

I joined the Creative Spirit Circle to explore the connection between creativity and individuation. This group has enhanced my search for meaning and wholeness. Twelve years of engagement with creative spirit has provided me with invaluable personal insight and wisdom. The first half of my career was invested in the sales and management of million-dollar performance improvement programs at Meridian Enterprises. I traveled worldwide overseeing sales and incentive programs. Later as a professor at a local business college, I taught courses in psychology, sociology, communications, conflict management, diversity, leadership, motivation, and team building. I am on the board and volunteer as a docent at the Campbell House Museum. My interest now lies in preserving the historical heritage of the Gateway to the West. I also mentor young women struggling with the challenges of motherhood. I am an avid traveler, reader, and lifelong learner.

Kim McCallum MD, FAPA

I was eager to awaken and nurture creativity, imagining the Creative Spirit Circle would help shape the next chapter of my life. My experience has exceeded expectations. I have been inspired by our topics...aging, soul, transitions, love. There is a special energy and calm that emerges from our process, allowing us each to grow in deeper ways than we would on our own. I am excited to share this process, which has been a joyful and central part of our lives for the past twelve years. A psychiatrist and psychotherapist, my career path was built on early interests in the mind–body connection. A

neuroscience major, I received my MD from Yale, psychiatry training at UCLA and the STL Psychoanalytic Institute, and Child Psychiatry training at Washington University. Throughout my career I have been passionate about integrating mindfulness practice into psychiatric care, especially the treatment of eating disorders.
Email: kimberli.mccallum@icloud.com

Nancy Williger, PhD, MSW
When the opportunity came to join a small creativity circle focusing on spiritual development through an expressive arts process, I was eager to join. The Creative Spirit Circle has added a new and unexpected dimension of creativity to my life, for which I am grateful. Professionally I have a Master's in Social Work and a PhD in Psychology. For most of my career, I have been in a private practice focused on helping people get divorced in a non-adversarial manner. For the last twenty years, I have helped to grow a charity, Mitrata Nepal Foundation for Children. The organization sponsors children in Nepal to get an education and become self-sufficient. I am retired from clinical work and currently work with non-profit organizations and teach mediation to lawyers and other mental health professionals. In my spare time, I enjoy creating with paint, polymer clay, and beads in my home studio and staying connected to friends.
Email: nawillgr@aol.com.